Crime

Explaining Crime

GWYNN NETTLER
The University of Alberta

McGRAW-HILL BOOK COMPANY
New York St. Louis San Francisco Düsseldorf Johannesburg
Kuala Lumpur London Mexico Montreal New Delhi
Panama Rio de Janeiro Singapore Sydney Toronto

Explaining Crime

234567890BPBP7987654

This book was set in Times Roman by Black Dot, Inc.
The editors were David Edwards, Ronald Kissack, and Susan Gamer;
and the production supervisor was Thomas J. LoPinto.
The printer and binder was The Book Press, Inc.

Library of Congress Cataloging in Publication Data

Nettler, Gwynn.
  Explaining crime.

  Bibliography: p.
  1. Crime and criminals. I. Title.
HV6025.N46   364   73-16076
ISBN 0-07-046298-4
ISBN 0-07-046297-6 (pbk.)

74855

Contents

Preface

"The seeds of every crime are in each of us," Leo Tolstoy believed. The point of Tolstoy's aphorism is to indicate a possibility common to all of us. The poverty of his statement is that it does not describe how the criminal seeds are germinated. On this, we dispute, and the victim in the cartoon on the cover of this book is no more confused in his response to crime than many of us.

Professional students of crime, like laymen, quarrel about which wrongs should be considered crimes. We vacillate between sympathy for the criminal and concern for his victim. We argue whether "the violence of conditions" justifies the violence of persons, and we debate whether crimes "understandably motivated" should be excused by the force of their circumstances.

Intellectuals—the occupationally thoughtful—as well as other citizens can be heard praising and condemning arson, theft, and murder depending upon their agreement with the political motives of the offenders and their approval or disapproval of the victims. On the right, the Governor of California tells us that the Watergate burglars and their accomplices are not "really criminals." On the left, defenders of campus arsonists and urban guerrillas tell us that the goodness of their ends and the meanness of conditions transform their acts from crimes to "social banditry."

The general public, as usual, is in the middle. It thinks it knows what it means by "crime." Both its definition of crime and its sense of justice remain more universal and more historical than the current claims of political advocates. However, when laymen turn to professionals for explanations of crime and guidance in policy, they receive a potpourri of answers that leaves them as "balanced," or as muddled, as the citizen in our cartoon.

Criminologists dispute what should be called "crime," and how to count crime. We quarrel, too, about where to lay the blame. Some explanations of crime hold the actor responsible for his behavior and look for the causes of crime in his difference from lawful people. Other explanations blame the actor's circumstances; still others blame the "moral entrepreneurs" who have the power to define crime and to enforce their definitions through police and courts.

These explanatory efforts will be described and criticized. Our standard of criticism is how adequately an explanation answers the questions about crime asked by most citizens. Our critical standard is concerned, first, with the *clarity* of concepts and hypotheses; second, with the *evidence* for a theory of crime production; and third, with the practical *consequences* of applying a theory. It will be apparent that some theories of human behavior that appear plausible on paper do not work well with people.

All the explanations to be described contain some truth. The prices we pay when we believe one explanation rather than another vary, however. Our criticism concludes with a statement, a rare one, of the conditions that generate crime. This roster of criminogenic conditions provides a partial account of the costs of reducing crime.

ACKNOWLEDGMENT

Fellow students have read portions of this work and have both corrected me and stimulated me. They are not to be blamed for my mistakes, of course, but they are to be thanked for their help. My appreciation is due Douglas Cousineau, John Hagan, George Kupfer, and Leonard Savitz.

GWYNN NETTLER

Explaining Crime

The Concern with Crime

There are at least as many explanations of "crime" as there are questions asked about it. How "good" any explanation is varies with the question that is asked and with the assumptions embedded in the question. For each reader, the adequacy of any explanation of crime is a matter of what he already believes about human beings, which kinds of crime he is interested in, and the quality of his concern with criminal behavior. The quality of one's concern with crime influences the kind of test to which each person puts the explanation he prefers. For example, predicting behavior is one test of the soundness of an explanation. The explanations that increase foresight, however, are not always those that increase insight and understanding, and neither the test of increased predictive power nor the test of "better understanding" will necessarily satisfy the requirements of political policy or moral judgment (Nettler, 1970). In short, accurate explanations may not be "good" ones.

As we attend, then, to the various theories that are given to explain crime, it is advisable to gauge the adequacy of each against the tests it can pass. The explanatory tests chosen depend, we have said, upon the nature of our concern with crime. Most of us pay attention to crime out of the desire to protect ourselves and our loved ones against the harm others may do. It is the threat to one's *person and property* and, secondarily, to the institutions that protect person and property that Everyman has in mind when he thinks of crime.

THE QUALITY OF POPULAR CONCERN WITH CRIME

The quality of popular concern with crime is *more restricted* than is the attention given to crime by professional students. The *legal* definition of a crime, to be discussed in the next chapter, encompasses a *wider* range of wrongs with more qualifications than the average citizen has in mind when he thinks of "crime." This point is important because it justifies our looking at the explanations of crime through the eyes of the majority of those who ask the questions about it—through the eyes of "people in general" rather than from the perspective of specialists.

This narrowed focus justifies examining the explanations of a limited category of criminal conduct, that kind of conduct that has been deemed wrong universally. This limitation of attention makes it unnecessary to try to explain all acts which, at some time, in some place, may have been criminal. The criminal law changes, and the acts it condemns are not always those the public considers "really wrong." In 1934, the American financier Samuel Insull expressed the point this way: "If two men had walked down Fifth Avenue a year ago—that would have been March, 1933—and one of them had a pint of whiskey in his pocket and the other had a hundred dollars in gold coin, the one with the whiskey would have been called a criminal and the one with the gold an honest citizen. If these two men, like Rip Van Winkle, slept for a year and again walked down Fifth Avenue, the man with the whiskey would be called an honest citizen and the one with the gold coin a criminal" (from Schultz, 1972, pp. 135–136).

Explanations of "crime" that would explain all the acts that have been legally proscribed as wrongs, sometime, someplace, would become diffuse and vague. They would come close to trying to answer the question, "Why is there sin?" They would become either descriptions of all the evils inflicted by man, or they would be reduced to a lamentation.

A narrower conception of "crime" is one that conforms to public concern about the topic. Public concern with crime is principally with those acts that have been universally condemned as "wrongs in themselves" (crimes *mala in se*). The motivation to attend to these crimes is as fundamental as survival. As we have said, it is, first, personal, and, second, societal. The concern is with protection of one's person and belongings and, after that, with the protection of those institutions and public properties which the citizen values. The concern is only slightly directed toward minor traffic violations, public drunkenness, vagrancy, or even toward the very expensive, but less visible, crimes against government and large corporations. If the organization is "big enough," and distant, popular guilt about stealing from it diminishes (Smigel and Ross, 1970).

The concern with crime, for most people, is an interest in those elements of public order that are perennial. It is expressed in the timeless desire to be able to move about freely without being robbed or beaten. It is witnessed in the universal wish to preserve one's property against theft and one's body against invasion. It is indicated by the shame and anger most citizens feel when their valued edifices—courts and universities, police stations and communications outlets, libraries and government buildings, department stores and banks—are willfully damaged. It is measured, in part, by public opinion surveys that reveal American disapproval of attacks on their police and riots in their streets (Erskine, 1968–1969; Robinson, 1970). It is gauged by such indicators as the poll in one American city (Harris, 1968) that asked a representative sample of citizens to select from a list of ten domestic issues "the single most serious problem [that they] would like to see the government do something about." Of the ten items, the one ranked "most serious" by the most respondents was "crime and lawlessness." This finding is matched by a Gallup Poll report in 1968 that, for the first time since it began publishing

33 years earlier, "crime is the nation's no. one domestic concern." (*Time,* 1968). The concern continued to be expressed by Americans in 1972, an election year (*Time,* 1972b, pp. 22–23).

Directing one's attention toward these public concerns does not in the least deny that there are other varieties of harm, criminal and noncriminal, that we do to each other. There *are* styles of fraud, deceit, insult, and denigration *not* included within the definitions of burglary, robbery, assault, and homicide. There *are* expensive crimes, committed with such sophistication and such protection as to evade public notice; examples are income tax evasion, fraudulent business practices, professional dishonesty, bureaucratic malfeasance, and the common thefts from big business, big education, and big government.

These many modern styles of theft and personal affront come to public attention only sporadically, however. Since their effects are spread among a host of anonymous victims, they are less likely to provoke indignation. Diluting the damage among numbers of victims is apt to reduce resentment—unless the crime has some symbolic significance, as does an attack upon a cherished institution. Further, if the crime is carried off with flair, and if the prey is big government or big business, the act is less likely to be considered criminal and more likely to be thought of as belonging to some other category of sin or adventure.

A measure of this differential definition of some "big" crimes is that neither their perpetrators nor large segments of their audiences seem to regard them as "criminal." Thus the first American skyjacker to parachute with an extorted fortune immediately became a type of folk hero, his name emblazoned on T-shirts and his act imitated by others. When such acts are imitated, they may of course come to be considered criminal.

So, too, "the con-man of the year" (*Time,* 1972a) who attempted unsuccessfully to bilk a book publisher out of $750,000 by palming off a fake biography is reported to have said, upon his conviction, that he had not believed his fraud was a crime.

A less glamorous example is a book (Hoffman, 1971) describing how to cheat universities, steal from department stores, and make bombs in one's basement; its publication was defended as coming under the right of free speech (Rader, 1971), and the crimes it recommends were redefined as "socially useful."

There is, then, a tug-of-war among intellectuals as to what should and should not be called "criminal," and even as to whether the long-standing definitions of "theft" and "murder" ought not to be reassessed if the victim is despised or dispersed and if the offender's motives seem moral. Despite these debates, the major theories of crime causation, like the concerns of the citizenry, are more strongly directed toward the explanation of the perpetual "serious offenses" against person and property—the more visible, predatory crimes—than they are toward the newer "administrative" or "public interest" crimes. This turn of attention does not lessen the social effects of these other wrongs. It simply leaves them aside, as this book will also do.

THE APPARENT INCREASE IN CRIME

Canadians, Americans, and residents of other industrialized nations believe that visible and serious attacks upon person and property have been increasing during recent years. Their belief is supported by business records and by some government statistics. For example, sales in the United States of protective devices for the home, principally electronic burglar alarms, increased over the past decade; and the number of American companies selling security services and equipment jumped from some 100 to 900 during the late 1960s (*U.S. News & World Report,* 1970e). A study by the Rand Corporation (Malloy, 1972) found that expenditure by citizens for private security forces in the United States increased by 150 percent during the last decade. In America there are now more private policemen than public ones.

In addition, retail merchants reported an increase of shoplifting in North America and in Sweden (Elmhorn, 1965, p. 137); and a panel of book merchants, pondering how to shore up store security, decided that "stealing is no longer a deviant way of life in America" (*Newsweek,* 1972, p. 87).

Meanwhile, "internal theft"—stealing by employees—continues to exact a heavy price from businesses and their customers. A sampling of American department stores with sales of $37 *billion* annually yielded an estimate of "inventory shrink-age," a polite term for the mysterious disappearance of stock, of 2 to 3 percent of sales. Discount stores estimated their "shrink-age" at from 3 to 5 percent of total sales (*U.S. News & World Report* , 1970f). A business survey (*Business Management,* 1968) concluded that three-fourths or more of all employees have at some time stolen from their employers; and a psychologist (Zeitlin, 1971) estimated the loss from such internal thieving in the United States to range between $1 *billion* and $4 *billion* annually. Zeitlin suggests that this kind of theft is now regarded as one of the perquisites of a job and a bolster of morale. His interpretation gains plausibility in the light of figures compiled by the U.S. Bureau of Domestic Commerce, which show crimes against business to have increased threefold during the 1960s (*U.S. News & World Report,* 1972).

Norman Jaspan (1960), the head of an engineering consult-ing firm which also investigates stealing by employees, found that "in more than 50 per cent of assignments involving engineering projects with no hint of dishonesty, white collar crime was uncovered. In addition [in 1959 alone] our staff has uneartherd more than $60,000,000 worth of dishonesty with more than 60 per cent attributable to supervisory and executive personnel" (p. 10). When he was interviewed more recently, Jaspan (1970) said he believed that American firms suffer a "better than 50 per cent chance" of being the victims of "sizable dishonesty."

Jaspan's opinion is seconded by surveys within the Ameri-can construction industry. Such studies lead to the belief that on-the-job larcenies have been increasing in recent years and that some 1 to 6 percent of the net worth of a contractor's equipment is stolen each year. No successful method of combating such crime has been worked out, and contractors are reported to be alarmed at indications that organized crime may be becoming involved (Mayer, 1972a).

Another area of business shows a similar recent rise in crime. The American Bankers' Association has compiled one of the longest continuous records of a specific crime, bank robbery. Their tallies, which were begun in 1931, show that bank robbery rates, calculated either by population or by the number of banks, rose during the 1960s, although the rate has not exceeded that of the worst years of the Depression (Mudge, 1967).

While all this normal larceny ebbs and flows, new crimes are invented and, once invented, copied in quick order by persons of diverse motivation. Aerial piracy, "skyjacking," began in the early 1960s with the occasional kidnapping of a flight to Cuba. By the middle of the decade aerial piracy had become a political instrument of the many deadly quarrels around the world, with passengers held hostage and flights diverted to "Hawaii, Egypt, Jordan, Italy, Argentina, and the Bahamas, as well as Cuba" (Boltwood et al., 1972). In 1966, the United States directed legislation specifically against this menace and made aerial piracy a crime carrying a sentence of from 20 years imprisonment to death. Aircraft of the United States alone experienced 106 incidents of skyjacking between 1968 and mid-1971, of which 80 were successful (U.S. Department of Transportation, 1971). By 1972 aerial piracy was not only a part of international and civil warfare but was also an outlet for neurotic hostility and a novel form of high-priced robbery (Hubbard, 1971).

These many business reports and journalistic accounts of recent increases in some kinds of crime are substantiated by the Uniform Crime Reports compiled annually by the U.S. Federal Bureau of Investigation. As will be seen in Chapter 3, there are many critics of these official figures, and the figures must not be taken as exact. However, these figures do confirm the business indicators of a rise in crime. The "serious" or "index" crimes tabulated by the FBI are murder, forcible rape, robbery, aggravated assault, burglary, larceny $50 and over in value, and automobile theft. Figures 1, 2, and 3 show an increase of these offenses during the 1960s, both in terms of the number of violations reported to the police and as a rate of crimes per 100,000 persons. The early 1970s are seeing a decline in the *rate* of increase in such crimes in the United States (FBI, 1971), but the volume of crime remains high and remains an issue of domestic concern.

Is the apparent increase real? The apparent increase in crime and delinquency during the 1960s has been criticized by some criminologists as artificially produced by the statistics makers. It is charged that crime rates have been inflated by the

Percent change
over 1960

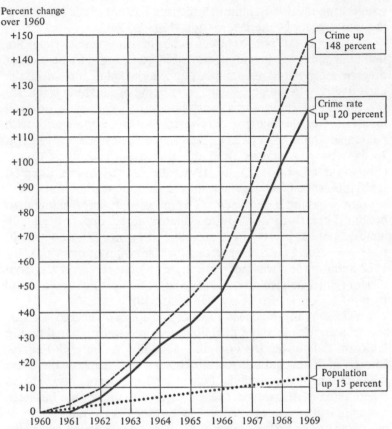

Figure 1 Crime and population, 1960-1969. "Crime" refers to index offenses; "crime rate," to the number of offenses per 100,000 population. (F.B.I. chart.)

police and the mass media and that the public perception confuses an increase in some crime with an increase in all crime.

For example, in Canada, McDonald (1969a) has shown from official data that, contrary to popular belief, the measures of serious crimes (indictable offenses) did *not* increase between 1950 and 1966, nor did sentences become more lenient. There had been an increase in the size of Canadian police forces relative to the population and an increase of police activity in the control of automobile traffic; charges of parking violations constituted a major source of the increased police work.

While McDonald's study shows that the Canadian public may have been premature in its perception of an increase in crime, the official statistics for the remainder of the 1960s confirm the popular belief that the rates of grave offenses have been increasing. Table 1 shows the rates of the more serious crimes per 100,000 population 7 years of age and over, year by year from 1965 through 1970. Most of these crimes have shown a steady recent increase in Canada, as they have in the United States.

A more dramatic change is reported for England and Wales, where violations both of property and of person have increased steadily since World War II, with an acceleration of the rate of increase during the 1960s. McClintock and Avison (1968, p. 38) calculate an increase in indictable offenses against the person of 82 percent between 1955 and 1965. This represents, in particular, an increase in malicious wounding and indecent assaults against

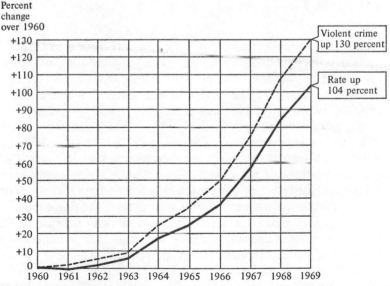

Figure 2 Crimes of violence, 1960–1969; limited to murder, forcible rape, robbery, and aggravated assault. (F. B. I. chart.)

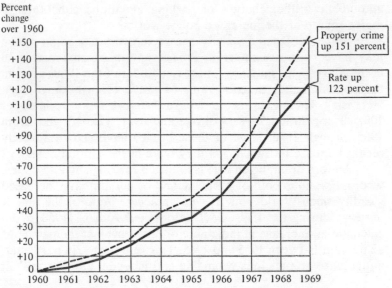

Figure 3 Crimes against property, 1960-1969; limited to burglary, larceny of $50 and over, and automobile theft. (F. B. I. chart.)

women. Even more striking increases are recorded for crimes against property. Robbery and breaking-and-entering offenses, for example, increased 239 percent during this decade (p. 42). Juvenile cases before the courts in England and Wales *doubled* between 1955 and 1968 (Power et al., 1972).

This trend continued in England and Wales through the late 1960s and had not abated as of the early 1970s. The year 1970 saw a rise of 6.0 percent over the preceding year in convictions for all indictable offenses among males and a slightly higher increase of 7.8 percent for females. The increase in convictions for crimes of violence was even greater than this overall rise. The proportion of convictions of males for violent attacks in 1970 increased 12.2 percent over 1969, and this increase was more than matched by a rise of 16.5 percent in convictions of females for violent crimes (Command Paper #4708, 1970, tables 13 and 15a).

Chapter 3 will note that counting crime is difficult and that these figures may be challenged. The challenge is based on the fact that there is no way of ascertaining the "true amount of crime" or of distinguishing an "actual increase" from a "registration increase" in official crime rates. Nevertheless, the "unobtrusive measures" of crime, such as sales of defensive devices, confirm the official records. The publicly noticeable predatory crimes are both *reported and perceived* to have increased worldwide in recent years. The reported increase has been associated with the rising affluence of industrialized countries in Europe and Asia, and with the movement of tribal peoples from the hinterlands to the cities of such changing African states as Ghana, Nigeria, and Zambia. The perceived short-run increase is cited for rich, egalitarian, and recently peaceful nations like Sweden, and for rich, authoritarian, and recently belligerent nations like Japan (Toby, 1969). It is apparently experienced in democratic, new societies like Israel (Shoham, 1966), and in democratic, old societies like Great Britain. Worldwide, if one can judge from records compiled by the United Nations (1960, 1965a), the apparent increase in delinquency and criminality has been experienced principally by free, rich, developed countries and has been less noted among underdeveloped nations (with the exception of those undergoing rapid urbanization) and totalitarian nations. The concern with crime is a shared domestic sentiment among affluent societies.

Table 1   Crime Rates per 100,000 Population Age 7 Years and Over, Canada, 1965–1970

Offense	1965	1966	1967	1968	1969	1970
Murder (includes capital and non-capital murder)	1.5	1.3	1.6	1.8	1.9	2.3
Attempted murder	0.7	0.8	0.8	1.0	1.2	1.4
Violent rape	3.9	3.9	4.5	5.0	5.6	5.8
Wounding	5.0	5.8	5.9	7.3	9.0	8.8
Robbery	34.0	34.0	41.6	47.1	55.1	62.5
Offensive weapons	20.0	21.7	23.7	28.2	30.6	34.6
Breaking and entering	588.5	607.9	688.0	814.6	888.3	954.9
Theft—Motor vehicles	232.2	236.0	258.0	290.7	327.1	337.5
Theft over $50	414.1	451.4	500.7	557.5	657.9	806.1
Frauds	197.5	225.0	239.1	272.0	317.5	361.5

Source: Summarized from *Crime Statistics,* 1967 and 1970. Ottawa: Dominion Bureau of *Statistics.*

SOCIOLOGICAL VERSUS PSYCHOLOGICAL QUESTIONS

The public question in response to this concern is, "Why is there so much crime?"—or, better, "What accounts for changes in crime rates and differences in crime rates between populations?"

This kind of question is a sociological one. It asks for an explanation of the behavior of aggregates. It need not receive the same kind of answer, then, as the psychological question that asks "Why did he do it?" Questions about a personal career or about the motivation and best treatment of an individual are psychological questions.

It is true that the sociological answer to a sociological question may rest, implicitly, upon some assumptions about human psychology. It is also true that some plausible explanations of collective behavior are offered in psychological language. It remains an open issue, however, whether the kinds of theories offered as explanations of individual behavior help or hinder the building of sound theories of collective events. Just as the movement of clouds may be explained without reference to the molecules of moisture within them, so too may the behavior of aggregates be understood without reference to the characteristics of the individuals within them. For example, the conclusions of Chapter 10 are statements about the conditions associated with increases or decreases in crime rates. It will be noted that most of these propositions are sociological. They are descriptions of the behavior of aggregates that do not require psychological terminology to make them true.

In evaluating the answers given by criminologists to the public's question, it should be borne in mind that it is the intent of the citizen's question not merely to satisfy curiosity, but also to seek ways to reduce criminal activity. A test of the explanations to be described is whether, with adequate evidence, they point to conditions or events changes in which would reduce crime.

The Meaning of Crime

"Crime," it has been said, means more than that which Everyman has in mind when he uses the word. *As defined by law,* a crime is an intentional violation of the criminal law, committed without defense or excuse, and penalized by the state (Tappan, 1947). This definition encompasses a wide range of acts from being vagrant, boisterous and drunk; to blocking traffic; to selling the sexual use of one's body or that of others; through all the ways in which people steal from each other; and on through the varieties of damage and death that members of a society inflict upon each other. This *legal* definition of crime is at once more broad than the popular image of "crime" and more limited and more precise than the *moral* definition, which uses the word "criminal" as synonymous with "sinful," "wrong," "bad," or "evil." At law, a "crime" is an intentional act that violates the prescriptions or proscriptions of the criminal law under conditions in which no legal excuse applies and where there is a state with the power to codify such laws and to enforce penalties in response to their breach. This definition says several things that require amplification. It holds that (1) there is no crime without law and without a state to punish the breach of law; (2) there is no crime where an act that would otherwise be offensive is justified by law; (3) there is no crime without intention; and (4) there is no crime where the offender is deemed "incompetent," that is, without "capacity." Each of these elements has its own history, its peculiar difficulties, and a range of implications.

NO CRIME WITHOUT LAW

The legal idea of a crime restricts its meaning to those breaches of custom that a society has recognized in either its common or its statutory law. This restriction acknowledges that there can be no crime without a *state* to define it and punish it. A state, an organization with a monopoly of power, is required to enforce the law and to attach penalties to its violation. Laws that are not backed by force are less than law and more like agreements or aspirations. Laws without penalties are hollow. By this token, "war crimes" are figures of speech rather than legally constituted crimes.

Law and Liberty

The conception of crime that places it within the boundaries of *law* has strong implications for civil liberties. The maxim that there can be "no crime without a law" means that people cannot be charged with offenses unless these have been defined. The protection of citizens against vague charges depends upon this ideal—that there must be a clear statement setting the limits of one's conduct in relation to others and defining the limits of the state's power to interfere in our lives.

This ideal has promoted other considerations having to do with the formulation of "good law" as opposed to "poor law," particularly as good and poor laws are perceived in the Anglo-American tradition. These additional ideals are that the criminal law must be *specific* and that it must be *applied uniformly*. Good laws *specify actions* that are criminal and *specify penalties* for each breach. Poor laws are omnibus condemnations such as one from a dead German code which prohibited "behaving in a manner contrary to the common standards of right conduct." This kind of phrasing lacks the specificity that is an ideal of Western criminal jurisprudence.

Similarly, it is an objective of modern jurisprudence that laws be framed and enforced so as to guarantee their uniform application regardless of the extralegal characteristics of the offender. As we shall see, this ideal is easier to express in general terms than it is to assess in particular instances.

Not All Wrongs Are Crimes

The legal conception of crime as a breach of the criminal law has an additional implication. It narrows the definition of wrongs. Not all the injuries we give each other are recognized by law, nor are all the injuries recognized by law called "crimes."

For example, North American and European law recognizes *breaches of contract or trust,* so that people who feel themselves thus harmed may seek a remedy from the law. Similarly, the law acknowledges other injuries to person, reputation, and property, called "torts," which, while not breaches of contract, may entitle one person to compensation from another. The distinction between the *wrongs defined by contract and tort law* and *wrongs defined by criminal law* is "who pursues the offense." A crime is deemed an offense against the public, even though it may have a particular victim and a particular complainant. It is the state that prosecutes crime, but it is individuals who "pursue" offenders against tort and contractual laws.

NO CRIME WHERE AN ACT IS JUSTIFIED BY LAW

A second category of "defense or excuse" against the application of the criminal law consists of legally recognized justifications for committing what otherwise would be called a crime. Both literate and preliterate societies recognize the right of an individual to defend himself and his loved ones against mortal attack. The injury or death that may be inflicted against one's assailant in self-defense is thereby excused.

Similarly, all states accord themselves the right of self-defense. With the French philosopher Sorel (1908), states distinguish between *force,* the legitimate use of physical coercion constrained by law, and *violence,* its illegitimate use.[1] The damage that occurs through the state's application of force is excused from the criminal sanction. Thus homicide committed in the policeman's line of duty may be deemed "justifiable" and the injury defined as noncriminal.

NO CRIME WITHOUT INTENTION

As a result of our moral and legal history, the criminal law tries to limit its definition of criminal conduct to intentional action. "Accidents" supposedly do not count as crimes. As the American jurist Oliver Wendell Holmes, Jr., put it, the law attempts to distinguish between "stumbling over a dog and kicking it." If "a dog can tell the difference between being kicked and being stumbled over," as Justice Holmes believed, so too can judges and juries.

This assumption seems plausible, but it gets sorely tried in practice. It gets tested and disputed because, in real life, some "accidents" are still defined as the actor's fault. "Negligence" may be criminal.

All criminal laws operate with some psychological model of man. According to the model prevalent in Western criminal law, the "reasonable person" ought to use judgment in controlling his behavior in order that some classes of "accidents" will not occur.

[1]People *do* use these words as Sorel said they did. Legitimate injury is called "force," or some other term less loaded than "violence." Injury that is deemed illegitimate is "violence." For example, Blumenthal and her colleagues (1972) studied the opinions of a representative sample of American men between the ages of 16 and 64. Among the findings were these:

(a) "Fifty-eight per cent of American men think that burning a draft card is violence, in and of itself."
(b) "Thirty-eight per cent think student protest is violence."
(c) "Twenty-two per cent feel sit-ins are violence."
(d) "Only 35 per cent of American men define 'police shooting looters' as violence."
(e) "Only 56 per cent define 'police beating students' [as violence]" (pp. 1300–1301).

For example, the reckless driver may not have intended to kill a pedestrian, but his "accident" is judged to have been the probable consequence of his erratic driving. The person licensed to manipulate an automobile is assumed to know the likely results of his actions. He is assumed, further, to be able to control his actions, and he is held accountable, therefore, regardless of his lack of homicidal intent.

Western criminal law is based upon this changing, and challenged, set of assumptions. It therefore qualifies its desire to restrict "crime" to intentional breaches of the criminal code. This qualification is accomplished by distinguishing between classes of crime—impulsive rather than premeditated, accidental rather than intentional. Since the law wishes to hold able, but negligent, people to account, it includes the concept of "constructive intent," a term that stretches "intent" to cover the unintended, injurious consequences of some of our behavior. The penalties for doing damage through negligence are usually lighter than those for being deliberately criminal, yet the term "crime" covers both classes of conduct.

Intention and Motivation

Motivation is sometimes used by lawyers to prove intention. The two concepts are not the same, however.

An intention is that which a person "has in mind" when he acts. It is his purpose, the result he wishes to effect. The criminal law is particularly concerned to penalize illegal intent when it is acted upon.

A motive is, strictly speaking, that which moves a person to act. The word may apply to an intention, but it need not. Intentions are but one of the many motors of action.

Intention is narrow and specific; motivation is broad and general. A jewel thief may *intend* to steal jewels; his *motive* is to become richer than he is. The motive is widespread and does not distinguish one thief from many others. His intention, to steal jewels, is more peculiar, and but one possible way of satisfying his motivation.

An intention may or may not move a person. It may remain

a wish, a plot, a dream. *A criminal intention, without the action, is not a crime.*

Motives, on the other hand, may move men haphazardly, purposelessly, without the focus of intent. A motive may be purely physiological and variously gratified. It may even be "unconscious," if we believe the psychoanalysts. *An intention, however, is only something cognitive.* The word "intention" is reserved for thoughts, for verbalizable plans. It does not refer to those subterranean urges or those physiological fires that may have kindled the ideas.

Since "intent" is part of the definition of crime, prosecutors in Western countries must establish such purpose in the actor, and they sometimes try to do this by constructing "the motive." The strategy of demonstrating intention from motivation calls for showing the "good reasons" why a person might act as the accused is alleged to have done. The good reasons, the alleged motives, may all have been there, however, without the actor's having formed the criminal intent which the prosecutor is attempting to establish. This is simply because "good reasons" are not always the real ones.

The distinction between the movers of action and intentions becomes important as criminal law takes heed of another qualification in its definition of crime, the qualification that people shall be held responsible for their actions, and hence liable to the criminal law, *only if* they are mentally competent. The legal meaning of "intention" is embedded in the concept of competence.

NO CRIME WITHOUT CAPACITY

The condemnation that is implicit in calling actions "criminal" is based on moral premises. It is part of our morality to believe that a person ought not to be blamed for actions that are beyond his control. The notion that behavior is within or beyond one's control rests upon conceptions of "capacity" or "competence." These conceptions, in turn, are cultural. They vary in time and with place, and they remain disputed today. The dispute concerns the criteria of competence, but it does not challenge the legal and moral principle that a person must be somehow "able" before he can be judged culpable.

Among modern states, the tests of competence are cognitive. They look to *mens rea,* the "thing in the mind," as definitive of the ability to form a criminal intent and as the regulator of one's actions. *Until* "the mind"[2] is sufficiently well formed to control the actor's behavior, and *unless* it operates in normal fashion, Anglo-American criminal law *excludes* the agent from criminal liability. Actors are considered "not responsible" or "less responsible" for their offenses if the offense has been produced by someone who is (1) acting under duress, (2) under age, or (3) "insane."

Crime Under Duress

The first exclusion consists of criminal deeds performed "against one's will." The law recognizes circumstances in which a person may be forced into a criminal action under threat. Since intent and the capacity to act freely are diminished when this is the case, so too is legal responsibility.

Age and Capacity

A second application of the moral principle that people must have some minimal mental capacity before they ought to be held legally accountable has to do with limitations of age. Laws of modern nations agree that persons below a certain age must be excluded from criminal liability. The number of years required to attain legal responsibility varies by jurisdiction, but the legal principle persists in declaring individuals "under age" to be "incompetent." *Nonage* means just that, that a person is a "legal infant." He may be protected by laws, but he is not subject to the criminal law. In most Anglo-American jurisdictions a child under the age of seven years cannot be held responsible for crime.

[2]Placing the word "mind" in quotation marks indicates its vagueness. As with many other useful terms, "mind" has many meanings. It may be interesting to consider how you use the word.

The Idea of Juvenile Delinquency Above the age of 7 and below that of 21, young people in literate lands are variously categorized as to their legal responsibility for crime. In the common law of English-speaking states, it was assumed that a "legal infant," someone between the ages of 7 and 14, did not have the capacity to form a criminal intent, although in cases of serious crimes this assumption might be refuted by showing that the actor could distinguish right from wrong. Between the ages of 14 and 21 years, the common law assumed capacity adequate for legal responsibility, but this assumption, too, was open to legal rebuttal. Beyond 21 years, age was no longer a defense against liability for one's criminal acts.

As the common law became codified, these assumptions were carried into effect, with qualifications, of course, in particular jurisdictions. The statutory laws of the "developed" countries have come to define a special status of offender called a "juvenile delinquent." The upper age limit of juvenile delinquency is 18 years in most Western jurisdictions. Beyond this age, a person is treated as an adult in regard to the criminal law. This age limit varies, however, with the jurisdiction and, sometimes with the sex of the youth. In the province of Alberta, for example, the upper age limit for treating girls as juvenile delinquents is 18 years. For boys this limit is 16 years. This "reverse sexism" not only ignores the fact that girls mature earlier than boys; it also produces some fascinating anomalies. "For example, in Alberta, one sixteen-year-old boy was convicted of *contributing to juvenile delinquency* and sentenced to a short term in the Fort Saskatchewan gaol. His 'offence' was that he was guilty of having sexual intercourse with his steady girl friend, a young woman who was nearly eighteen" (Cousineau and Veevers, 1972, pp. 246–247; italics added).

The tendency in most industrialized countries has been to raise the age limit so that more young offenders might be treated as delinquents rather than as criminals. There are some jurisdictions in which a legal borderland is defined, commonly between the ages of 16 and 18, within which youths may come under the jurisdiction of both juvenile and adult courts, or either, depending upon the gravity of their offenses.

The justification of a special status for youthful offenders rests, again, upon the moral premise that people ought not to feel the full force of the criminal law unless they are "responsible" for their actions. This moral maxim has been bolstered by a practical concern that seeks to *protect* children from harmful influences, *prevent* their waywardness, and *guide* them into acceptable patterns of conduct when they have given indication of deviation that might become chronic.

This mixture of legal purposes has meant that the definition of delinquency in Anglo-American law includes the commission of crime, but it also includes as the object of legal attention some noncriminal conduct and some noxious circumstances. Among the varied jurisdictions of the United States, for example, an "underage" person may be treated as a delinquent for such matters as:

Being habitually truant
Being incorrigible
Growing up in idleness or crime
Immoral or indecent conduct
Habitually using vile, obscene, or vulgar language in public
Attempting to marry without consent in violation of the law
Being given to sexual irregularities
Using tobacco or alcoholic beverages or being addicted to drugs
Habitually wandering about railroad yards or tracks or wandering about the streets at night (Sussman, 1959, p. 20.)

It is apparent that the extension of the word "delinquency" to cover more than youthful *criminal* activity increases the risk that the law may be vague and that efforts to protect children may violate their civil liberties. It is notable that the laws of Asian, Middle Eastern and Latin American countries include *only* criminal conduct in their attention to youthful offenders (United Nations, 1953, 1958a, 1958b, 1965b). The legal responsibility of juveniles may be diminished under these statutes, but the status of "a delinquent," if it is defined at all, refers to one who has broken the criminal law.

The federal law of Canada reads like a blend of definitions.

On the one hand, it restricts delinquency to violations of the criminal law, but, on the other hand, it extends the definition to cover "any other act" that might get one into trouble with provincial laws. It defines a delinquent as "any child who violates any provision of the Criminal Code or any Dominion or provincial statute, or of any by-law or ordinance of any municipality, or who is liable by reason of any other act to be committed to an industrial school or juvenile reformatory under the provisions of any Dominion or provincial statute" (Duhamel, 1962). In its application, then, this definition is broadened by the various provinces that may make separate provisions for the segregated court treatment and differential sentencing of juveniles.

It is here, as in the debate about insanity as a defense, that the legal profession battles with the "helping" professions. Social workers, psychiatrists, and some judges would use the judicial system as part of a welfare system that tries to meet "children's needs." Lawyers, on the other hand, are chary of expanding the power of state agencies to control children under the guise of helping them, unless adequate legal safeguards are built in. The attorneys' caution derives from the fact that many of the juvenile delinquency statutes do not satisfy the legal ideal that *actions* be specified before state control can be applied. "Having done something" is more readily determinable than "being something." Just as we should not want the criminal law to apply to those of us who are "in a state of criminality," lawyers are generally opposed to the idea of charging children with being "in a state of delinquency" (Cousineau and Veevers, 1972, p. 244).

In Summary All definitions of crime mark off some ages below which people are deemed not to have the capacity for crime. In addition, the literate countries tend to define a borderland, occupied by youths, within which legal liability is acknowledged, but diminished, and in which the stigmatizing effect of the criminal sanction is avoided or attenuated by special treatment.

Insanity as a Defense

A third excuse by which one may reduce or escape the application of the criminal law is the claim that the offender's capacity to control his behavior has been damaged. The locus of the damage, the "place" in which one looks for this incapacity, is, again, the mind.

Defects of the mind seem clear in the extremities of senility, idiocy, and the incapacitating psychoses. They are clear, too, as one is able to link abnormal performance to lesions of the central nervous system. However, it is in the gray area between these extremities and more normal behavior that citizens, lawyers, and their psychiatric advisors dispute the capacity of offenders.

It bears repeating that this dispute rests upon moral considerations. The quarrel is stimulated by the belief that only people who "choose" their conduct deserve punishment for their crimes, that "accidents" and "irresistible impulses" do not count, and that other classes of behavior beyond one's control should not be penalized. The philosophical questions opened by this debate range beyond our present concern. These questions include, at a minimum, the ancient issues of free will and determinism, of the justice and the value of praise and blame, and of the proper ends of the criminal law.

These questions intrude upon the law and ensure that attempts to define mental competence are all imperfect. They are less than perfect because moral conceptions of the "causes" of behavior color the assignment of responsibility to actors. They are less than perfect, also, because the boundaries of the defense of insanity move with the justifications of the criminal law. That is, who we believe to be "incompetent" before the law varies with what we want the law to do. These points will be amplified as we consider the tests of incapacity and their relationship to the justifications of the criminal law.

Tests of Insanity   The criminal law attempts to evaluate capacity from signs of sanity. "Sanity" refers to soundness, to wholeness. Being less than whole, being of "unsound mind," is, therefore, a legal defense against accountability to the law.

The definition of insanity is difficult, however, and an embarrassment to a profession which, like the law, depends so heavily upon the precision of its terms. The word "insane" has poor credentials among psychologists and psychiatrists. Nevertheless, the law has looked to these students of the mind for help in assessing the competence of defendants. In the Netherlands, Denmark, Norway, and Sweden, the test of insanity is simply the testimony of such medical experts. In Belgium, France, Italy, and Switzerland, the test is psychiatric judgment concerning the ability of the offender to understand what he was doing at the time of his crime and to control his behavior. Anglo-American law has attempted to guide judges, juries, and psychiatrists in assessing the competence of defendants by formulating more specific tests that have been used alone or in qualified combinations. The most popular of these guidelines are the *M'Naghten rule, the "irresistible impulse" rule, and Durham's rule.* As with all regulations that seek to implement moral sentiments, none of these principles is perfectly clear. All three contain ambiguities, and all three have been under attack. However, they remain, in various forms, the principal rules by which judges and juries under Anglo-American law attempt to distinguish between sane offenders and insane ones.

The M'Naghten rule This provides the only definition of insanity in Great Britain and 31 of the United States. The rule, promulgated in an English trial in 1843, is

> that every man is to be presumed to be sane, and . . . that to establish a defence on the ground of insanity, it must be clearly proved that, at the time of the committing of the act, the party accused was labouring under such a defect of reason, from disease of the mind, as not to know the nature and quality of the act he was doing; or if he did know it, that he did not know he was doing what was wrong [Goldstein, 1967, p. 45].

Here, as elsewhere, common words become cloudy when one attempts to use them with precision, and each of the key terms in the M'Naghten formula has been debated. "Disease of the mind" is vague. "Wrong" may mean morally so or legally so. The meaning of the phrase "the nature and quality of the act" has been disputed, and the simple verb "to know" is troublesome. Critics of the M'Naghten rule have argued that "knowing" may refer only to intellectual awareness and have wanted to substitute a psychiatric sense of "knowing" that would include emotional appreciation as well as cognitive understanding. As employed in Canada, the "knowledge test" within M'Naghten's rule has been broadened so that "the act must necessarily involve more than mere knowledge that the act is being committed; there must be an appreciation of the factors involved in the act and a mental capacity to measure and foresee the consequences of the violent conduct" (Royal Commission, 1955, pp. 12–13).

As the professions of psychology and psychiatry developed and grew in authority, they attacked M'Naghten's rule for the ambiguities in its language and added to this attack the claim that under M'Naghten's tests psychotic persons could be and had been declared sane. An American judge, J. Biggs (1955), has documented cases of this sort. For example, in *The People v. Willard,* 1907, Willard was formally declared insane by a California court, became enraged at the commitment proceedings, and killed a sheriff who tried to block his escape. Under M'Naghten's rule, then applicable, Willard was judged to have known the nature and quality of his act and that it was wrong, and he was hanged as a legally sane person despite a diagnosis of "alcoholic paranoia."

With the popularizing of psychiatry and, in particular, of the ideas of psychoanalysis, legislators have taken account of the possibility that "knowledge of right and wrong" is only one test of capacity. It is now recognized that some psychotic individuals may be moved by beliefs which we regard as false, but which they believe true and over which they seem to have no control. When such a delusion can be shown to have caused a crime, some jurisdictions excuse the agent as incompetent. Canada, for example, adds the defense of *delusive incapacity* to the M'Naghten rule in defining insanity (Duhamel, 1962, sec.16), but it qualifies this excuse by saying that "a person . . . shall not be acquitted on the ground of insanity *unless* the delusions caused him to believe in the existence of a state of things that, if it existed, would have justified or excused his act or omission" (italics added).

The "irresistible impulse" or "control" test This test represents a similar qualification of M'Naghten's rule that is applied in 18 of the United States and in the American federal courts. A defense against criminal conviction on the grounds of insanity is made first by using the M'Naghten rule and then by applying a control test. Such a test acknowledges that there are "mental diseases" in which cognition is relatively unimpaired but volition is damaged. Some people who know the difference between right and wrong seem, nevertheless, to be unable to control their actions.

The trouble with this principle is, of course, that its application requires a wisdom beyond the skills of psychiatrists. It requires finer psychological tools than are presently available to be able to distinguish reliably between behavior that is *uncontrollable* and behavior that is *uncontrolled.* On this issue, as with other situations in which psychiatric experts are called on to determine "mental disease," the battles between the experts testifying for the prosecution and those testifying for the defense do not promote confidence in their science (Hakeem, 1958).

Durham's rule   This rule represents a further extension of psychiatric influence on the definition of insanity. Durham's rule enunciates a principle which had been recommended in 1953 in a report by the British Royal Commission on Capital Punishment and which has been amplified in a series of American trials. The principle holds that the mind which controls human beings is a functional unit in which emotion and reason are blended, and that the separation of knowing from feeling and willing, apparently required by M'Naghten's rule, is false to our knowledge of man. Durham's rule would hold people responsible for their conduct only when their emotions, their "will power," and their thoughts appeared to be normal. In *Durham v. United States,* a trial held in the District of Columbia in 1954, Judge Bazelon wrote the opinion that "an accused is not criminally responsible if his unlawful act was the product of mental disease or mental defect."

On its face, Durham's rule appears more humane and more modern than the M'Naghten principle. In practice, however, it turns out to be vague. The difficulties in applying its test of sanity account for the fact that only the District of Columbia, Maine, and the Virgin Islands have adopted it.

The rule is vague because it does not equate a "mental disease" with a psychosis, as the latter is understood by psychiatrists. It provides no standard, therefore, by which to judge the capacity of a defendant to control his behavior. Judges and juries are left dependent upon the unreliable estimates of psychiatric experts (Arthur, 1969; Ash, 1949; Eron, 1966; Goldberg and Werts, 1966; Mehlman, 1952; Schmidt and Fonda, 1956; Zigler and Phillips, 1965). The poorly articulated notion of a mental disorder allows such fuzzy categories of character as "psychopathy," "sociopathy," "character defect," and " emotionally unstable personality" to be certified as evidence of a person's lack of responsibility for his crimes. As part of the "mental health" movement, the Durham principle encourages the tendency to regard disapproved deviations, like homosexuality or addiction to narcotics, as constituting in themselves signs of "mental disease" (Goldstein, 1967, p. 246). Finally, the criminal act itself can be, and has been, used as evidence of the "mental sickness" which is alleged to have caused it and which, it is argued, should excuse the offender. This is particularly so with bizarre crimes. Here, for example, is a verbatim exchange between a defense counsel and the prosecution's psychiatrist, debating the sanity of a 17-year-old boy who had murdered and dismembered a young woman previously unknown to him (Nettler, 1970, p. 71):

Defense Counsel: "Whether one calls him insane or psychotic, he's a sick man. That's obvious."

Psychiatrist: "I should think that's largely a matter of terminology."

Defense Counsel: "Do you mean to suggest that a man could do what that boy has done and not be sick?"

Other tests The kind of thinking that calls criminal conduct "insane" if the crime is sufficiently bizarre has been attacked in the Model Penal Code drawn up by The American Law Institute (1953). The Institute's proposed redefinition of "responsibility," adopted in a revised form by Vermont, holds that a person shall not be held accountable for a crime "if at the time of such conduct as a result of mental disease or defect he lacks substantial capacity either to appreciate the criminality of his conduct or to conform his conduct to the requirements of law." This proposal adds, however, that "the terms 'mental disease or defect' do *not* include an abnormality manifested *only* by repeated criminal or otherwise anti-social conduct" (ALI, 1953, sec. 4.01; italics added).

The debate continues as to who should be held responsible for his actions. It is a debate that moves with the moral tides. The subjective character of definitions of insanity and the intrusion of moral preconceptions upon legal categories are demonstrated by the fact that, while in England one-third to one-half of homicide offenders are classified as legally insane, in the United States only 2 to 4 percent of these offenders are so classified (Wolfgang and Ferracuti, 1967, pp. 201–202).

Psychiatrists versus lawyers   Attempts to expand the defense of insanity to include all those defects of the mind that discomfort us have run into opposition from lawyers, courts, and the psychological professions themselves. Simon and Shackelford (1965) surveyed opinions of the defense of insanity among a national sample of American lawyers and psychiatrists. While 77 percent of the psychiatrists expressed confidence in their expert testimony in criminal trials, only 44.5 percent of the lawyers expressed confidence in psychiatric expertise. A large majority of the attorneys (72 percent) approved of the system of using experts to challenge experts, but only a minority of psychiatrists (31 percent) agreed. As might be expected, the two professions disagreed also on the relationship between "serious criminal activity and mental illness." Table 2 shows that *half* of the psychiatrists believed that "anyone who commits a serious crime is mentally ill" or "most people who commit serious crimes are mentally ill." Only a *third* of the lawyers agreed. Only 15 percent of the physicians, but over a third of the lawyers, believed that there was *no relationship* between mental illness and serious crime.

The continuing resistance of the law to psychiatric intrusion has been documented by Krash (1961), who studied cases in the District of Columbia in which the Durham rule was pleaded but rejected. His research adds to the catalogue of judicial skepticism about the scientific status of psychiatry and of judicial reluctance to view most crime as a symptom of sickness. Judges and juries continue to believe in "free will," in holding people accountable

Table 2   Psychiatrists' and Lawyers' Opinions On the Relationship Between Criminal Activity and Mental Illness

Which best states the relationship between serious criminal activity and mental illness?	Percent of	
	Psychiatrists	Lawyers
a. Anyone who commits a serious crime is mentally ill.	8.0	3.7
b. Most people who commit serious crimes are mentally ill.	41.8	29.2
c. Most people who commit serious crimes are *not* mentally ill.	25.1	20.3
d. There is no relationship between mental illness and serious crime.	15.1	34.2
e. No answer.	10.0	12.6

Source: Reprinted, with permission, from Simon and Shackelford, 1965, p. 417.

for their wrongs, and in the efficacy of punishment as a deterrent.

At the same time that courts have been hesitant to absolve "mentally diseased" offenders of responsibility for their crimes, there have been voices within the psychiatric profession claiming that the very idea of "mental illness" is a myth (Szasz, 1961). It has also been argued that allowing psychiatrists to judge who is and who is not accountable for his unlawful conduct usurps the role of juries and runs the risk of violating the civil liberties of defendants. Both the Soviet Union and the United States have been accused of using "mental hospitals" as substitutes for prisons for persons distasteful to the regime (Bukovsky, 1972; Gorbanevskaya, 1972; Medvedev, 1971; Szasz, 1957, 1958, 1963). Some novelists, and other observers of the social scene, have been alert to the manner in which punishment may be disguised as "treatment." The English philosopher C. S. Lewis phrased the possibility this way: "If crime and disease are to be regarded as the same thing, it follows that any state of mind which our masters choose to call 'disease' can be treated as crime, and compulsorily cured" (1953, p. 224).

In summary   The various tests of sanity are fallible and can never be made perfect. They reflect our changing conceptions of human nature and of morality. The current vogue, sponsored by the social sciences, has been to shift the burden of responsibility from individuals to their environments, to place the blame for offensive acts not on the criminal, but on the social forces that presumably shaped him (Nettler, 1972a). The Durham rule expresses this train of thought, the logical conclusion of which is to regard all undesirable conduct as "sick" and subject to "treatment" by physicians of the body social. However, until a "brave new world" is reached in which all deviance is engineered out of us (cf. Huxley, 1960), it may be expected that states will continue to hold citizens responsible for broad ranges of their behavior, and the defense of insanity will not be available to most of us.

Some personal comments on "treatment" It is doubtful whether being "treated" by the state for one's crimes is better for one than merely being restrained. The stigma of being officially "crazy" is at least as great as, or greater than, that of being officially criminal. Further, there is evidence that judges and probation officers who are oriented toward treatment perceive more facets of deviance, lawful or not, as ominous. Practitioners of psychic rehabilitation are sensitized to the supposed symptomatic meaning of abnormalities and regard more of them as premonitory of graver offenses to come. There is also reason to believe that those who prefer to treat offenders rather than to punish or restrain them may favor *longer* incarceration (Cousineau and Veevers, 1972, pp. 257–258).

To examine the possibly punitive nature of the orientation toward treatment, Wheeler and his colleagues (1968) interviewed "police chiefs, police juvenile bureau officers, juvenile probation officers, juvenile court judges, and psychiatrists who work in juvenile court settings" in 28 court jurisdictions within the Boston Metropolitan Area (p. 34). The interviews were supplemented by structured attitudinal measures designed to assess the respondent's orientation to delinquency and its control. Contrary to expectation, it was found that

> the judges who take the more severe actions are those who read more about delinquents, who read from professional journals, who do not wear their robes in court, and who are more permissive in outlook. They are also the younger judges (who characteristically express more liberal attitudes on these and other issues) and the

judges who rank their own experience with delinquents as of relatively less importance than other factors in influencing their views.

Severity of the sanctions, therefore, appears to be positively related to the degree to which a judge uses a professional, humanistic, social welfare ideology in making his decisions. . . . Judges who are most favorably disposed toward the mental health movement and least committed to more traditional doctrines of punishment and deterrence tend to take what is commonly regarded as the most severe actions regarding delinquents [pp. 55–56].

A similar finding is reported by Wilson (1968) who compared two large American police departments to find out whether "professionalization" made any difference in the handling of juvenile offenders. Wilson's conclusion is that "a 'professionalized' police department tends to expose a *higher* proportion of juveniles to the possibility of court action, despite the more 'therapeutic' and sophisticated verbal formulas of its officers. . . . " (p. 19; italics added.)

Given the severity of "treatment," some personal advice follows: never let yourself fall into the hands of the "official helper." You won't like it.

CAPACITY AND THE JUSTIFICATIONS OF THE CRIMINAL LAW

The guidelines for judging the capacity of offenders are imperfect. They continue to be debated because our moral beliefs find the causes of human behavior in different locations. These beliefs move responsibility between the actor and his environment so that "who is to blame" and who deserves punishment are points endlessly disputed. Dispute is fostered, too, by the fact that *justifications* of the criminal law are supported by assumptions about the conditions under which human beings can control their own behavior. What we want the law to do and what we believe it does have bearing upon whom we are willing to excuse from criminal liability.

The criminal law is justified by what it supposedly does. If the law is to be respected for what it does, it must be applied in ways that achieve specific ends—or, more accurately, it must be applied in ways that are *believed* to achieve these ends.

The law serves a changing mixture of objectives, however, and this instability of its objectives encourages the continuing quarrel about who should, and who should not, be held responsible for his conduct.

The criminal law is commonly considered to be useful in achieving five ends, some of which are in conflict. These objectives receive various titles, but they can be recognized as attempts to reform the offender, to restrain him, to deter others, to revive communion symbolically, and to achieve justice. All these functions are relevant to the issue of who should or should not be excused for "incompetence."

Rehabilitation

It is popularly assumed that the criminal law is applied, or ought to be applied, to correct the offender. If the law is employed to improve the criminal's conduct, then it is believed that the candidate for rehabilitation must be capable of recovery with the attention the law provides. This means, to the conventional way of thinking, that the offender must have a mind capable of guiding his behavior and amenable to education. The idea implicit in this justification of the law is that, just as one does not pummel the hydrocephalic idiot for failing at mathematics, so one does not penalize the criminal who "can't help himself."

Restraint *— Segregation*

The law is also used to restrain a person from injuring others. As regards this objective, there need be no concern for correcting the offender. Indeed, too, there need be no concern with punishing him. Attention is given, rather, to controlling him.

Definitions of capacity enter into the problem of achieving restraint principally in determining *how* the lawbreaker is to be repressed. Recently it has been our practice to restrain sane criminals in prisons and insane ones in mental hospitals. The growing emphasis upon the rehabilitative function of "correctional institutions" has meant, however, that some prisons now have as many psychotherapeutic facilities as do mental hospitals (Goldstein, 1967). How frustrating incarceration in prison is, as compared with incarceration in a hospital, is an open question (Goldstein, 1967; Kesey, 1964).

Deterrence

A major justification for the criminal law is that its application will deter you and me from committing the crime for which someone else has been punished. This justification assumes that you and I are sufficiently normal to get the message. It is further assumed, with some good evidence, that you and I will get the message more clearly, the more closely we identify ourselves with the miscreant. It is believed that the more we resemble the punished person, the more forcefully his penalty threatens us and deters us. It is assumed that, if we have felt the same desires as the punished person and have come close to committing similar crimes, the punishment provides us with a deterrent example. If, however, we healthy people observe "sick minds" being punished, then, presumably, the law's lesson is lost on us; in such cases, the deterrent example is diluted because we perceive the offender as different from ourselves.

The determination of capacity is considered to be important, therefore, as a means of increasing the efficacy of the law as a deterrent. It is not *known* how effective this determination is in increasing deterrence, but some jurists *believe* it to be very important.

Morals seem more important here than *consequences*. Our moral beliefs find it cruel and unjust to punish persons who are "not responsible for their actions," regardless of the societal ends that such punishment might serve. The test of capacity tries, in a fumbling manner, to define persons who are sufficiently different from us that they may be excused from accountability under the criminal law.

Symbolism

A neglected, but important, function of the criminal law is symbolic. Exercise of the criminal law reaffirms what we are for and what we are against. Thus the courtroom becomes one of the various educational theaters every society uses.

Capacity is part of this legal drama because, again, the drama depends upon identification. One must be able to feel himself in the roles portrayed if the dramatic lesson is to be apprehended. The symbolic and the deterrent functions of the law use capacity in the same way: it is, presumably, the "normal mind," not the defective one, that can appreciate the threats and the symbolism of the law.

Retribution

The oldest conception of justice is balance: the idea that evil ought not to go unpunished, that the wrong a person does should be returned to him in equal degree, if not in kind.

Today it is unpopular to defend retribution as such. The idea of retribution runs against some facets of the Christian ethic and is opposed by "enlightened" opinion. It is also held that retribution is impractical: revenge, it is said, costs too much (Nettler, 1959b, p. 384).

Despite the unpopularity of retribution as a stated objective of the criminal law, the impulse to take revenge persists. This impulse is part of a perennial and universal sense of justice. Although we no longer use the harsh phrasing of the code of the Babylonian king Hammurabi (1760 B.C.), which recommended "an eye for an eye," people are still moved to demand that wrongs be punished.

We seem to feel this urge more strongly as the crime comes closer to home, or as it reaches heinous proportions (genocide, for example). After World War II, the Nürnberg trials and the trial of the Japanese General Yamashita were justified on rational grounds, as deterrents, but that there was also an element of vengeance was not lost on the defendants, their supporters, and some international observers (Minear, 1972).

Justifications of revenge may be couched in pragmatic terms, but the motivation appears moral. The moral roots of the sense of justice, affirmed in the law, require this balance, this compensation, so that evil does not seem to go free. The idea is well put by the philosopher Arendt in her study of the trial of the Nazi Eichmann by the Israelis. Arendt justifies the trial and the hanging of Eichmann by saying, "To the question most commonly asked about the Eichmann trial: What good does it do?, there is but one possible answer: It will do justice" (1964, p. 254).

To repeat, the law is not merely practical; it is also symbolic. *It expresses morals as well as it intends results.*

It is part of the morality being expressed that people should be held accountable only for what they have "chosen" to do. If Eichmann had been defined as an idiot or a lunatic, justice would not have required his execution. The same sense of justice that calls for retribution also demands some quality of capacity in the offender.

DEGREES OF CRIME

The legal conception of crime not only acknowledges degrees of responsibility in the offender but also recognizes degrees of gravity in his offense. Neither citizens nor their laws regard all crimes as equally serious. The punishment that is to "fit the crime" is weighed according to the moral indignation the crime evokes. One way of speaking of these grades of offense is to divide them into offenses that require a formal charge, or *bill of indictment,* before prosecution can be initiated and offenses of lesser gravity that can be judged in a *summary proceeding* without the requirements of a formal trial. This classification in Anglo-Canadian law approximates the American division of crimes into *felonies* and *misdemeanors.* In both cases the penalties are usually, but not necessarily, heavier for the indictable offenses.

Another way of ranking the gravity of offenses and of distinguishing between the public image of "crime" and its legal definition is the division of crimes into those "wrong in themselves" *(mala in se)* and those deemed wrong because they intrude upon others' rights as these rights have come to be defined by law *(mala prohibita).*

The crimes "wrong in themselves" are characterized by universality and timelessness. While the specific legal definitions vary from time to time and from jurisdiction to jurisdiction, every civil society legally calls some kinds of killing "murder," some kinds of coercion "kidnapping," some kinds of fighting "assault," some kinds of sexual abuse "rape" or "incest," some kinds of damage to property "malicious mischief," "vandalism," or "arson," and some kinds of appropriation of property "theft."

The definitions of such acts—that is, the boundaries demarcating acts given such names—change. So do the weights assigned to the seriousness of the acts.[3] Nevertheless, with this qualification it can be said that social concern with crime is largely with crimes *mala in se* and only slightly with some of the newer "administrative crimes" like traffic offenses or weights-and-measures violations. Polls of citizens of Western nations, particularly citizens of the United States, report that concern is with collective and individual violence, robbery, rape, and arson; burglary and highjacking; drug addiction and moral decay (Biderman et al., 1967; Harris, 1968; *Life,* 1972; McIntyre, 1967; President's Commission, 1967a; *U.S. News & World Report,* 1970a, 1970b, 1970c, 1970d).

CRIME AND OTHER EVILS

The idea that some crimes are "wrongs in themselves," while other crimes represent less definitive wrongs that have been made illegal, points up the connection between law and morality, between what is officially proscribed and what is publicly condemned. The criminal law has evolved with morality. It *expresses* moral beliefs, it *codifies* them, and it attempts to *enforce* them. The criminal law is effective, therefore, insofar as it is supported by morality. It becomes less effective, both as a dramatic expression and as a social defense, when its moral underpinnings are weakened.

The changing relationship between a people's moral beliefs

[3]An illustrative study is Coombs's comparison (1967) of the judged gravity of 19 crimes with the rankings given to these offenses 40 years earlier in the United States (Thurstone, 1927). Coombs found that there was *more* agreement about the judged seriousness of crimes 40 years ago. He also found that offenses against the person were judged to be *more* serious in the 1960s than in the 1920s, while offenses against property, with the exception of arson, were judged to be *less* serious.

and the criminal laws of their state allows criminologists to dispute the proper content of their discipline. The student who attends principally to the common conceptions of crimes *mala in se* will be accused of neglecting the study of other, greater injuries, be they legal, quasi-legal, or illegal. Thus the radical sociologist will want more attention paid to "crimes against the public interest" such as industrial pollution, racial and sexual discrimination, and misleading advertising. On the other hand, the conservative sociologist will want more attention paid to the "subversive crimes," such as the traffic in pornography and narcotics; treason; and intrusion by the state upon the individual's religious, educational, and property rights.

Crime and Sin

The debate among criminologists as to the proper focus of professional attention is evidence that the concept of crime has its origin in the larger concept of sin. There is a popular tendency to call any disapproved behavior—usually that of the other person—a "crime." This usage has literary precedent. For example, the *Oxford English Dictionary* adds to its legalistic definition of crime a moralistic meaning: "2. more generally: an evil or injurious act; an offence, a sin; *esp.*, of a grave character."

The trouble with broadening the definition of crime in this manner is that the explanations which will be advanced to account for all evil will be *generally applicable* only at the cost of being *specifically vague*. A broad span of attention promotes the use of "elastic hypotheses" which can be stretched to explain everything that happens and which, therefore, can never be refuted by any particular fact. Every account of crime, including that of this book (Chapter 10), is vulnerable to this common criticism. The partial remedy lies in narrowed attention and clearer focus.

This point is made in repetition of our theme: that the adequacy of a theory depends upon *what* it is used to explain and upon the *use* to which the student will put it. The explanation that satisfactorily tells us why rates of robbery change will not necessarily tell us why rates of fraud, murder, or treason change.

If to these offenses one adds others—violations of civil rights, "loan sharking," and "war crimes," for example—any single explanation of all of them runs the risk of being so full of faith as to be impervious to fact.

A Division of Criminological Attention

A way out of the dispute over the proper focus of criminological attention is to divide the study into three broad topics: (1) the sociology of law, (2) theories of criminogenesis, and (3) studies of social defense.

The Sociology of Law   The sociology of law tries to understand why some acts, but not others, are made the subject of the criminal law. It is concerned with how continuing social groupings come to define their expectations of behavior that shall receive formal, public attention. Among literate peoples, the sign of "formal, public attention" is codification in law. Within the field of criminology, only those laws are pertinent that describe the behavior of notice as an injury to the *society*—that is, as crimes. Students of the sociology of law are interested in such questions as these:

1 What seem to be the determinants of definitions of behaviors as worthy of, or irrelevant to, legal notice?
    a   What factors seem to be correlated with changes in these definitions?
    b   What consequences may be attributed to such changes?
2 How does the social group implement its criminal law? This question promotes study of courts, judges, and juries, of the differential administration of law, of the consequences and determinants of differential sentencing practices, and of the occupations concerned with processing the law (the police, lawyers, corrections officers, and others).

Theories of Criminogenesis, or "Crime Causation"   Such theories are concerned with understanding changes in crime rates and with the characteristics of individuals and groups that do, and do not, violate specific bundles of criminal laws.

This study deals with the methodological issues inherent in

finding out the characteristics of violators, victims, and nonviolators. It attends, also, to the theories constructed to explain both individual involvement in crime and historical and comparative variations in the rates of various kinds of crime. This is the part of criminology to which the following chapters are addressed.

Social Defense   This is a European phrase for an interest in what has also been called "penology," "corrections," and "societal response." It is the study of the measures societies take in response to violations of their formal, public expectations. Research in this area is interested in the consequences of different styles of social defense, in the justifications given for these differing reactions, and in the determinants of both the reactions and their consequences.

"Criminalizing" and "Decriminalizing" Sin[4]

The tripartite division of criminological attention is difficult to maintain; the three areas of interest overlap. Recently, there has been a tendency, more common among American criminologists than among their colleagues on the European continent, to submerge theories of crime causation in theories of *definition* of crime. This tendency moves attention from theories of criminogenesis toward the sociology of law, emphasizing who has the power to call which acts and which actors "criminal" (see pages 202–212).

This diversion of attention has also influenced ideas about social defense. A principal recommendation that has followed from this shifting focus has urged that many acts be decriminalized while others be criminalized. In particular, it has been recommended that "crimes without victims" be removed from legal concern while other wrongs whose victims are deemed defenseless be recognized as crimes.

"Crimes without victims" have been variously defined by different advocates as such sometime offenses as abortion,

[4]Sociologists make up words to describe what is not yet in dictionaries. The verb "to criminalize" will not be found in standard English dictionaries, but it will be found in sociological writing (see, for example, Kadish, 1967). The term seems a useful neologism to signify bringing an act or a situation within the purview of the criminal law. Henceforth this term will appear without quotation marks.

homosexuality, and drug addiction (Schur, 1965). Some have suggested decriminalizing prostitution, incest, keeping a bawdy house, statutory (noncoercive) rape, and the production and distribution of pornography. Others are in favor of eliminating the crimes of suicide and attempted suicide, gambling, drunkenness, disorderly conduct, vagrancy, some kinds of speeding, and the sale and possession of gold.

On the other side of this coin, other advocates are making various suggestions about criminalizing certain behavior. It has been recommended that new categories of "victims" be defined and protected by the criminalization of such heretofore lawful acts as manufacturing, advertising, and distributing products considered "harmful," such as alcoholic beverages, aspirin, tobacco, detergents, some kinds of cosmetics, and ill-designed automobiles. The noxious atmosphere of many modern cities has led to the enactment of laws with criminal sanctions against "pollution" by the emission of noise, fumes, and liquid and solid waste by corporations and by individuals and their animal pets. So, too, concern with population increase has moved some people to advocate that bearing more than two children be made a crime, with the law to be enforced by the tattooing, compulsory sterilization, and compulsory abortion of the excessively fertile (Willing, 1971).

It has also been urged that the dissemination of "hate literature" be made criminal, along with the practice of discrimination in housing, education, or occupation by reason of age, sex, race, creed, national origin, tested intelligence, or income; and in some jurisdictions such legislation has been enacted. Apropos of discrimination in education, Thomas (1972) has advocated that "certain acts committed by school people" should be redefined as criminal and that a legal strategy be developed "for actually documenting and charging that teacher or principal or administrator with being an accessory to *whatever crime the child commits in later life* as a result of a teacher's or administrator's cruelty" (pp. 179 and 182, italics added).

The Limits of Criminalization   The capacity of a society to decriminalize some "crimes without victims" and criminalize other actions whose victims are classes of people, rather than individuals, has a limit. One determinant of the limits of criminalization is the clogging of the courts.

It is notable that most police work against crime involves minor offenses. In the United States in any recent year, more than 5 million persons were charged with minor crimes (misdemeanors), *not* counting traffic offenses, whereas some 350,000 were charged with major crimes (felonies). Of the minor violations (excluding traffic offenses), about one-third are cases of public drunkenness. It has long seemed a waste of judicial energy to prosecute as criminal what might as well be regarded as merely a nuisance or as evidence of sickness. Certainly, the "revolving door" alcoholic, the person repeatedly arrested for drunkenness, is not rehabilitated by being jailed, nor does his incarceration deter other inebriates (Pittman and Gordon, 1958). A Presidential task force studying this problem in the United States (President's Commission, 1967c) has recommended that "drunkenness, when not accompanied by disorderly or otherwise unlawful conduct," be removed from criminal proceedings and that civil detoxification centers be established.

This type of recommendation will probably be extended to other presently criminal but minor wrongs as research demonstrates the ineffectiveness of the criminal law in changing the rates of these misdemeanors, as the courts become more and more overworked, and as civil rights receive an expanded definition. In the United States, for example, the Supreme Court recently decreed (12 June 1972) that defendants charged with misdemeanors for which they might be sent to jail must be provided with legal counsel if they are too poor to pay for such aid. This decision, in the case of *Argersinger v. Hamlin,* followed upon an earlier ruling, *Gideon v. Wainwright* (1963), in which the requirement of counsel was established for indigents charged with indictable offenses. The Argersinger decision now extends this right to all poor defendants charged with minor offenses that carry a possible jail sentence. This ruling will affect some 90 percent of all defendants charged with drunkenness (Mayer, 1972b).

The expected reaction to this decision is twofold: states can set up systems of public defenders, and they can rewrite the thousands of misdemeanor statutes so as to eliminate the threat of jailing. A mixture of both responses will probably occur. In this way, at the trivial end of the spectrum of crime, some wrongs will be decriminalized.

While some crimes not "wrong in themselves" may be erased, and while other "administrative crimes" may be created, predatory attacks upon person and property persist as matters of universal concern. The explanation of these kinds of crime requires that we know something about who commits them and about the conditions under which their rates of commission vary. This kind of knowledge requires the reliable and valid counting of criminal conduct. As the following chapters will show, counting crime is not easy.

Chapter 3

Counting Crime —Officially

Explanations that would aspire to the term "scientific" are created with facts and some assumptions to account for variations in other facts. One trouble with theories of crime causation is that they are built upon shaky facts to explain imperfectly known events. To the extent that one is uncertain about *what* he is explaining, he loses confidence in his ability to distinguish a good explanation from a poor one.

It is a rule of thumb that any measure of human action becomes less representative of all the events it might have gauged as it is filtered through social sieves. To put it another way, the more the records used as measures of crime are "socially processed," the less accurate they are as indicators of all criminal acts. This source of distortion affects in various degrees all attempts to count crime and leads to another criminological "axiom": every measure of crime for an aggregate[1] of individuals probably *underestimates* its actual amount. This would not be an obstacle to understanding crime causation if the underreporting were random or systematically biased in some known manner. However, if the difference between crimes committed and crimes recorded is biased in some *unknown* way, then many competing explanations can claim to be plausible. As will be seen, there is competition among explanations, and what kind of criminogenic theory one is apt to find most satisfactory is only in part a function of the facts one believes. How satisfactory an explanation seems is also affected by one's philosophy of social life and what one wants to see accomplished.

Four kinds of tallies have been used in counting crime: official statistics and three types of unofficial measures. The unofficial tallies, to be discussed in Chapter 4, include counts through direct observation, surveys of victims, and self-report measures.

As might be expected of attempts to count complex activities in varied settings, none of these measures is without error. Each has its distinctive set of disadvantages. Each is insensitive to some segment of the range of all possible wrongs. It will be the conclusion of this book, nonetheless, that these different measures point toward similar zones of crime causation, and that this result allows a reasoned choice to be made among explanations of crime.

THE NATURE OF OFFICIAL STATISTICS

The most popular measure of crime is official statistics of offenses reported to the police, or of arrests made, or of convictions obtained. Since there is a large loss in numbers as one moves from complaints to the police to the making of an arrest and, again, to the conviction of an offender, the most accurate tally of the amount of crime among these official statistics is the count by the police of complaints made to them.

These "crimes known to the police" are corrected by

[1]This qualification has to be added because some measures of an *individual's* criminal activity may *overestimate* the actual amount of his offensive conduct (see pages 93–94).

subtracting from all complaints those which, upon investigation, are judged to be "unfounded." For example, the figures for the United States discount on the average about 4 percent of the allegations of "serious offenses," according to the FBI's Crime Index. Such discounting ranges from about 3 percent of larceny complaints to around 18 percent of forcible-rape complaints[2] (FBI, 1970, p. 4).

WHAT DO OFFICIAL STATISTICS MEASURE?

Criminal statistics, like every other public measure, are constantly disputed. They should be. The critical citizen's doubts about the validity of public figures has never been better summarized than by an English economist who was long accustomed to their use. Sir Josiah Stamp (1880–1941) advised us that "the government are very keen on amassing statistics. They collect them, raise them to the nth power, take the cube root and prepare wonderful diagrams. But you must never forget that every one of these figures comes in the first instance from the village watchman, who just puts down what he damn pleases."

Stamp's warning applies today. It means that the "real" amount of criminal activity is never known. Differences in police activity, for example, make a difference in the swelling and receding of crime rates. Thus, upon the death of the anti-pornography laws in Denmark in the 1960s, some "sex crimes" were reported to have declined. It would be more accurate, however, to say that while human sexual behavior probably did not change much in Denmark, the law did, and with it police activity.

A difference in vigilance by the police is apparent, too, in the English experience with changes in laws concerning homo-

---

[2]Under the influence of the "women's liberation movement" and sociological studies of discretion by the police in making arrests, investigators' judgments that this high a proportion of forcible-rape complaints are without foundation is being challenged (*National Observer*, 1971). Still, rape remains, in the words of Lord Hale, "an accusation easily made, hard to be proved, and still harder to be defended by one ever so innocent." As a result of this combination of difficulties, most persons accused of rape are not convicted. In the United States in 1970, about 70 percent of men *arrested* for forcible rape were *prosecuted*. Of all those prosecuted, only 36 percent were *convicted* of rape, while about 18 percent were found guilty of lesser offenses (FBI, 1971).

sexual offenses. The Wolfenden Committee on Homosexual Offences and Prostitution was initiated in 1954. Within a year or two, it was common knowledge that this Committee would recommend not using the criminal law to interfere with the private sexual behavior of consenting adults. Walker (1971, p. 27) notes that by 1966 the number of recorded homosexual offenses had dropped to *half* that of 1955 even though no change in the law had occurred. Behavior had undoubtedly not changed all that much, but police activity had.

CRITICISM OF OFFICIAL STATISTICS

Official tallies of criminal activity are questioned, therefore, as to (1) what is collected, (2) how it is collected, and (3) how the numbers are manipulated.

What Counts?

An occurrence called a "crime" may have one offender, or many; one victim, or many; and one breach of the criminal law, or more. A political assassin may kill the President and wound two bystanders. An embezzler may steal $1,000 a month for eight years before he is caught, and he may forge some documents in the process. A father may have intercourse with his daughter several times before he is apprehended. One robber can hold up ten men in a tavern, take their money, shoot and kill the bartender, and make his getaway in a stolen car.

In each of these examples a decision will be involved as to how many crimes to count. The rule in England and Wales for attacks on a person is "one victim, one crime." Canada and the United States follow a similar practice. For offenses against property, the English have as yet no clear rule for counting; the Americans and Canadians try to call "one operation, one crime." In North America, when more than one crime occurs in an "operation," as in our example of the holdup in the tavern, the most serious of the offenses is counted, the gravity of an offense being determined by the maximum legal penalty it carries.

It is apparent that measures of criminal activity can attend to different matters. *Official statistics* record "crimes" as though they were single events. Surveys of the *victims of crime* count each victim separately, transfer the count to a "household," and try also to count criminal incidents. Crime surveys by *direct observation* and *self-report* procedures attempt to record each breach of the law for each individual. Some of these self-report measures assign a "crime score" to each person by weighting the gravity and frequency of his admitted offenses.

The concerned citizen does well to attend to *what* has been counted when interpreting *all* official figures. Such attention sometimes provides a new view of social reality. It is, for example, a healthy exercise to find out what is counted by the official recorders in one's community as they compute such "social indicators" as unemployment, suicide, per-capita income, mental health, and educational opportunity.

Continuing Issues in Counting Crime   Another question regarding the calculation of criminal statistics is whether certain kinds of offenses should be counted at all and which violations should be included in any index of crime. For example, it has been argued that the FBI's reference to "larceny $50 and over" as one of the serious crimes has failed to allow for monetary inflation. In a country that has been experiencing an estimated loss of 5 percent a year in the value of its money, a $50 larceny, according to this argument, no longer represents what it did in 1950 or 1960. In brief, what this argument says is that in this case the FBI's standard of seriousness of an offense is not the critic's, and perhaps not the public's. Canadian law had met this criticism and caught up with inflation as of mid-1972 by raising the lower limit of an indictable larceny from $50 to $200.

In a similar vein it has been argued that "automobile theft," one of the FBI's "index crimes," does not represent a homogeneous kind of crime. Some of it is "borrowing" for "joyriding," some is impulsive theft, and some is an organized business. The critics of official statistics do not believe that such diverse situations should be lumped together as equally serious. Doleschal (n.d., p. 13), for example, doubts whether joyriding belongs in the category of serious crime, since "nine out of ten 'stolen' cars are returned to their owners." However, when we consider the fact that the police *recover* a high proportion of stolen vehicles, a rather different interpretation of the phrase "are returned to their owners" is suggested from that which Doleschal's statement at first implies. The quotation marks around the word "stolen" are Doleschal's. Again, this is a critic's estimate of the gravity of "borrowing" automobiles—not necessarily the victim's or the public's. What is needed in response to such a criticism is some measure of the publicly perceived gravity of offenses.

The S-W Index: A Delinquency Index[3]   The American criminologists Sellin and Wolfgang (1964) have proposed a way of doing this that would also answer the earlier question about counting "one crime" in an occurrence which contains several criminal offenses. These investigators have devised a measure of delinquency which is based on a broader range of crimes than is included in the FBI's report and which is calculated by the *degree of publicly judged seriousness of offensive events.* In this index, a criminal occurrence is given a score based on a weighing of all the offenses that occurred during an "index event." The score is the sum of the judged gravity of these offense according to the standards prevalent in the community subject to the criminal law. In contrast to present recording procedures used by the police, the Sellin-Wolfgang measure, known as the S-W index, considers "each violation of the law occurring during an event [as] a component thereof, and in the evaluation of an event account [is] taken of all its components and not merely of the most serious one" (p. 297).

This measure is currently being tested. If adopted by police departments, it would of course require calibration for each population for which it is used and recalibration with the passage of time. The Sellin-Wolfgang index represents an improvement over present official records because it attempts to weigh a wider range of the legal violations that occur during a criminal event,

---

[3]More accurately, this measure should be called a "criminality index." We follow the authors in their title, however, with the proviso that "delinquency" and "criminality" may be used interchangeably here.

and because it scores these violations according to their judged gravity. It therefore provides a more sensitive measure of who is doing how much harm to whom.

Applications of the S-W index, comparing its results with those of official statistics, are as yet few. In one such test, however, the greater sensitivity of the S-W measure to the injury inflicted in a criminal event reveals some differences between it and the official diagrams. Normandeau (1969) compared robberies known to the police in Philadelphia in the seven years from 1960 through 1966 as perceived by the Uniform Crime Reports (UCR) and by the S-W index. The differences between the two profiles are shown in Figure 4. According to the S-W index, the robbery rate, when assessed for the seriousness of the harm inflicted, *decreased* from 1960 to 1962; the UCR figures, on the other hand, show an *increase*. After that, the S-W measure describes an *increase* year by year, whereas the UCR diagram shows *decreases* in 1963 and 1966 over preceding years. Overall, the S-W index reports that the 1966 robbery rate for 1966 had increased 13.6 percent over 1960, while the UCR figures report an increase of 18.1 percent. The disparity in the measures occurs because the S-W index pays greater attention to the *injury* component of a robbery than do the UCR figures, which attend only to the *theft* element.

An interesting sidelight of Normandeau's study derives from a separate analysis of the robberies by juveniles in a test of the popular hypothesis that youthful robbery may be "nasty, but not serious." As measured by the S-W index, this hypothesis was contradicted by the finding that "seriousness per juvenile event or juvenile offender is consistently greater (although not significantly so) than for all robbery events taken together" (p. 154).

Who Does the Counting, and How?

Official criminal statistics not only are imperfect because of *what* they do and do not count, but are also criticized for imperfections in the *accountant.* This kind of criticism of official records reaffirms Sir Josiah Stamp's skepticism. If human beings are doing the counting, they themselves are a variable and a source of

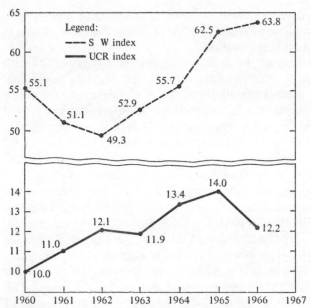

Figure 4 Trends in robberies known to the police as shown by the S-W and UCR indexes: 1960-1966, Philadelphia. Rates are per 10,000 population according to census adjustments. Reprinted with permission from Normandeau, 1969: Figure 1 in T. Sellin and M. E. Wolfgang, eds., *Delinquency: Selected Studies,* copyright John Wiley & Sons, Inc.

unreliability in the tallies. The question, then, concerns the biases of the recorders and the procedures by which they come to record a crime.

Official statistics on crime are generated by the police in two ways—in response to complaints made to them and through their own surveillance. In both cases, a decision is involved as to whether a crime has been committed and whether it is worth acting upon.

The vigilance with which a police department responds to complaints and records them is a variable with unknown, but estimated, movers. Vigilance varies, for example, with the organization of the police department, with the discipline of its personnel, and with the political pressures upon it. In New York

City, for instance, the involvement of the police in the federal government's Uniform Crime Reporting program in 1933 was followed by a year-by-year decline in the number of crimes recorded. There was evidence that some complaints to the police were being "referred to Detective Can"—that is, filed in the wastebasket. Civic bodies took action and, with a change in departmental administration in 1950, some kinds of crime immediately received a higher score on the police blotter, obviously as a result of tightened record keeping (Institute of Public Administration, 1952).

Studies of Police Discretion The fact that criminal conduct must be socially perceived and socially processed before it becomes part of the official record has stimulated studies of the differential selection of offenders, particularly juveniles, for arrest and referral to court. These studies do not give evidence of any striking extralegal bias in the treatment of the more serious offenders.

Goldman's research Goldman (1963) examined arrest records for 1,083 juveniles from four communities in Allegheny County, Pennsylvania, to ascertain whether there were any extralegal factors operating in the referral of these youthful offenders to court by the police. Goldman found what other studies have confirmed: that the majority of police contacts with juveniles are handled informally without referral to court. Sixty-four percent of the apprehended youths were treated without being sent to court. The response of the police varies, of course, with the offense, so that while only about 5 percent of the arrests for "mischief" were placed before the court, 91 percent of the arrests for automobile theft were placed before the court. *The gravity of the crime is a principal factor in determining a decision by the police to proceed with judicial action.*

Interestingly, Goldman discovered a higher arrest rate in the wealthiest of his four towns, but there the arrests were mostly for minor offenses that were settled out of court. In the poorer communities, arrests were for the more serious offenses and resulted in a higher proportion of court referrals.

In Goldman's data, the decision of the police to refer

juveniles to court was not influenced by the sex of the offender, but it did vary with age. The older the offender, the more probable a court referral was. Unfortunately, Goldman did not control in his analysis for the relation between age of offender and the number of previous offenses, and it may be suspected that this variable accounts for the differential disposition of cases involving older youths.

A similar situation is found in Goldman's analysis of ethnicity as a factor in court referral. He reports that "there appears to be little difference in the disposition of cases of white and Negro children who were arrested for serious offenses. However, there does appear to be a statistically significant difference in the disposition of minor offenses. A Negro child arrested for a *minor* offense has a greater chance of being taken to juvenile court than does a white child" (p. 44; italics are Goldman's). Again, it is impossible to interpret this finding as evidence of extralegal discrimination because there is no control for the number of previous arrests.

McEachern and Bauzer's study (1967) These investigators studied a random sample of 1,010 records drawn from the juvenile index of the Los Angeles County Sheriff's Department and 7,946 police contacts with juveniles contained in the Santa Monica records for 1940 to 1960. As in Goldman's study, these data were analyzed to ascertain what factors affect the disposition of juvenile offenders by the police. The answer of these investigators is that, with samples of this size, "almost everything is significantly related to whether or not a [court] petition was requested. Sex, age, number of the offense in the youngster's delinquent history, whether or not he comes from an intact family, whether or not he is on probation, and the year in which he was born all apparently have some influence on the police disposition. To balance these findings, the nature of the offense, the police department, and the year in which the incident occurred are also all very significantly related to whether or not a petition is requested" (pp. 150–151).

The one exception to these factors, and a surprising exception in the light of some public charges, is the lack of importance of the child's ethnicity. After apprehension by the police, there was no systematic or consistent difference in the proportions of Negroes, Mexican-Americans, or "Anglos" referred to juvenile court.

Policemen on patrol: The Piliavin-Briar study A deficiency of much of the research on the generation of official statistics is that the research starts *after* a police contact has been made and the first step taken on the judicial escalator. It would be of interest to observe how arrests are made, as well as to count what happens after the arrest. To this end, some sociologists have gone along on police patrols to ascertain how the police use their discretion.

One such investigation was carried out by Piliavin and Briar (1964). They observed the behavior of some 30 policemen in the juvenile bureau of the police department of an American industrial city. A large number of encounters between police and boys were observed, and systematic data were collected on 66 of these cases. The issue to which Piliavin and Briar addressed themselves was whether police discretion in arrest was influenced by the characteristics of the youth or whether it was solely a function of what the youth had done. In the minority of encounters (about 10 percent of the encounters) in which the offense was a *serious* one such as robbery, homicide, aggravated assault, grand larceny, automobile theft, rape, or arson, police discretion was minimally affected by the personal or social characteristics of the offender. However, the majority of the encounters involved *minor* offenses, and in these cases the policeman's assessment of the youth's character affected the decision to arrest or dismiss. In brief, boys whose "group affiliation, age, race, grooming, dress, and demeanor" signified that they were "tough guys" and disrespectful toward the police were more likely to be arrested than boys whose bearing in similar situations was judged less "delinquent." Piliavin and Briar conclude that, for juveniles, and for the large range of minor offenses, police patrolling may be "discriminatory" and may result in legal decisions based more on the "juvenile's character and life-situation than [on] his actual offending behavior" (p. 213).

One qualification should be made here. The Piliavin-Briar study ought not to be generalized into the conclusion that prejudice on the part of the police significantly affects official crime rates. This research was based on detailed observation of 66 encounters in the atmosphere of a "delinquency prevention" program. The policemen assigned to the juvenile bureau were selected partly on the basis of their "commitment to delinquency prevention" and they performed "essentially as patrol officers [cruising] assigned beats" (Piliavin and Briar, p. 207). However, in the industrialized democracies, most major crimes come to the attention of the police as a result of citizens' complaints rather than as a result of police patrols. "Modern police departments employ primarily a *reactive* strategy," say Black and Reiss, and "the majority of the cases handled . . . originate with mobilizations by citizens" (1967, pp. 2–3; italics added).

   The Black and Reiss study   As part of a recent survey by the United States government of crime and law enforcement in American cities, Black and Reiss (1967) directed a research in selected precincts of Boston, Chicago, and Washington, D.C., during the summer of 1966. Thirty-six trained observers were assigned to record detailed descriptions of the behavior of policemen and citizens. Incidents requiring attention by the police were divided into (1) "calls for service" or "dispatches," (2) "on-view mobilizations," in which officers initiated contacts in response to events that occurred in their presence, and (3) requests for action by the police from "citizens in the field." More than 5,000 situations involving over 11,000 individuals were observed. The "types of mobilization" of the police were then tabulated by the race and social status of the citizens involved and by the gravity of the offense.

   Eighty-one percent of all the occasions for police action were "calls for service"; 14 percent were "on-view" situations; and only 5 percent were initiated by "citizens in the field." In sum, the alerting of the police to crime comes principally from victims and witnesses of crimes. The decision as to the appropriateness of a response by the police is, then, more frequently the citizen's than it is the policeman's.

   The persistent allegation—made more strongly in Canada and the United States than in Europe—that the police respond to offenses and offenders in a prejudiced manner was *not* borne out

by the investigation made by Black and Reiss. With one qualification, there was no evidence of racial or class discrimination in
attending to crime throughout these many observations of interaction between citizens and the police. Unprofessional conduct
among the policemen did not vary significantly with the race or
social status of the citizen. "If anything," Black and Reiss write,
"police officers appear less hostile and brusque toward Negroes
and to ridicule them less often than whites" (p. 32).

To this finding, as has been noted, there is one major
qualification. In response to the serious offenses (felonies), the
American police were observed to be *more* vigilant when the
complaints were made by "white collar" citizens than when they
were made by "blue collar" citizens. This was *not* found to be the
case for the misdemeanors. The police were particularly attentive
when a white-collar complainant reported himself the victim of a
felony by a blue-collar offender and they "discriminated against
blue-collar citizens who feloniously offended white-collar citizens by being comparatively lenient in the investigation of
felonies committed by one blue-collar citizen against another"
(Black, 1970, p. 746). What this bias entails, of course, is a
lowering of the blue-collar arrest rate.

These findings refer to juvenile and adult offenders combined. In a special analysis, Black and Reiss (1970) examined
police encounters with juveniles only; 281 contacts with suspects
under 18 years of age were examined for type of police mobilization and for signs of discrimination by the police. The findings for juveniles parallel those for adults. The preponderance
of police encounters with juveniles was initiated by complaints
from citizens (78 percent of nontraffic violations) rather than
by police on patrol (22 percent of nontraffic violations). There
was no difference between these types of mobilization as
regards the race of the suspect. There was, however, a difference
in arrest rate when a complainant was present. "In not one
instance did the police arrest a juvenile when the complainant
lobbied for leniency," say Black and Reiss (1970, p. 71). "When a
complainant explicitly expresses a preference for an arrest,
however, the tendency of the police to comply is also quite
strong." A portion of the higher juvenile arrest rate among blacks

is a result of the fact that more serious crimes were charged against them than against whites, and of the fact that blacks were more frequently involved in encounters where there were complainants, themselves predominantly black.

Terry's research A similar finding of fairness in the official tallies is reported by Terry (1967) who analyzed over 9,000 juvenile offenses committed in a midwestern American city over a 5-year period. Terry was concerned with the possibility of discriminatory treatment by each of three agencies of social control: the police, the probation department, and the juvenile court.

As in the investigation by Black and Reiss, the overwhelming majority of the offenses noted were *not* a result of police surveillance. Over 83 percent of Terry's cases were reported by persons other than the police. Furthermore, the severity of the treatment of juvenile offenders did not vary with their sex, race, or socioeconomic status *when the gravity of their offenses and their records of previous offenses are considered.* Holding constant the seriousness of the crime and the juvenile's record of previous violations, Terry found no indication that the court, the police, or the probation department treated boys differently from girls, poorer adolescents differently from richer ones, or Anglos differently from Chicanos or blacks. Again, there is one qualification: when girls were "processed" beyond the police and probation departments and arrived before the court, they were more frequently sent to institutions than were boys.

Parallel studies With some variation, other studies of a smaller scale than those by Black and Reiss and Terry yield results that counter the charge of prejudice in the American judicial system. Weiner and Willie (1971) examined the decisions of juvenile officers in Washington, D.C., and Syracuse, New York, in search of racial or class bias. They found no such effect. Arnold (1971) studied the operation of one court in a middle-sized American city and found no ethnic discrimination in the actions of the probation officers. Once the juveniles were referred to court, however, the two judges in this jurisdiction sent fewer Anglos than Negroes and Chicanos to a correctional facility. Arnold interprets this more as "letting Anglos get off easy" than as "uncalled-for treatment of the minorities." He recognizes that, given the protective philosophy of the juvenile court, judges must consider the probability of continuing delinquent behavior as suggested by the offender's home and neighborhood. The impact of these variables upon a judge's decisions requires further study and may lead to suggestions for better ways of responding to youthful criminality.

In summary Getting arrested is an interactional process. The police force, the policeman, *and* the offender do make a difference—up to some limit—in determining what is recorded as crime. The question is whether this interaction systematically biases the official statistics of a particular jurisdiction for a particular period. The best answer seems to be that official records in the democracies reflect the operation of a judicial sieve. What are counted, finally, as crimes are the more obvious offenses, the more serious offenses, offenses whose victims have brought complaints, and offenses some of whose victims are dead—those crimes, in short, for which the public put pressure on their police to make arrests. A recent survey of research on the uses of police discretion in North America concludes that "police powers seem to reside, for better or worse, in the hands of the people" (Hagan, 1972, p. 11).

For those localities in which the matter has been studied, official tallies of arrests do not seem to be strongly biased by extralegal considerations. These studies confirm common sense. They indicate that if you are apprehended committing a minor crime, being respectful to the policeman may get you off. If you are apprehended committing a minor crime and you talk tough to the policeman, the encounter will probably escalate into arrest. If you are apprehended committing a more serious offense—if, for example, you are caught robbing a bank—being respectful to the police is not likely to make much difference to your being arrested.

How Are the Official Numbers Manipulated?

Counting behaviors of social concern is difficult; interpreting the tallies compounds the difficulties; and transforming simple tallies into rates compounds the difficulties further.

Statistics, like any other information, become more or less

adequate *in terms of one's purposes.* Much depends upon what
one wants to do with what he knows. Thus, for some purposes,
absolute numbers—straight counts—are good enough. Learning
that so many thousands of people died of lung cancer last year or
that motoring fatalities on a holiday reached a certain number
may be sufficient for one's concern. To use the demographer
Petersen's illustration, "the datum that the Chinese are increasing
by 15 million a year . . . could hardly be put more forcibly" (1969,
p. 79). The number stands on its own.

However, when we want to make comparisons for a population over a period of time, or comparisons between groups or
between treatments, then absolute numbers become less satisfactory. This is so because we are seeking a choice among hypotheses in an attempt to increase our predictive ability. We
therefore prefer to think in terms of ratios, proportions, or rates,
rather than absolute numbers.[4] This preference leads to questions
about the bases upon which rates are computed.

The Bases of the Rates   A criticism of the FBI rates, such
as those plotted in Figures 1, 2, and 3 in Chapter 1, is that the
population base in the United States is known with some certainty only for a decennial year. For each succeeding year within a
decade, the national population can only be estimated. If the
estimate is low, the reported rate is inflated, so that the crime
rates for, say, 1969 are given a spuriously high number in
comparison with rates for the census year, 1960.

The question of the appropriate population base to be used
in statistics does not end, however, with the problems of counting
people. Since not all persons are equally vulnerable to the events

---

[4]Students of populations distinguish between ratios, proportions, and rates.

A *ratio* compares one segment of a population with another where both numbers come
from the same tally. The relation is usually reduced by some convenient constant. For
example, $a/b\ k$ expresses a ratio in which a is one portion of a population, say, males; b is
another sector of that population, females; and k is a constant—in a sex ratio, usually 100.

A *proportion* describes the relation between a part of a population and the whole. It looks
like this: $a/(a+b)\ k$ where, again, a = males; b = females; k = a constant.

A *rate* compares events during a specified time against some population base. It takes the
form $m/P\ k$, where m is a measure of some occurrence, P is a population count, and k is a
constant. An important feature of a rate is that m and P do *not* come from the same records.
This is an additional source of error in official accounting.

that interest us, the *composition of a population* becomes important. Under conditions of *unequal vulnerability,* it is possible that changes in the composition of a population, rather than changes in behavior, may account for variations in the incidence of events. For example, if adolescents are more frequently involved in automobile theft than people of other ages, then a difference in the number of such crimes committed in two populations may reflect a difference in their age composition rather than a real difference in behavior. Just by looking at the age composition, we should expect less automobile theft in a retirement community than in a neighborhood with a large population of young people. Similarly, since males commit murder more frequently than do females, then again a comparison of the homicides in two populations requires some control for differences in the proportion of males in the two populations.

The rationale for the computation of rates is a predictive one. Its ideal is to express the relationship between "the actual and the potential," as Petersen puts it (1969, p. 79). To increase the accuracy of forecasts, a rate should be "refined" so that it includes in its denominator *all those persons and only those persons who are at risk* of whatever kind of event is being tallied in the numerator.

To refine a rate in this manner means that one must know something about these relative risks. Sometimes the population at risk is obvious; sometimes it is not. For example, the chance of being killed while traveling by automobile requires that one be *in* such a vehicle. (The hazard of being killed *by* an automobile is still another matter.) Official figures of traffic mortality are not computed on this basis, however. In North America the number of traffic fatalities per year is compared with the midyear population of a region or of the country. Sometimes this is refined by guessing from gasoline consumption the number of passenger miles traveled. Nevertheless, no one knows how many people travel how many miles by automobile in specific zones. This means that a jurisdiction with a small residential population but a large transient population, like the state of Nevada, will have an artificially inflated rate of deaths in automobile accidents. Traffic mortality rates are, in this sense, "crude."

Crime rates are similarly crude approximations of the calculated risk that individuals, groups, or localities will experience different rates of offense. At a minimum, we should expect crime rates to be refined by controlling for age, sex, and density of population. Infants and the aged are not likely to be offenders. Males and females *do* differ in their conduct. Much crime is a function of things to be stolen and of people meeting people. Comparisons between populations become more accurate, then, when the rates employed are age-specific, sex-specific, and density-specific.

Having said this, however, one runs into dispute. Should the statistician refine his crime rates further—for example, by making them race- and class-specific? The answer depends on the assumptions with which one approaches his data. If it is assumed that, for a given society, people of different ethnic groups and different social status run equal risks of being arrested, then there is no need to refine rates in acknowledgement of the various population sectors. If, however, the "potential" for apprehended crime varies with income or ethnic group, then comparisons become more accurate as rates are made class- or ethnic-specific. For example, a definition of "embezzlement" calls it a criminal violation of financial trust. Obviously, a condition of being able to embezzle is being *in* a trusted, financial position. The embezzlement experience of two populations—say, that of Switzerland and that of the Soviet Union—may be expected to vary with the proportion of their people who are entrusted with others' money and property. The comparative crime rates should thus be occupation-specific.

SUMMARY

The major charge against the use of official statistics as data for criminological theory is that they are biased, and biased principally against poor people and against visible minorities. This accusation is more common in Canada and the United States, with their numerous minority groups, than it is on the European continent. However, the belief that rich people can get away with crimes for which poor people are hanged is universal. It is a belief substantiated by the fact that money buys legal defense and by the fact that the kinds of theft available to trusted business and government officers are less public than strong-arm robbery. The act of fraud is more clever, less readily apparent, and more difficult to discover than a burglary or a rape. Apart from the discovery of the *crime*, however, there is also the matter of the discovery of the *criminal*. Here the burglar may have an advantage over the embezzler. It is more difficult to catch an external thief than an internal one.

The question of bias in official records can be raised, but it cannot be definitively answered. It is a charge that could only be verified if there were accurate tallies by segments of societies of the *proportions* of people committing *various offenses* of ranked *seriousness* and known *frequency.*

The *gravity* of the prevalent offenses is one element in evaluating judicial bias. The *number of offenses* and the *proportion of a population* committing them are two additional, and different, measures of criminality. No presently employed measure of criminal activity, official or unofficial, is sensitive to the full range of crime and, at the same time, sensitive to variations in the judged gravity of these crimes while it counts how many persons in each stratum of society commit how many crimes. This fact allows political preference to affect the choice of measures of crime and their interpretation.

The confidence one has in public records increases as other modes of measurement yield similar results. If each method of counting crime gave widely different results, no theories of crime causation could be well supported. As will be seen, however, the various imperfect measures of the serious crimes point in the same general direction for their social location.[5] For answers to the *sociological* questions about crime, this is all that is required.

---

[5] An interesting test of the convergence of public and private measures in mapping the social location of crime has been conducted by Price (1966). This investigator assumed that the premium rates of insurance against loss of property ought to bear some relation to official statistics. He found such validation and concluded that police figures on offenses against property "are highly correlated with premium rates on the most appropriate insurance coverages" (p. 220).

Chapter 4

Counting Crime
—Unofficially

The imperfections of official statistics on crime have led sociologists to invent other ways of counting violations of the law. It cannot be said, however, that these measures *improve* upon the official tallies. Where the unofficial measures disagree with official statistics, no one knows which is the more valid. Where the official and unofficial tabulations agree, one is more confident of the facts with which explanations of criminality are built. Fortunately for theories of criminogenesis, official and unofficial counts of crime are in general agreement in mapping the social locations of the serious offenses.

The unofficial procedures for measuring crime include (1) direct observations of criminal activity, (2) surveys of the victims of crime, and (3) studies of confessions of crime.

1 OBSERVATIONS OF CRIMINAL ACTIVITY

An interesting way of counting crime is to live with a group of people and to keep a log on their criminal conduct. This procedure is obviously expensive, restricted in its application, and subject to variations traceable to differences in attention and recording on the part of the observer. The few attempts to count crime in this manner in literate societies have been limited to areas with a high rate of crime. Their findings are important, however, because they mesh with the results of official tallies and surveys of victims.

The Cambridge-Somerville Youth Study

This research was based on a delinquency-prevention project started in 1937 in two crowded, industrial cities near Boston, Massachusetts. The project was curtailed in 1941 by the entry of the United States into World War II, but the research persisted with some changes until 1945. In 1955 Joan and William McCord (1959) brought the information up to date and reexamined the findings. Over these years a tremendous dossier was developed for each of the 650 boys originally in the project. The McCords comment that "seldom has so large a group of children been so carefully studied over such a long period of time. Social workers investigated the neighborhoods and recorded the school progress of each boy. Perceptive investigators visited their homes, talked with their parents, and observed their families. Psychologists and psychiatrists measured intelligence and analyzed the personalities of the children. The social and psychological observations . . . told about their boyhood homes, their families, their neighborhoods, and their personalities" (pp. 13–14).

As a part of getting to know the boys, caseworkers maintained records of observed and admitted crimes, whether officially recorded or not. What is of importance for our purposes is, again, the enormous amount of "hidden delinquency" and the *relation between the persistence and gravity of offenses committed and action by the police.* In a special study of 101 of these youths, Murphy and his colleagues (1946) noted that 61 of the boys had committed a variety of delinquencies without being sent to court.

Another 40 boys did appear in juvenile court. Table 3 shows the relation between the number and kinds of offenses observed and official response. It is apparent that boys who commit the more serious crimes, and more of them, run a higher risk of appearing in official statistics. What is not revealed in the chart, but appears in Murphy's report, is that of the more than 6,416 offenses observed, only 95 (about 1.5 percent) resulted in court action. The boys who became "officially delinquent" had committed from 5 to 323 violations each, with a median of 79 crimes. By contrast, the "unofficial delinquents" had committed on the average 30 offenses each.

We may all have broken some criminal laws, but some of us have done so more frequently and more seriously than others. Frequency and gravity of offense are among the strong determinants of official notice.

Thieving Gangs

Under the direction of Walter B. Miller (1967) field workers have become intimate with American urban gangs of males and females and have counted three classes of their larcenous conduct: "behaviors in some way oriented to theft, arrestable acts of theft, and appearance in court" on charges of theft. As is true of all comparisons between official statistics and hidden crime, Miller's workers observed a large amount of criminal activity going unrecorded. "There were three and one-half theft-oriented

Table 3   Offenses Committed by Official and Unofficial Delinquents

Type of offense	Unofficial delinquents (N = 61)	Official delinquents (N = 40)	Both groups (N = 101)
City-ordinance offense	739	655	1,394
Minor offense	1,913	2,493	4,406
Serious offense	174	442	616
Total	2,826	3,590	6,416

Source: Reprinted with permission from Murphy et al., 1946, p. 688, table 1.

behaviors for every 'hard' act of arrestable theft, and about ten theft involvements for every court appearance on theft charges. This is a rather surprisingly high ratio of court appearances to acts, but it still means that during the study period well over 300 incidents of theft were observed for which no official action was recorded" (p. 33).

The significant results of this research show that

> theft [is] a culturally patterned form of behavior. It was mostly place theft [as opposed to theft from persons] with peak frequencies occurring during the fourteen to seventeen age period; it had a strong utilitarian component; it was far more frequent than any other form of crime; it was predominantly a male activity; its frequency bore little relation to being White or Negro; [and] its patterning was so decisively related to social status that status differences as small as those between lower class 2 and 3 had marked influence on its frequency [p. 37].

In Summary

Observations of people obeying and breaking criminal laws reinforce the common-sense impression that violations are common, that they vary by kind and amount with different social locations, and that the policing process operates like a coarse net that is more likely to catch the repetitive, serious offender than it is to catch the incidental, minor offender.

2 SURVEYS OF VICTIMS

Another measure of the amount and kind of crime being committed is derived from surveys of the victims. In conjunction with the work of the President's Commission on Law Enforcement and Administration of Justice, a pilot study of victimization was conducted in the District of Columbia by the Bureau of Social Science Research under the direction of Biderman and his colleagues (1967), and a nationwide survey was conducted by the National Opinion Research Center and reported by Ennis (1967). A smaller study, limited to victims of sex crimes in Copenhagen,

Denmark, was prepared by Kutschinsky (1970) for presentation to the U.S. Presidential Commission on Obscenity and Pornography.

The Bureau of Social Science Research Study

Trained interviewers sampled selected police precincts of Washington, D.C., in 1966. For each respondent, they ascertained:

1 Whether he personally had been a victim of specific crimes since January, 1965.
2 Whether any member of his household had been victimized.
3 The "very worst crime" that had ever happened to him.
4 The "very worst crime" that had ever happened to anyone currently living with him.

Five major findings resulted from this poll:
1 Respondents believed that the crime problem in their city was serious, that it had been growing worse, and that it was of immediate personal concern to them (p. 119).
2 Official statistics ("crimes known to the police") greatly *underestimate* the total amount of crime to which people say they have been subjected. As Table 4 shows, over 9,000 criminal incidents were said to have been experienced; but only some 400 such incidents were "known" to the police—a difference of the order of 23 to 1.
3 The discrepancy between police statistics and reports by victims varies with the type of offense. Again, from Table 4 it appears that about 11 times as much rape occurs as is known to the police, 20 times as much burglary, and more than 30 times as much robbery and criminal homicide. (The discrepancy in the enumeration of murders is difficult to believe. If the people accurately perceive so much more murder than is known to the police, Washington is an even more dangerous city than has been thought.)
4 According to this survey, the discrepancy between official figures and victims' claims is not due to the failure of citizens to report their injuries as much as it is due to variations in

Table 4 Offense Classes in Survey and Police Data, Precincts 6, 10, and 14

Class of offense	Incidents mentioned by survey respondents		Actual offenses known	
	N	%	N	%
Part I:				
Criminal homicide	31	*	1	*
Rape	46	*	4	1
Robbery	1,082	11	35	8
Aggravated assault	457	5	20	4
Burglary	2,174	22	110	25
Larceny	1,832	18	116	26
Auto theft	1,381	14	21	5
Part II:				
Other assaults	675	7	30	7
Arson, vandalism	112	1	47	10
Fraud, forgery, ombezzlement	143	1	8	2
Other sex offenses	48	*	12	3
Offense against family	3	*	-	-
All other offenses	2,009	20	39	9
Total	9,993	100	443	100

*Less than 1%

Source: Reprinted with permission from Biderman et al., 1967, p. 34.

attention by the police. Biderman notes, "If we accept what our respondents say, the discrepancy presumably involves the police, not reporting what people report to them in much greater degree than the nonreporting of offenses to the police by the public" (p. 118).

5 Despite the discrepancies between the *amount of crime* gauged by police statistics and by this survey of victims, the *rank order* of the frequency of the crimes reported is quite similar for the two measures.

If one looks only at the FBI's "index crimes," the ordering of the frequency of these offenses by both measures is identical. However, a kind of crime not included in the "index offenses" was found by this survey of victims to be the third most frequently mentioned violation: malicious destruction of property (p. 33).

The National Opinion Research Center Study

This polling organization asked a representative sample of Americans about their experiences as victims of crime and about their opinions of the police and of their own personal security. The survey was concerned principally with *crimes against individuals and their property.* It did not intend to inquire about citizens' experiences with gambling and violations of game laws, with abortion, or with violations of liquor and drug laws. This inquiry was not used as a confessional instrument, as self-report measures are. Furthermore, it is clear that a study of *individual victims* omits from its tally crimes against corporations and other institutions.

The findings of interest in the present context are these:

1 As appears from all unofficial measurements of deviant behavior, much more crime is committed than is recorded. Again, the discrepancy between the number of people who say they have been victims of crime and the number of crimes known to the police varies with the type of offense. Forcible rape, robbery, aggravated assault, burglary, and larceny over $50 are all experienced far more frequently than they are reported to the police. Depending on the city and the kind of crime, individual victims say they have suffered from 3 to 10 times the number of offenses that are recorded by the FBI's Uniform Crime Reports. Only automobile theft and homicide appear to be more frequently reported to the police than to survey interviewers. (The finding that citizens are *less* aware of murder than the police are confirms the doubts about the validity of the District of Columbia finding mentioned on page 66.) Overall, about twice as much crime, major and minor, was recorded through this survey of victims than appeared on official logs. Table 5 compares the estimated rates of the "index crimes" with their official rates as calculated by the FBI.

2 A second finding, in agreement with that of the study by the Bureau of Social Science Research, is that, despite the

Table 5 Estimated Rates of Part I Crimes (see Table 4): 1965–1966

Crime	NORC Sample Estimated Rate per 100,000 Population	Uniform Crime[a] Reports: 1965 Total per 100,000 Population	Uniform Crime[b] Reports: 1965 (Individual or Residential Rates) per 100,000 Population
Homicide	3.0	5.1	5.1
Forcible rape	42.5	11.6	11.6
Robbery	94.0	61.4	61.4
Aggravated assault	218.3	106.6	106.6
Burglary	949.1	605.3	296.6
Larceny ($50+)	606.5	393.3	267.4
Vehicle theft	206.2	251.0	226.0[c]
Total	2,119.6	1,434.3 N . . (32,966)	974.7

[a]*Crime in the United States, 1965 Uniform Crime Reports*, Table 1, p. 51.

[b]*Crime in the United States, 1965 Uniform Crime Reports*, Table 14, Page 105, shows for burglary and larcenies the number of residential and individual crimes. The overall rate per 100,000 population is therefore reduced by the proportion of these crimes that occurred to individuals. Since all robberies to individuals were included in the NORC sample regardless of whether the victim was acting as an individual or as part of an organization, the total UCR figures were used as comparison.

[c]The reduction of the UCR auto theft rate by 10 per cent is based on the figures of the Automobile Manufacturers Association (*Automobile Facts & Figures*, 1966), showing 10 per cent of all cars owned by leasing-rental agencies and private and governmental fleets. The Chicago Police Department's auto theft personnel confirmed that about 7–10 per cent of stolen cars recovered were from fleet and rental sources and other non-individually owned sources.

Source: Reprinted, with permission, from Ennis, 1967, p. 8.

underreporting characteristic of official counts of crime, *the rank order of the frequency of these serious offenses reported by their victims is, with the exception of vehicle theft, identical to that of the Uniform Crime Reports.*

3 The crimes most frequently experienced, according to these victims, are theft of property worth less than $50 and malicious mischief.

4 The probability that one will be a victim of a crime varies with the kind of crime and where one lives.

The centers of American cities are the more probable sites of violent crimes. Forgery, fraud, and other cheats do not vary with type of community. "Petty theft and malicious destruction of property are reported most often in the suburbs" (Ennis, 1967, p. 23). "As one moves from the central city to the suburbs out into smaller towns and rural areas, the crime rates decline, but much more drastically for crimes against the person than for property crimes. The metropolitan center . . . has a violent crime rate about *five times* as high as the smaller city and rural area but a property crime rate only *twice* as high" (pp. 29–30).

Contrary to some professional and popular opinion, the southern United States do not report the highest rates of violent crimes. When community size is controlled for, the West is the most violent area, according to victims there (p. 29).

5 "At all levels of income, Negroes have higher rates of victimization for serious crimes against the person compared to whites. Property crimes show a more complex relationship to both race and income. For whites, there is a general decline of burglaries as income rises, but an *increase* of larcenies and car thefts with income. Among Negroes, the trends are less clear, but they mirror the patterns for whites with an important exception. Burglaries rise with income" (p. 30).

6 The serious offenses of aggravated assault, forcible rape, vehicle theft, grand larceny, and robbery are most likely to occur "close to home and secondarily on the public streets" (p. 40).

7 The NORC investigation found, in disagreement with the pilot study reported for Washington, D.C., that the major reason for a discrepancy between surveys and official statistics on crime is *the failure of citizens to report offenses.* About half the instances of victimization were not reported to the police.

Willingness to report a crime varies with the seriousness of the offense and with the victim's estimate that reporting will have some result. The high proportion of automobile thefts reported is a consequence of the necessity of filing a complaint with the police as a prerequisite to making an insurance claim. Other serious crimes tend not to be referred to the police principally because the victim believes the police cannot be effective. Secondary reasons given for failure to complain about a crime are the feeling that the affair was "a private matter" and the wish to protect the offender (Ennis, 1967, chap. 5).

Sex Crimes in Denmark

Kutschinsky and his associates interviewed a representative sample of residents of Copenhagen concerning their sexual victimization. This survey was greatly restricted as regards the number of victims studied (about 400), the locale, and the kinds of violations under scrutiny. However, within its limited and often ambiguous area of "sex crimes," this research is of interest for its similarities to the findings of the American investigations:

    1 Crimes reported to the police are but a small portion of crimes experienced.
    2 The rank orders of the frequency with which various kinds of sex offenses are experienced and the frequency with which they are reported to the police are highly correlated (p. 116).
    3 The *less* serious sex offenses are the most common.

For males in Copenhagen, the most frequently mentioned offense was "minor homosexual interference or attempts." The second most frequently mentioned offense was exhibitionism (p. 115).

Danish women were most frequently victims of exhibitionism and second most frequently victims of "indecent approaches" by other females. The rarest crimes reported by these women were rape and incest.

In Summary

Every measure of a social behavior has its critics, and all the criticism has some substance. If official counts of crime, held up against some criterion of perfect information, may be accused of invalidity, so too may tallies of victims and, as will be seen, measures of confessions.

Surveys of victims suffer from all the handicaps of any public opinion poll—doubts about how representative the sample is, refusals of some potential respondents to participate, bias and cheating by interviewers, and the perennial difficulty of assuring that the same question means the same thing to respondents in widely varying social positions.

In addition, asking people about the crimes they have suffered runs into the problem of how good their memories are and whether people of diverse status have equally good memories for events of possibly different importance to them. Then, too, there is the question of honesty or, if you will, of "openness." Individuals do differ in their willingness to talk about themselves—whether on paper to an anonymous questionnaire or in person to a strange interviewer. The reluctance to disclose various things about oneself is aggravated when confessions of crime are asked for, as in self-report measures, but it is also a possible source of distortion when people are being asked about their victimization.

All these criticisms would be of importance if, in the *social location* of the major crimes, the surveys of victims revealed striking differences from the map drawn by official figures. One would not know, then, what to believe about crime, and any explanation of crime would be as good as another. If a student cannot use the statistics of aggregates of individuals to locate the sites of different kinds of crime, then he cannot speak reasonably of what causes crime. (It must be remarked that the difficulties in finding the facts about who commits which crimes, and where, do not prevent politicians, journalists, and even criminologists from advancing hypotheses about the causes and cure of crime.)

Fortunately, as has been noted, despite the repeatedly discovered fact that more crime is committed than is recorded, when crimes are ranked in order of occurrence, the ordering is very much the same no matter which measure is used. Furthermore, the social conditions associated with high rates of serious crimes known to the police are also, with some qualification, associated with high rates of reported victimization. Both measures of criminality show higher rates of burglary, robbery, and serious assaults "in areas characterized by low income, physical deterioration, dependency, racial and ethnic concentrations, broken homes, working mothers, low levels of education and vocational skill, high unemployment, high proportions of single males, overcrowded and substandard housing, high rates of tuberculosis and infant mortality, low rates of home ownership and single family dwellings, mixed land use, and high population density" (President's Commission, 1967a, p. 35).

It must be pointed out, again, that these conditions are *correlates* of high crime rates, not necessarily their *causes*. Nevertheless, it is among such factors that criminologists have searched for the roots of crime; and it is of significance here that for most serious crimes, the *pattern* of their incidence as expressed by complaints made to the police is similar to that expressed by reports of victimization to interviewers.

3 SELF-REPORT MEASURES OF CRIMINALITY

The fact that surveys of victims and official crime statistics produce parallel findings has only slightly reduced skepticism about the validity of the official tabulations. Doubt remains, and it has moved criminologists to attempt to find out who has committed how much of which crimes by asking people to confess. Measures based on such "self-reports" have been devised in a number of ways:

1 By asking people to complete anonymous questionnaires (Akers, 1964; Christie et al., 1965; Clark and Wenninger, 1962; Dentler and Monroe, 1961; Elmhorn, 1965; McDonald, 1969b; Nettler, 1959a; Nye and Short, 1957; Porterfield, 1943, 1946; Wallerstein and Wyle, 1947).

2 By asking people to complete anonymous questionnaires, identified in a circuitous fashion, and validated against later interviews or police records (Forssman and Gentz, 1962; Voss, 1963).

3 By asking people to confess to criminal acts on signed questionnaires validated against police records (Hirschi, 1969; McCandless et al., 1972).

4 By having people complete anonymous questionnaires, identified by number, and validated against follow-up interviews and the threat of polygraph ("lie-detector") tests (Clark and Tifft, 1966).

5 By interviewing respondents (Belson et al., 1970; Gold, 1966; Reiss and Rhodes, 1961; Waldo and Chiricos, 1972).

6   By interviewing respondents and validating their responses against official records (Erickson, 1971; Erickson and Empey, 1963).

All these procedures provide imperfect measures of what people have done. Whether they are better or worse indicators of criminal activity than official records and victimization surveys is an open question. The findings of the many studies that have used confessional techniques run from consensus to complete disagreement.

Consensus Among the Confessions of Criminality

The numerous international studies that have employed self-report scales agree on these rather obvious findings: (1) that almost everyone, by his own admission, has broken some criminal law; (2) that the amount of "hidden crime" is enormous; and (3) that people who commit crimes are better described as representing a continuum, as having committed more or less crime, rather than simply being "delinquent" or "nondelinquent." As with most behaviors controlled by social norms, the graph of criminal conduct is a unimodal (one-humped) curve that looks like a "J" or an "L," depending upon how it is drawn. For example, Figure 5 is a graph of "delinquency scores" for Stockholm schoolchildren, 9 to 14 years of age, who responded to an anonymous questionnaire (Elmhorn, 1965). The delinquency score represents a weighting for each child of the *frequency* and the *seriousness* of his confessed criminal conduct. This chart is similar in form to others drawn from a variety of studies of antisocial behavior, all of which tell us that most people commit some minor infractions of the criminal code and that a few individuals commit many offenses and more serious offenses. For example, on Elmhorn's delinquency index, the highest possible score is 375 points. The average score is about 20; the median is approximately 8.

The number of individuals who exceed these central tendencies decreases as one moves toward the extremity of committing many crimes and more serious crimes. While some criminality is normal, persistent and grave violations of the law are the

Distribution of delinquency index

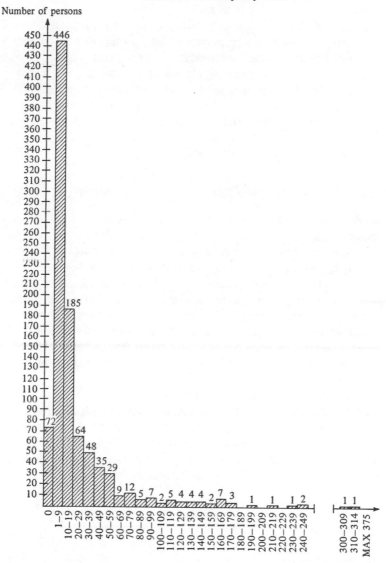

Figure 5 Self-reported delinquency among schoolchildren. Reprinted with permission from Elmhorn, 1965, p. 129.

experience of a minority. *This holds true whether the measure is confession or official statistics.*

Furthermore, there is a relationship in both measures of criminality between being *persistent* as an offender and being a *serious* offender. These data indicate that the more frequently one breaks the law, the more likely he is to commit more grave offenses. The finding of a skewed continuum of admitted delinquencies is in agreement with the distribution of criminal activity indicated by court records. This finding of a small minority of repetitive, serious violators justifies the picture of the incorrigible tough guy, the "hard-core" delinquent.[1]

Disagreement among the Confessions of Criminality

Research with confessional data provides mixed results when one inspects scores of criminal conduct for their relationship with the correlates of criminal behavior usually given by official statistics. (These correlates are summarized in chapter 5.) The presumed value of asking people about their offensive behavior is that it gives a clearer picture of the social location of crime, a picture undistorted by the alleged biases of a judicial system. However, it is not at all certain that self-report measures provide a more accurate description (pages 86–96); and—what is equally disturbing—the pictures drawn from admissions of criminality vary with who is drawing them.

In the United States, at least seven "social locators" have been correlated with scores from confessional instruments. Sociologists have explored the association between self-report measures and sex, age, socioeconomic status, ethnic group, religion, rural or urban residence, and family relationships. A consistently reported relationship is found between admissions of delin-

---

[1]The image of the "hard-core" juvenile delinquent is also substantiated by research on the background factors that, in some degree, differentiate more and less delinquent boys. For example, Eleanor and Sheldon Glueck (1970), who have been studying this subject for years, describe what they call "core delinquents" from poor scores on measures of maternal supervision, maternal discipline, and family cohesiveness. The Gluecks report that such delinquents, when grown to young adulthood, show a somewhat greater tendency than other types of youthful offender toward residential mobility, poor work habits, low occupational status, the use of social service agencies, and failure to be self-supporting.

quencies and differences in age, sex, family relations, and rural or urban residence. Disagreement occurs, however, when this extensive research looks at the association between self-report scales and socioeconomic status and ethnicity, including religion. Some American studies find class and ethnic differences in admitted offenses; some do not. Hardt and Bodine provide a summary of these investigations as of 1965 (table 1, pp. *vii–ix*), a summary that has not been seriously emended by later research.

From the point of view of an outsider, this mixture of findings could be attributed to an "experimenter effect," the possibility that investigators find what they believe they will find. The impulse to employ self-report scales has been "democratic," in the sense that official crime statistics and the judicial system out of which they flow have been charged with bias against poor people and ethnic minorities. The search has been, therefore, for a more accurate measure of misbehavior, one which might challenge the assumption that criminality varies with class and nationality. It is notable here that European scholars are *less* reluctant to believe the official records when these records link crime rates to class and ethnicity. "From the American studies," McDonald writes " . . . evidence . . . both supports and denigrates the theory that the working class is more delinquent than the middle class . . . [whereas] almost all of the literature on delinquency in Britain is in favour of the view that the working class is more delinquent" (1969b, p. 19).

Given these disagreements, it is instructive to examine the findings of two of the bigger and better investigations of the class and ethnic correlates of admitted delinquency, one conducted in the United States, the other in England.

Hirschi's Research (1969)   Hirschi used the facilities of the Survey Research Center on the Berkeley campus of the University of California to question a sample of some 4,000 junior and senior high school students in the San Francisco Bay area. A three-part questionnaire was employed to ascertain attitudes toward school, teachers, neighborhood, friends, parents, and human relations. Questions were also asked about work and money, aspirations and expectations, the use of leisure, and participation in school activities. Six items in the questionnaire were used as an index of admitted violations (Hirschi, 1969, p. 54):

1 Have you ever taken little things (worth less than $2) that did not belong to you?
2 Have you ever taken things of some value (between $2 and $50) that did not belong to you?
3 Have you ever taken things of large value (worth over $50) that did not belong to you?
4 Have you ever taken a car for a ride without the owner's permission?
5 Have you ever banged up something that did not belong to you on purpose?
6 Not counting fights you may have had with a brother or sister, have you ever beaten up on anyone or hurt anyone on purpose?

In addition to these data, school records, including grade point averages and academic achievement scores, were collected for each respondent. Police records were also examined, but only for the boys in the sample.

To each of the six questions in the delinquency index, respondents were able to reply that they had "never" committed the offense; that they had committed the offense "more than a year ago"; that they had committed the offense "during the last year"; or that they had committed the offense "during the last year *and* more than a year ago" (p. 56). Replies structured in this manner reflect more than one dimension of behavior. They assess the *recency* of a delinquency, the *persistence* with which one has broken the law, and, in an indirect fashion, the *frequency* of delinquent acts. Among the various indices that might be constructed by weighting recency, persistence, and frequency, Hirschi chose an index based on the "number of acts committed during the previous year" (p. 62). In interpreting Hirschi's data, it should be noted that this index is *not* the same as the so-called "standard index," used by most investigators of confessed crime, which totals all delinquencies ever committed and admitted. Hirschi believes his choice of index to be justified, although the standard index bears a slightly higher relation to other indicators of juvenile misbehavior. Table 6 shows the coefficients of correlation between the "recency," "persistence," and "standard" indices and admissions of truancy, suspension from school, apprehension by the police, and police records for part of Hirschi's sample. The standard index has a slightly higher association with these "outside variables" than the other measures.

Summarizing Hirschi's findings provides the following map of the social location of delinquency:

1   "Forty-two per cent of the Negro and 18 per cent of the white boys in the analyzed sample had police records in the two years prior to administration of the questionnaire. When other measures of 'delinquency' are used, the difference between Negroes and whites is sharply reduced. For example, 42 per cent of the Negro and 35 per cent of the white boys report having been picked up by the police; 49 per cent of the Negro and 44 per cent of the white boys report having committed one or more delinquent acts during the preceding year" (pp. 75–76). Table 7 plots the relation between race, official offenses, self-reports of apprehension by the police, and self-reports of delinquencies.

2   "Negroes are more likely to report 'non-delinquent'

Table 6   Correlations Among Alternate Self-Report Indexes and Selected Outside Variables, White Boys Only[a]

	Recency	Persistence	Standard
Recency	1.00	.90	.76
Persistence		1.00	.92
Standard			1.00
Truancy[b]	.39	.42	.42
Suspension[c]	.33	.35	.35
Police contact[d]	.42	.47	.50
Official record[e]	.27	.29	.30

[a]The number of cases upon which these correlations are based is not less than 1,300.

[b]"During the last year, did you ever stay away from school just because you had other things to do?"

[c]"Have you ever been suspended from school?"

[d]"Have you ever been picked up by the police?"

[e]Scored as total number of delinquent acts recorded by police.

Source: Reprinted with permission from Hirschi, 1969, p. 63.

Table 7   Number of Official Offenses, Number of Times Picked up by Police, and Number of Self-Reported Delinquent Acts, by Race (percent)

Number of acts (or reported contacts with police)	(A) Official offenses		(B) Self-reported police pickup		(C) Self-reported delinquent acts	
	White	Negro	White	Negro	White	Negro
None	81	57	65	57	56	51
One	10	19	18	20	25	25
Two or more	8	23	17	22	19	24
Totals	99	99	100	99	100	100
	(1335)	(888)	(1302)	(833)	(1303)	(828)

Source: Reprinted with permission from Hirschi, 1969, p. 76.

offenses involving interaction with and requiring definition by officials other than the police . . . They are, for example, more likely to report having been sent out of a classroom and having been suspended from school" (p. 79).

3   Hirschi used the father's occupation as his principal measure of socioeconomic status. When the connection between self-reported delinquency and father's occupation is examined (Table 8), only "a very small relation [is found] that could easily be upset by random disturbances of sampling or definition" (p. 69).

Table 8 shows the socioeconomic pattern of admitted delinquency for white boys only. Hirschi explains his decision to base his analysis on the information from white males on the grounds that the data for Negroes were less reliable and that "most independent variables had the same relation to official and self-reported delinquency among Negroes as among whites . . . . The major difference was that the relations among Negroes were consistently smaller, an attenuation apparently due to greater unreliability of response" (p. 79, fn. 23).

This kind of exclusion of data points up one of the criticisms of the self-report technique, which will be amplified on pages 86–96. Interpretation of some facets of Hirschi's study becomes difficult, then, because the omission of information from females and from blacks weakens the impact upon delinquency of some of the factors presumed to be associated with misconduct.

4 "Boys whose fathers have been unemployed and/or whose families are on welfare are more likely than children from fully employed, self-sufficient families to commit delinquent acts" (p. 72).

5 "The educational and occupational expectations of delinquents tend to be low" (p. 185). "The less a boy cares about what teachers think of him, the more likely he is to have committed delinquent acts" (p. 123). "The greater the value the student places on grades, the less likely he is to be delinquent" (p. 223). "Academic ability and school performance influence many, if not most, of the variables that turn out to be important predictors of delinquency. The causal chain runs from academic incompetence to poor school performance to disliking of school to rejection of the school's authority to the commission of delinquent acts" (pp. 132, 134).

6 Respect for and attachment to one's parents is a strong correlate of immunity to delinquency. According to Hirschi, "the fact that delinquents are less likely than nondelinquents to be closely tied to their parents is one of the best documented findings of delinquency research" (p. 85). Hirschi's data support

Table 8 Self-Reported Delinquency by Father's Occupation— White Boys Only (percent)

Self-reported acts	Father's occupation[a]				
	Low 1	2	3	4	High 5
None	62	53	56	49	61
One	16	26	25	28	25
Two or more	23	21	19	23	14
Totals	101	100	100	100	100
	(151)	(156)	(390)	(142)	(282)

[a]1 = Unskilled labor; 2 – Semi-skilled labor; 3 – Skilled labor, foreman, merchant; 4 – White collar; 5 = Professional and executive.

Source: Reprinted with permission from Hirschi, 1969, p. 69.

this finding and show that "the child attached to a low-status parent is no more likely to be delinquent than the child attached to a high-status parent" (p. 108).

Many of these conclusions are repeatedly found in other studies *whether they employ official records of criminality or confessions of delinquency.* The principal question at issue among investigators who use self-report tools has to do with the class and ethnic distribution of criminal misconduct. Hirschi's research strongly reduces the significance of socioeconomic status for young boys' behavior. Except for the sons of professionals and executives, who were disproportionately free of both admitted and official criminality, Hirschi found little association between confessed delinquencies and the remaining strata of income, education, and occupation. Hirschi locates the causes of lawful conduct in attachment to the prevalent order (parents and schools), positive attitudes toward personal achievement, and belief in the validity of conventional legal and moral rules. Conversely, delinquency is associated with a lack of these characteristics.

This causal attribution need *not* be denied if other studies, using other instruments on different populations, find different patterns for the connection between *class* and illegitimate conduct. As will be argued (pages 106–107, 116–117, and 145–147), there is no necessity for "social class" to have a uniform significance regardless of the milieu in which it is experienced. McDonald's English study, for example, finds a different class distribution of admitted delinquency from that which Hirschi reports. However, other correlates of delinquency, particularly the school correlates, hold true in England as they do in Canada and the United States.

McDonald's Research (1969b)   McDonald distributed anonymous questionnaires to almost 1,000 schoolboys in and about London in middle- and working-class areas and in secondary modern schools and the more traditional grammar schools.

McDonald, like Hirschi, inquired about boys' aspirations and attitudes toward aspects of their lives, although she did not probe as extensively as Hirschi in this area. However, Mc-

Donald's questionnaire included about eight times as many delinquency items as Hirschi's.

Responses were analyzed by *frequency* of admitted offense and were correlated separately and in clusters of crimes for their association with four social-class categories: "upper middle, lower middle, upper working, and lower working." The clusters of delinquencies included seven questions about serious theft, twelve questions about petty theft, four questions about vehicle theft, twelve questions about "misconduct" such as truancy and running away from home, seven questions on vandalism, and five questions about violent behavior.

McDonald's findings agree with most of the pictures of delinquency drawn by American self-report studies, with the exception that there is a clearer association in England between measures of socioeconomic status and confessions of crime. McDonald's data may be summarized as follows:

1   When the *proportions* of boys in the four social classes are compared with respect to the *frequencies* with which they admit to the various delinquencies, there are consistently higher rates for working-class boys. This association varies by cluster of offenses. The correlation is particularly strong between socio-economic status and admissions of vandalism and violence. For example, Table 9 shows the distribution by social class of admissions to five items of violent behavior: being in a fist fight, starting a fist fight, beating someone up without provocation, possessing a weapon, and participating in gang fights. An overall "violence" score is also assigned, and the probability of this

Table 9   Admissions of Violence by Social Class

Offence	UM	LM	LW	LW	P
			(Percent admitting)		
Violence	60	64	71	78	< .005
Fist fight	72	75	81	83	< .05
Fight start	44	42	50	57	< .05
Assault	24	22	32	33	< .05
Gang fights	33	39	49	51	< .001
Weapons	16	30	22	24	< .02

Source: Reprinted with permission from McDonald, 1969, p. 88.

distribution's occurring "by chance" is listed under "P" in the table.

The petty-theft and misconduct measures are less clearly distributed by social class. Again, as in other surveys of such peccadilloes, everyone has done so many of these things so often that class makes little difference. In England the majority of these schoolboys say they have stolen things from their schools and done some small shoplifting. Middle-class boys apparently steal more frequently from their parents than do working-class boys, while working-class boys more frequently admit to having pinched fruit and accepted stolen articles.

Of all the clusters of crimes examined by McDonald, the category of admitted "serious theft" showed the weakest relation with social class. Since the number of boys admitting these more grave offenses was small, it becomes difficult to interpret this finding. Among the various kinds of "serious theft" assayed, only larceny and a composite score of "vehicle theft" showed significant differences in the expected direction among the social classes (Table 10).

Overall, McDonald reports differences in the *proportions* of the social classes admitting to delinquencies and differences in the *frequencies* of their confessed crimes.

2   The type of school attended was associated with differences in admitted delinquencies. Grammar school children re-

Table 10   Admissions of Theft by Social Class

Offence	UM	LM	UW	LW	P
Serious theft (percent admitting)	33	34	35	37	> .80
Shoplifting	8	9	10	12	> .10
Larceny	6	9	13	17	< .005
Breaking & entering	22	22	23	22	> .50
Taking car	4	6	7	5	> .70
Car possession	6	8	10	11	> .20
Taking cycle	3	7	8	9	> .05
Taking scooter	4	7	6	11	> .05
Vehicle theft	12	15	16	22	< .05

Source: Reprinted with permission from McDonald, 1969, p. 83.

ported fewer offenses than did boys in the secondary modern schools, and this difference persisted when their social class was held constant. "Amongst middle-class children those attending grammar schools admitted to less delinquency than those attending modern schools. And the same occurred with respect to working-class children" (p. 164).

3 As in Hirschi's American study, self-reported delinquency and school achievement were also correlated in England. When school achievement is judged by the "stream" in which a boy has been placed, "children of lower streams . . . have higher rates of delinquency than children of higher streams, holding class and school type constant" (p. 164).

4 McDonald examined official records of court appearances to ascertain whether the same distribution of offenses by classes obtained. This was done on a school-by-school basis, rather than by checking on the court appearances of the individual respondents. Such an area, or ecological, analysis, does not provide strong validation of self-report measures. However, McDonald was interested in ascertaining whether, among the schools surveyed, the pattern of confessed crime resembled the pattern of officially noticed crime. It did:

> The correlation of numbers of working-class boys per school and numbers of court appearances per school was extremely high . . . As in the admitted delinquency survey the simple social-class variable, father's occupation, was the variable most associated with rates of delinquency [p. 165].

Type of school was also associated with official delinquency, as it was with admitted offenses. While not so important a variable as social class itself, "the rates of court appearances . . . produced a very high and significant correlation" with type of school (p. 166).

In Summary

Self-report measures seem to confirm or disconfirm official records of criminality depending upon where one looks and the kinds of observational instruments one uses. The hope that

asking people about their crimes would provide criminologists
with better data than official figures cannot be said to have been
fulfilled. Where self-report measures *confirm* official statistics,
observational studies, and surveys of victims, one can have some
confidence in them. Where confessions of criminal conduct
disagree with these other tallies of delinquencies, it will be
political preference or "social philosophy," rather than good
reasons, that determines which statistics one chooses. This is so
because *asking people questions about their behavior is a poor
way of observing it.*

Criticism of Self-Report Measures

Sociologists, this one included, continue to ask people questions.
It is one thing, however, to ask people their *opinions* about a
matter. It is quite another task to ask people to recall *what they
have done,* and it is particularly ticklish to ask people to recall
their "bad" behavior.

Confessional data are at least as weak as the official
statistics they were supposed to improve upon. Self-report studies have been criticized on three grounds: (1) that their tools are
poor and varied, (2) that the research designs have often been
deficient and conducive to the drawing of false inferences, and (3)
that the social settings in which the studies have been undertaken
are so varied as to provide inconclusive tests of hypotheses that
challenge other ways of counting crime.

Weakness of Instruments   Among the qualities one seeks
in a measuring tool, two prime requisites are *reliability* and
validity. "Reliability" refers to the *consistency* with which a
yardstick yields a measurement. A ruler that reports different
sizes upon repeated measurements of the same object is unreliable.

"Validity" refers to the *accuracy* with which a measure
gauges the concept being studied. A measure of length ought to
calibrate the construct "length," and not some other quality, like
heat. A measure of criminal acts ought to gauge criminal acts
rather than something intermediate like what the police do or
what people say.

Measuring instruments that are unreliable cannot be valid. If the ruler expands or contracts haphazardly each time it is used, it cannot accurately measure the relatively constant reality to which it is applied. However, a reliable instrument may still be invalid. Measuring tools, like people, can lie consistently.

Reliability of self-reports Several measures of reliability have been invented. Some of these are tests of the internal consistency of a scale; others are assessments of the retest consistency of a measurement. Because of the special circumstances under which confessions of criminality are collected, the internal consistency of these measures has been proved more frequently than their retest reliability. For both types of reliability, however, the results are mixed.

If a self-report measure were internally consistent, it would mean that respondents who score criminally on the more serious items would do so also on the more trivial ones. When *scaling* techniques are employed in the construction of self-report measures, their internal consistency is assured by the method of construction (Nye and Short, 1957). These scaling procedures weed out questions that do not "hang together" for the population being studied. When an index of criminal activity is thus "scaled," there is some assurance that individuals who get a high score on the serious offenses also score high on the more trivial offenses. Scaling a self-report index is rather like assuring that "tall people are taller than short people." On the other hand, an unscaled index might reveal that "some tall people are shorter than some short people"—that is, an individual who scores high on the serious offenses might score low on the light offenses.

Unscaled self-report measures yield a mixed pattern of internal consistency. For example, Hirschi reports modest correlations among the admissions to the six kinds of crime he measured. According to Table 11 these correlations range from a low of .20 between having stolen $50 or more and having deliberately beaten someone up, and a high of .48 between having stolen $2 to $50 and having stolen $50 or more. These associations are low for several reasons, including the fact that the time span covering these delinquencies was not necessarily the same for all respondents.

Table 11   Correlations Among Self-Report Items, White Boys Only

	1	2	3	4	5	6
1. Theft ($2)	1.00	.45	.26	.27	.28	.27
2. Theft ($2–$50)		1.00	.48	.30	.26	.27
3. Theft ($50 or more)			1.00	.32	.21	.20
4. Auto theft				1.00	.23	.22
5. Vandalism					1.00	.28
6. Battery						1.00

Source: Reprinted with permission from Hirschi, 1969, p. 56.

Some investigators report higher reliability for *retests* of admissions of criminality. Clark and Tifft (1966) found that 18.5 percent of the confessions originally given on a questionnaire were changed when the respondents were threatened with a "lie-detector" check on their veracity. Under such duress, the consistency of response, 81.5 percent, is probably quite adequate.

Dentler and Monroe (1961) report a very high reliability of response (.955) on a retest of their questionnaire, and a similar finding (.98) has been published by Kulik and his colleagues (1968). Kulik's study is of additional interest because it demonstrates that anonymous questionnaires are not necessarily more reliable than signed ones. Although *more* antisocial behavior was disclosed anonymously, the differences between anonymous and signed confessions were slight. The differences were more pronounced for the *minor* infractions than for the serious offenses, and they did not change the rank order of individuals on a measure of their delinquency.

Validity of self-reports   The reliability of self-report measures is not questioned as much as is their validity. The crucial questions are whether self-report instruments are valid and, in particular, whether they are more valid than police statistics or surveys of victims. Validation of criminal confessions has been attempted in three ways: (1) by checking admissions of crime against self-reports of other antisocial behavior, (2) by comparing the self-reports of "known groups," and (3) by comparing these scores with official records.

(1) *Self-reports validated by self-reports.* The first procedure correlates admissions of delinquency with admissions of other

misconduct like truancy, school suspension, or "contacts" with the police. This is, of course, a redundant form of validation—self-report against self-report. One would expect a high degree of association among such measures. The reported correlations are, however, low. Hirschi found that individual items in his self-report index correlated between .24 and .33 with truancy, between .18 and .28 with admitted school suspensions, and between .28 and .39 with admitted "contacts" with the police (p. 57).

(2) *Known-group validation.* The second procedure, "known-group" validation, looks at the pattern of scores from verbal reports of criminality that are made by segments of the population "known" to have behaved differently. For example, the self-report scores of "official" delinquents, like boys in "training schools," are compared with a sample of "nondelinquents." When this has been done, significant differences are reported on the confessional instruments between "known delinquents" and less offensive populations (Nye and Short, 1957; Voss, 1963).

This form of validation assumes, of course, what the self-report technique was to have tested, namely, that official delinquents really do behave differently. Such convergent validation gives some assurance that both official statistics and unofficial confessions are measuring the same thing. This convergence does not, however, permit a conclusion about the greater validity of one measure over another. This can be said, too, about the third procedure for validating self-report instruments: checking admissions of crime against police or court records.

(3) *Self-reports and official records.* It is paradoxical that critics of official records of criminal activity should revert to them as validators of data from questionnaires and interviews. It is difficult to know what kind of finding would constitute a validation and yet justify the preferred use of confessions. Without an informed hypothesis framed in advance as to the expected relation between what people say they have done and what they get arrested for, the investigator has no way of deciding how strong a correlation is required to validate the confessions he collects. If the association between admitted crime and official records approaches zero, presumably the self-reports are invalid.

If the association approaches unity, then one measure may be substituted for the other. Between these poles, how much association, or dissociation, proves validity, and of which instrument?

Despite these unanswered questions, students who have used self-reports of criminality have sometimes checked the replies they have received against official data. The results, again, have been mixed. Four of the better investigations of this matter, in descending order of the validities discovered, are those of Erickson and Empey, Voss, Hirschi, and McCandless and his associates.

The Erickson-Empey study (1963). Erickson and Empey interviewed boys between the ages of 15 and 17 in Utah. They had a sample of 50 randomly selected high school boys who had never been to court, a sample of 30 boys who had been to court once, a sample of 50 randomly selected repeat offenders who were on probation, and a sample of 50 randomly selected incarcerated offenders. After the interviews, the names of all respondents were checked against court records. "None of those who had been to court failed to say so in the interview, nor did anyone fail to describe the offense(s) for which he was charged" (p. 459).

The high coincidence of appearance in court and confession lends confidence to, but does not prove, the validity of the admissions that may *not* have resulted in arrest. However, a finding significant for our understanding of the meaning of official statistics is Erickson and Empey's demonstration that the *frequency* with which laws are broken is a significant factor in determining arrest and appearance in court. The distinction between *frequency* of violations and the *proportions* of persons who have committed an offense is important, say Erickson and Empey, in helping "to avoid the pitfall of concluding that, because large *proportions* of two different samples—i.e., students and institutionalized delinquents—have committed various offenses, the samples are equally delinquent in terms of total volume" (p. 462).

It appears, again, that the law operates like a coarse net; only the biggest fish are caught.

Voss's research. Voss (1963) was interested in testing whether official statistics distorted the representation of ethnic groups in delinquent activities. His locale was Honolulu, a multiethnic city, in which official records show a disproportionate number of Hawaiians, male and female, charged with delinquencies and committed to institutions and an underrepresentation of Orientals so categorized.

Voss selected a 15.5 percent sample of seventh-graders to whom a reliable delinquency scale was administered and its scores compared by ethnicity with both delinquent charges laid against these diverse groups and with their differential institutionalization.

Of the 620 respondents, 52 were known to the police and had been apprehended for 83 offenses. Of these 83 violations, only four were denied on Voss's questionnaire, a remarkable degree of validity. Given this kind of validity, it is not surprising that Voss found a strong convergence between charges laid, juveniles incarcerated, and confessions of delinquency. All three measures pointed to the same social locations of youthful crime.

Hirschi's study. Hirschi's work yields a more modest convergence of self-reports with official records. He found that 15 percent of the white boys in his sample who said that they had *never* stolen anything of medium value actually had police records (p. 57). Hirschi does not tell us what this 15 percent had done to get on the police blotter, so that it is difficult to assess the degree of invalidity this figure may represent. Similarly, Hirschi found that 46 percent of the boys who admitted having stolen something of medium value had police records. Again, it is not clear whether this expresses high or low validity.

A better test of validity in Hirschi's data is provided by answers to his question, "Have you ever been picked up by the police?" Fifty-five percent of the white boys who said they had been apprehended by the police did *not* have police records. Sixteen percent of the boys who said they had *never* been picked up by the police actually had records (p. 77). The figures are quite different for the black boys in Hirschi's sample. Among the Negro respondents, 24 percent who said they had been picked up by the police had no official records, while 36 percent of those who said they had never been arrested actually had police records. Hirschi attributes some portion of this discrepancy between confession and official record to failures of memory and to arrests that occurred after administration of his questionnaire.

The research of McCandless and his colleagues. An even less optimistic validation of self-report measures appears in the recent work of McCandless and his associates (1972). These psychologists studied institutionalized black and white boys, 15 to 17 years of age, who had been reared in impoverished environments in the southern United States. A self-report instrument was composed of 15 questions taken from scales developed by Nye and Short (1957) and Siegman (1966a). Answers given to the questionnaire were compared with official records from which an index of "committed delinquency" was calculated that weighed the *frequency and the seriousness* of the offenses known to have been committed by these boys. *The rank-order correlation between these overall measures of admitted and committed delinquency was a low .12.*

The investigators checked specific answers to particular items in the self-report measure against each boy's intake sheet. In the authors' words,

> "Forty of the 51 summary sheets contained information sufficient to check one or more of the *S*s' responses to the admitted delinquency questionnaire. Of the total of 69 clear-cut items that could be checked, 48 or 70 per cent were accurate, while 21 or 30 per cent were inaccurate. The large percentage of inaccurate responses is particularly surprising when one considers that the items selected for inspection concerned those offenses that the boys had either been apprehended for or had previously admitted to. Nineteen (almost 50 percent) of the 40 *S*s included in this subanalysis were found to have answered at least one item inaccurately" [p. 285].

What can be made of these diverse results—results that range from high to low convergence among measures? Where there is agreement among them, confidence in the information is increased. Where there is divergence among the tallies, the choice of the more correct map of social reality becomes a function of one's confidence in the cartographer and his instruments. Instruments built out of people's answers to our questions are always tricky. There are good reasons for listening skeptically to what people tell us they have done.

Sources of unreliability and invalidity in questionnaires and interviews Both the reliability and the validity of the answers people give to our questions are affected by a host of factors well known to social psychologists. For example, people give invalid responses to questions because the words and the phrases mean different things to them. The form of the question, the choice of words, and the position of the question in a series of items all affect what we think the question means (Nuckols, 1949–1950, 1953; Rugg and Cantril, 1942; Stember and Hyman, 1949–1950). In interviews, even vocal intonation affects the comprehension of meaning (Micklin and Durbin, 1968).

People also give invalid answers because their memories are inaccurate. The validity of memory varies with time, with the way in which the memory is evoked (recall versus recognition, for example), with a person's interest in remembering, with the emotionality of the subject matter (we tend to forget the unpleasant), and, of course, with personality traits (Alper, 1946; Haber, 1970; Waldfogel, 1948; Zeigarnik, 1927).

In addition to these many sources of error in answering questions about our criminal conduct, there are sources of error in the interrogator. Bias on the part of the interviewer in following instructions and in recording responses, and even cheating by the interviewer, are recognized distorting factors (Cahalan *et al.,* 1947; Gales and Kendall, 1957; Hanson and Marks, 1958; Smith and Hyman, 1950).

Finally, a difficulty in using confessions to measure criminality is the sad fact that people do not always tell the truth. We do not tell the truth for a variety of reasons. The "prestige" of a question, the "social desirability" of its content, has a well-documented impact upon the kind of answer given to it (Edwards, 1957). People sometimes lie to conceal their faults, even from themselves, and they sometimes lie when a confession of criminality gives them glamor. In addition to these motivations to deception, there is carelessness in attending to what is asked

and there is the delinquent's joy in "jiving" his "square" interrogator.

These multiple defects in counting crime from confessions
have been well summarized by the English psychologist Belson
and his colleagues (1970), who have taken care to develop more
sensitive methods of finding out who has stolen how much. These
procedures involve interviews in a depersonalized atmosphere in
which threat is removed and anonymity is assured. A list of
offenses is used after it has been tested for comprehensibility
among the samples to be studied. Interviewers are trained and
strictly regulated, and their note taking is reduced to a minimum.
The interview schedule also contains "trap questions" that serve
as validators of the replies. Belson's research with these im-
proved measures is in progress. It will be interesting to compare
his findings with the varied American reports.

Research Design and Fair Inference   The defects of self-
report measures of criminal conduct do not end with flaws in the
instruments. Research design has also been poor and has encouraged improper inferences from ambiguous data.

The trouble derives from the difficulties suggested earlier in
comparing official records with measures that are supposed to
correct them. Without an external criterion, independent of either
measure, against which to validate statistics, one can *quarrel* with
the relative accuracy of competing measures, but he cannot *test*
their correctness.

Suppose that students interested in the fruitfulness *(criminality)* of different regions *(classes, nations)* doubt whether
counting oranges *(crimes known to the police)* provides a fair tally
of fruitfulness. The skeptics propose that counting apples *(confessions)* may yield a more accurate estimate of fruitfulness. To
prove their case they compare the distribution of apples and
oranges in regions that produce both. Assume, now, that the
different regions are found to contribute different proportions of
apples and oranges. What has the exercise demonstrated?

A comparison of a new measure of uncertain validity
(self-reports) with old measures of moderate validity (official
records) tells us nothing about their relative accuracy *unless there*

is assurance that both instruments are designed to measure the same thing. However, questionnaires about delinquency have been heavily weighted with *trivial* offenses, the very kind that most of us have committed and that are least likely to result in arrest. These instruments have even included large numbers of noncriminal acts like "doing things my parents told me not to do" and "being out at night just fooling around after I was supposed to be home." (Clark and Wenninger, 1962).

From such incomparable measures false inferences can be drawn, and have been drawn, about the true distribution of delinquency among classes or races. The erroneous conclusions are stimulated through the artifice of the *shifting cutting point.* The investigator decides that scores above and below "x" on his self-report scale constitute, respectively, being "delinquent" and "nondelinquent." In one study, for example, it was decided that scores above the median constituted "delinquency" (Chambliss and Nagasawa, 1969). The researcher then compares the proportions of these so-called "delinquents" and "nondelinquents" among the social classes or ethnic groups with the proportions given by their official records. *Since it is not known what score on the questionnaire represents activities equivalent to those for which the same people were arrested, the cutting points are arbitrary.* By moving the cutting points from, say, the 50th percentile to the 70th percentile, different proportions of classes of people may be categorized as "delinquent." This arbitrary decision encourages false inferences.

By contrast with this poor procedure, a fair comparison between two such different measures of criminality requires that the frequency and the gravity of admitted offenses be correlated, *individual by individual* among the different classes or races, with the crimes for which these persons have been charged.

The Varied Social Setting It has been pointed out that the relation between confessions of criminality and some of the "social locators" of crime, like income and ethnicity, varies with the instruments used and the places studied. This is to be expected. Interpretation of the results of research with self-report tools must consider the social setting in which they have been employed. These settings have varied greatly. For example, Dentler and Monroe (1961) studied seventh- and eighth-grade students in three small Kansas towns, Voss (1966) asked for confessions of delinquency in a highly Oriental city (Honolulu), and Clark and Wenninger (1962) quizzed schoolchildren in four Illinois locations that varied from a rural farm setting to a Negro section of Chicago to one rich suburb and one industrial suburb.

Such variation of types of communities is an important qualifier of the impact of any variable, like money, upon the behaviors to be explained. If a student is trying to ascertain the effect of "social class" upon criminality, as is required by many theories of crime causation, he must consider that the ways of life of people categorized by their income, occupation, or education differ widely depending upon the social setting in which they live as rich or poor, learned or ignorant members of society. Being relatively poor in rural Scandinavia or rural Mexico has an altogether different meaning for one's style of life than being relatively poor in New York City. Being "working class" in an English town that is ethnically homogeneous, highly religious, and family-centered is a markedly different experience from being "working class" in a heterogeneous American metropolis. The community setting, then, makes a difference to the expected impact of possibly causal factors, like social status, upon misbehavior. This qualification affects the interpretation of *all* criminal statistics, of course, not just the self-report measures.

SUMMARY

Considerable attention has been paid to the utility of self-report measures of criminality because they have been devised and employed as correctives of the apparent deficiencies in official statistics. An evaluation of these unofficial ways of counting crime does *not* fulfill the promise that they would provide a better enumeration of offensive activity.

We know best where certain kinds of crime are generated when the major measures of criminality converge. Fortunately for those who would assess the competing explanations of crime, confessions of delinquency, surveys of victims, and judicial records point to similar social sites in industrialized nations as producing more murderers, muggers, rapists, robbers, burglars, and heavy thieves than others. We know something, too—although with less certainty—about the social locations of less visible crimes like shoplifting and embezzlement.

In describing these correlates of crime, it should be borne in mind that our defined scope concerns principally the more visible, predatory crimes, the crimes *mala in se,* and that our interest is in the explanations advanced in reply to the sociological, rather than the psychological, questions about these crimes. It bears repeating, also, that these correlates are not necessarily the causes of offenses, but simply the material with which the sociological explicator works.

Furthermore, in looking at these materials sociologically, it is not in the least necessary to "dehumanize" the groups of actors whose behaviors are under scrutiny. This is said because a common charge against study of the behavior of aggregates is that such study ignores the distinctiveness of the individual. On the contrary, facts having to do with higher probabilities of crime among certain categories of people, as these are outlined in the following chapter, do not deny that "every man may have his price," that we are all subject to criminal temptation, or that, given the right (or wrong) combination of opportunity, pressure, need, and passion, even an improbable crime may become part of our fate. One can agree with Tolstoy's humanistic dictum that "the seeds of every crime are in each of us" and yet hold, with the social scientists, that the seeds are germinated under different conditions that raise or lower the probability of their fruition.

Chapter 5

Some Correlates of the Serious Crimes

If attention is limited to the more visible, predatory crimes, criminologists can point to correlates of these offenses. Such correlates constitute some, but not all, of the facts with which explanations of these kinds of crime are built. In reviewing these associations it should be remembered that these correlations do not in themselves describe causes, and that the strength and the shape of these relationships vary with what surrounds them. The connections to be described are not absolutes; they do not operate in a vacuum. They are themselves variables whose meaning for behavior changes with the social setting in which the association occurs.

AGE AND SEX

Two of the most striking and persistent "conditions" associated with the risk of committing serious crimes are being male and being young. If one groups people by age and sex and then looks at their proportional contribution to arrest or conviction rates, the worldwide experience is that young men make higher contributions to crime than do old persons and women.

In England and Wales, for example, convictions for indictable offenses tend to peak among boys 14 to 16 years of age. This sex and age differential obtains despite the liberal use of cautioning by the police instead of arrest, particularly at the earlier ages. McClintock and Avison (1968) provide a picture of indictable offenses (Figure 6) that dramatically indicates the higher crime rates of teen-agers and of males. A similar pyramid of criminality appears in Sweden (Sveri, 1960); and the United States also exhibits this proclivity of young men to crime.

Compared with their proportions in the population, young Americans are arrested far more frequently than middle-aged or senior citizens. Table 12 shows that, while youths of both sexes aged 15 to 19 years constituted only 9.0 percent of the population, they accounted for 27.6 percent of the arrests for violent crimes and 41.0 percent of the arrests for selected offenses against property. After these older teen-agers, the group next most frequently arrested were men and women 20 to 24 years of age, who constituted 8.0 percent of the population but accounted for 23.8 percent of the arrests for violence and 15.6 percent of the arrests for certain kinds of theft. Table 12 also shows that children 10 to 14 years of age were arrested for these kinds of theft at a rate twice that of their representation in the population.

The association of age with criminal conduct varies, of course, with the kind of crime. In industrialized countries, burglary, automobile theft, and the "ordinary larcenies" tend to be teen-age crimes. The years during which one is most likely to commit murder tend to be the early twenties. The more "intelligent" larcenies like forgery, counterfeiting, fraud, and embezzlement peak at later years. In the United States, according to FBI figures (1970, table 28), these more clever larcenies are distributed among the age categories in a pattern similar to the pattern of arrests for forcible rape, murder, and manslaughter, all crimes that reach their zenith among people 20 to 24 years of age.

There are some interesting interactions between sex, the age

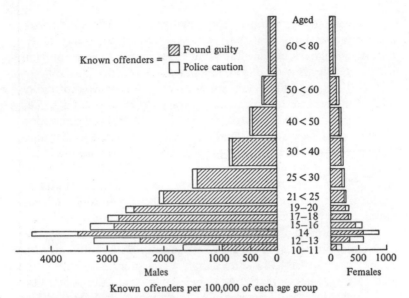

Figure 6 The proportion of known male and female offenders in each age group, indictable offenses only, England and Wales, 1965. Reprinted with permission from McClintock and Avison, *Crime in England and Wales,* 1968, diagram 7.

of one's introduction to crime, and repetition of crime. For example, when women get arrested for the "chemical offenses"—drunkenness, possession or sale of narcotics, violation of liquor laws, and driving while intoxicated—they tend to do so at earlier ages than men (FBI, 1970, table 26). On this point, too, there is evidence that, in Western cultures at least, females who become addicted to the popular chemicals do so at earlier ages than males, with graver consequences, and with less probability of reforming (Karpman, 1948). Regardless of this possible sex difference, the younger a person of either sex is when first arrested, the greater the likelihood of a second arrest and, in general, the shorter the time span between offenses (Mannheim and Wilkins, 1955; Sellin, 1958).

The types of crime that men and women tend to commit also differ in some rather obvious ways. It is only men who get arrested for forcible rape and it is principally, but not entirely, women who get arrested for prostitution and infanticide. Although males have consistently higher arrest and conviction rates than females, and although they have exhibited this proclivity over the years in a variety of cultures, *the disparity between the sexes fluctuates with class of crime, with time, and with the social setting.* For example, the rate for males of *crimes against the person* exceeds the rate for females in North America by more than 8 to 1, but the rate for males of *crimes against property* exceeds the rate for females by about half that, something in the order of 4 to 1 in recent years.

The influence of culture is strong here and affects the sex ratio of crimes exhibited at different times and places. For example, it must not be concluded that any men, anywhere, are always more murderous than any women, anywhere. As an illustration, Wolfgang's detailed study of homicide in Philadelphia (1958) reports that white males were convicted of criminal homicide 8 times as frequently as white females. The sex ratio for this offense among Negroes was half that, 4 to 1.

Table 12 Selected Serious Crimes (Arrests) by Age Group, United States, 1970

Age group	Percent of population	Percent of arrests for violent crimes[a]	Percent of arrests for offenses against property[b]
10–14	10.4	7.0	21.8
15–19	9.0	27.6	41.0
20–24	8.0	23.8	15.6
25–29	6.5	13.8	6.9
30–34	5.5	8.6	3.9
35–39	5.4	6.3	2.7
40–44	5.7	4.8	2.2
45–49	6.0	3.3	1.6
50–54	5.4	2.1	1.0
55–59	4.8	1.3	.7
60–64	4.2	.7	.4
65 and over	9.8	.7	.5

[a]Violent crime is offenses of murder, forcible rape, robbery, and aggravated assault. The percentages do not add up to 100, because of rounding and omission of ages under 10.

[b]Crime against property is offenses of burglary, larceny, and automobile theft. Percentages do not add up to 100 for the reasons specified in footnote a.

Source: Abstracted from U.S. Department of Commerce. Bureau of the Census, *General Population Characteristics*, 1970 P C(1)–B1, and Uniform Crime Reports, 1970.

However, the disparity in cultures was such that Negro females in Philadelphia had a recorded homicide rate 3 times that of the white males (p. 55).

It is true that men generally produce higher crime rates than women. However, the sex ratios for criminal activity are not constants. The shifting circumstances under which criminal behaviors among men and women change is an intriguing subject that would take us far afield. A description of the styles of criminality between the sexes and among the cultures would make its own book, which might expand upon the fascinating data Pollak (1951) has recorded in his study of the criminality of women. Pollak observes, for example, that where poisoning as a specific homicidal method has been recorded, as in Italy, it has appeared as a specialty of women, with a sex ratio during the late nineteenth century of 123 women convicted of the "Borgia practice" for every 100 men. What is of more importance is the conclusion Pollak draws from North American and European data: that if one looks at all the serious crimes for which men and women are convicted, the homicide rate among females constitutes a larger proportion of all female crimes than male murder constitutes of all male crimes.

Equality and Changing Sex Ratios in Crime

The most interesting hypothesis advanced to explain cultural differences in the sex ratios of criminal activities and changes in these ratios over time is the suggestion that as women become the equals of men in rights and privileges, they become their equals also in crime.

Cross-culturally, the more distinct and different the roles of the sexes, the wider the reported disparity between the crime rates of the sexes. As cultures approximate unisexuality, the disparity between the crime rates for the two sexes narrows. For example, Houchon (1967) calculated sex ratios in crime for nine regions of Africa and found that the crime rates for men exceeded the rates for women by differences ranging from 900:1 to more than 20,000:1. The cultures he studied draw distinct lines between male and female work and privileges. Findings of the same order are reported for Ceylon (1957), where almost all (98 percent) of juvenile probationers are male; and for prewar Algiers and Tunis, where men convicted of crime exceeded women by almost 3,000 to 1 (Hacker, 1941).

Such disparities contrast with the figures for North America and western Europe, where women more closely approach equality with men. For example, Wolf (1965) studied a representative sample of Danes and found that 18.8 percent of the men and 2.3 percent of the women had criminal records, a ratio of about 8 to 1. Similarly, British criminal statistics report that for England and Wales in 1970, the ratio of convictions of males to convictions of females for all indictable offenses was 6.1 to 1 (Command paper #4708, 1970).

Changes over time, as well as cross-cultural comparisons, support the hypothesis that, as women achieve equality in other spheres, they close the gap, too, between their crime rates and those of men. For example, in the United States during the 10 years from 1960 through 1969, the robbery rate for males under 18 years of age increased 170 percent while the rate for females of the same age increased 319 percent. Larcenies over $50 in value increased 79 percent for young men and 227 percent for young women; the rates for automobile theft increased 61 percent for young men and 132 percent for young women. During this decade, the overall increase in arrests for violent crimes was 142 percent for males under 18 years of age and 231 percent for females of the same age. The increase in arrests for all offenses against property was 73 percent for boys and 211 percent for girls. Table 13 summarizes this narrowing disparity in the criminality of American men and women.

The fact that sex ratios of criminality vary in time and with the social setting reduces, though it does not eliminate, the importance of biological factors in the explanation of crime rates. Men and women continue to be different biological organisms, and the recent reduction of the differences between them in delinquency is not expected to continue until their rates of offenses are equal.

Table 13 Total Arrest Trends by Sex, 1960-1970

2,528 Agencies; 1970 Population 98,698,600[1]

Offense charged	Males						Females					
	Total			Under 18			Total			Under 18		
	1960	1970	Percent change	1960	1970	Percent change	1960	1970	Percent change	1960	1970	Percent change
TOTAL	3,156,811	3,968,794	+25.7	439,929	870,460	+97.9	387,073	675,212	+74.4	77,110	234,483	+204.1
Criminal homicide:												
(a) Murder and nonnegligent manslaughter	4,137	8,582	+107.4	353	1,072	+203.7	871	1,527	+75.3	27	80	+196.3
(b) Manslaughter by negligence	1,769	1,613	-8.8	144	142	-1.4	199	211	+6.0	9	16	+77.8
Forcible rape	7,149	11,094	+55.2	1,284	2,380	+85.4						
Robbery	32,191	69,786	+116.8	7,996	23,737	+196.9	1,603	4,615	+187.9	389	1,813	+366.1
Aggravated assault	48,503	80,585	+66.1	6,041	13,421	+122.2	8,503	12,427	+46.1	689	2,265	+228.7
Burglary—breaking or entering	119,908	190,949	+59.2	57,232	97,200	+69.8	3,983	9,312	+133.8	1,751	4,450	+154.1
Larceny—theft	173,267	309,694	+78.7	85,986	157,911	+83.6	34,317	122,588	+257.2	14,703	56,009	+280.9
Auto theft	55,637	92,245	+65.2	34,043	50,633	+48.7	2,094	4,870	+133.0	1,344	2,784	+107.1
Violent crime [2]	91,980	170,047	+84.9	15,674	40,610	+159.1	10,977	18,569	+69.2	1,105	4,158	+276.3
Property crime [3]	349,012	592,878	+69.9	177,261	305,744	+72.5	40,394	136,779	+238.6	17,798	63,243	+255.3
Subtotal for above offenses	442,761	764,538	+72.7	193,079	346,496	+79.5	51,570	155,559	+201.6	18,912	67,417	+256.5

Offense										
Other assaults	118,484	+52.7	180,980	39,428	+155.2	13,004	27,833	+114.0	1,994	7,980	+300.2
Forgery and counterfeiting	17,884	+36.4	24,388	2,429	+102.6	3,447	7,918	+129.7	352	926	+163.1
Embezzlement and fraud	29,752	+43.9	42,816	1,536	+168.1	5,350	16,235	+203.5	161	642	+298.8
Stolen property; buying, receiving, possessing	9,247	+354.1	41,990	2,871	+389.9	878	4,437	+405.4	185	941	+408.6
Weapons; carrying, possessing, etc	31,718	+128.5	72,466	1,532	+75.3	1,827	5,194	+184.3	203	512	+152.2
Prostitution and commercialized vice	8,084	+17.2	9,473	311	+143.0	20,976	36,330	+73.2	297	726	+144.4
Sex offenses (except forcible rape and prostitution)	39,115	−18.7	31,809	5,006	−21.2	8,798	4,959	−43.6	2,915	1,533	−47.4
Narcotic drug laws	26,931	+734.3	224,694	−3,436	+2,956.7	4,680	41,040	+776.9	243	11,420	+4,599.6
Gambling	110,615	−37.5	69,162	1,393	−6.6	10,996	6,163	−44.0	42	49	+16.7
Offenses against family and children	36,940	−6.6	34,487	271	−31.7	3,433	3,642	+6.1	171	146	−14.6
Driving under the influence	139,246	+88.6	262,696	2,763	+157.5	8,573	18,854	+119.9	57	165	+189.5
Liquor laws	73,479	+61.7	118,790	36,057	+139.4	12,614	17,889	+41.8	2,502	7,658	+206.1
Drunkenness	1,181,259	−13.5	1,021,568	24,639	+110.1	100,444	75,692	−24.6	1,363	3,943	+189.3
Disorderly conduct	366,475	+.9	369,815	71,432	+66.3	58,368	67,047	+14.9	7,583	15,131	+99.5
Vagrancy	129,912	−50.2	64,661	7,739	+2.6	10,690	17,650	+65.1	914	1,686	+84.5
All other offenses (except traffic)	394,909	+60.7	634,561	222,341	+101.4	71,425	168,770	+136.3	39,216	113,608	+189.7
Suspicion (not included in totals)	105,563	−58.0	44,311	70,852	−43.7	13,095	7,453	−43.1	2,732	2,442	−10.6

[1] Based on comparable reports from 1,898 cities representing 81,246,000 population and 630 counties representing 17,452,000 population.

[2] Violent crime is offenses of murder, forcible rape, robbery and aggravated assault.

[3] Property crime is offenses of burglary, larceny and auto theft.

Source: Reprinted with permission from Uniform Crime Reports, 1970, table 26.

OCCUPATION, INCOME, AND OTHER INDICATORS OF SOCIAL STATUS

Of all the factors that condition our lives, money has become the most popular symbol. It is the sign of what ails us and what cures us. Sophie Tucker used to say, "I've been rich and I've been poor. Rich is better." One of America's most honored bank robbers, Willie "The Actor" Sutton, would have agreed. "Why do you rob banks?" an official helper once asked him. "Because that's where the money is," Sutton replied. The most persistent explanation of stealing, and of the violence connected with it, is that some people want what others have.

Given our belief in the allure of money and the things it buys, it is no surprise to find that developed countries show a *negative* association between measures of social position, like income and occupational prestige, and vulnerability to arrest, conviction, and imprisonment. Within each state, people with less money, with less schooling, with lower occupational status and measured intelligence are disproportionately represented in the statistics of the serious, predatory crimes (Cooper, 1960; Mack, 1964; Morris, 1957; Schmid, 1960; Wolf, 1962; Wolfgang *et al.*, 1972).

This association is most clearly represented when official records and surveys of victims are used to locate criminality. Although the association is challenged, as we have seen, by some American research using self report measures, it has been confirmed in varying degree by such studies in Sweden and England (Elmhorn, 1965; McDonald, 1969b). Furthermore, those American self-report investigations that have attended to the *frequency and gravity* of admitted offenses, rather than merely to the distribution of all offenses among the social classes, more frequently yield a negative correlation between status and crime.

A Parenthetical Caution

The research reporting this type of correlation shows that it is not fixed and that its shape and its strength vary by region, by type of offense, and over time. There are styles of being rich, poor, and middling, and the social setting in which ascribed status is experienced makes a difference to behavior. In short, we must be careful, once more, not to interpret the tendencies described by the reported correlations as uniformities or as causal connections. Locating crime socially is a step toward explaining it, *but the location is not the explanation.* Particularly, we should avoid confusing the *location* with the *cause.*

For example, we note, that in modern countries hospitals are the principal sites of deaths without concluding that hospitals *cause* dying. Similarly, we may observe areas of greater or lesser criminality without concluding that the area, or its defining characteristics, causes the differences in crime rates. Van den Haag (1968, p. 283) puts it this way:

> The crime rate in slums is indeed higher than elsewhere; but so is the death rate in hospitals. Slums are no more "causes" of crime than hospitals are of death; they are locations of crime, as hospitals are of death. Slums and hospitals attract people selectively, neither is the "cause" of the condition (disease in hospitals, poverty in slums) that leads to the selective attraction.

With this caution in mind, a sample of the international research may be summarized.

Ecological and Individual-case Studies of Status and Criminality

Some research on the relation between social status and criminality has used an ecological approach and some an individual-case procedure.

Ecological Studies The ecological method examines areas of a country or zones within a city for the association between measures of social position and criminal activity. Such area studies have been widely conducted since the nineteenth century and have repeatedly found an *inverse* relation between high status and rates of crime and delinquency.

In the United States, Shaw and McKay (1942) constructed indices of the economic status of residential zones in 20 cities and correlated these measures with official crime rates. The usual correlation of poverty and criminality was found, an association that held true for male and female delinquency and for youthful and adult crime. Other accompaniments of poverty, such as families dependent upon state aid and high rates of infant mortality, tuberculosis, and mental disorder went along with the higher crime rates.

A similar conclusion about the location of crime derives from an intensive investigation of the significance of social status in one American city. Warner and Lunt (1941) report for the city they called "Yankee City" a strong negative relation between social position and criminality, as shown in Table 14. "The two upper classes," according to Warner and Lunt, "accounted for less than three-fourths of one per cent of those arrested; the two middle classes, for about ten per cent; and the two lower classes for approximately 90 per cent of the crime in Yankee City" (pp. 375–376).

Such a topography of crime appears repeatedly among the cities of North America. Schuessler (1962) examined the clustering of types of crime with selected "social locators" for 105 American cities and found a strong relation among murder, assault, low income, crowded dwellings, and the nonwhite proportion of the population. Chilton (1964) compared data from Indianapolis, Baltimore, and Detroit to ascertain the relative importance of a host of variables in accounting for delinquency rates. Despite the differences in the size, location, physical plan, population composition, and historical traditions of these cities, Chilton reports a remarkable congruence in the maps of delin-

Table 14   Arrest Rates by Social Class in "Yankee City"

Class	Percent of Population	Percent of Arrests
Upper	1.45	0.43
Lower-upper	1.57	0.28
Upper-middle	10.30	1.84
Lower-middle	28.36	7.80
Upper-lower	32.88	24.96
Lower-lower	25.44	64.69

Source: Adapted with permission from Warner and Lunt, 1941, table 35.

quency for them all. Delinquency resides disproportionately in zones characterized by low income, low occupational skills, poor housing, overcrowding, and transience.

Similar findings derive from Bloom's detailed analysis (1966) of the distribution of "socially deviant behaviors" in an American middle-western city. He found the usual association of delinquency with certain "disruptive conditions," such as:

1 "Familial disruption," the proportion of adolescents not living with both parents.

2 "Marital disruption," the number of divorced and separated males per 1,000 married nonseparated males.

3 "Economic disruption," the percent of the male civilian labor force unemployed.

4 "Environmental disruption," measured by the first-response fire runs of the city fire department as a proportion of total housing units.

5 "Educational disruption," the number of public school dropouts per 10,000 population age 18 and under.

Shifting the focus from all juvenile delinquency to gang-affiliated behaviors in particular, Cartwright and Howard (1966) studied the characteristics of Chicago neighborhoods in which 16 delinquent gangs resided. They found these areas to have more youthful populations than less delinquent neighborhoods and to be characterized by a higher proportion of deteriorated, renter-occupied dwellings. The gang zones had a higher proportion of households headed by women, a higher proportion of separated women, and a lower "family net disposable income" than other neighborhoods. Contrary to the findings of some other investigations, however, the Chicago "ganglands" were *not* differentiated by higher rates of unemployment or by lower educational levels.

These kinds of observations are supported, with some qualifications, by Boggs's research (1965) in St. Louis. Census tracts within this city were rated for social rank, urbanization, and racial segregation. "Social rank" is an index of educational and occupational status. "Urbanization" is a measure based on the fertility ratio, the proportion of single-family dwelling units, and the proportion of women in the labor force, where it is assumed that childless or small families living in apartments and with the women working are more "urban" than their opposites. Racial segregation is measured by a "segregation index," which is the proportion of Negroes in each census tract.

An interesting facet of Boggs's study is the distinction she draws between the kinds of crime committed where the offender lives and the kinds of crime that attract offenders from other areas. Businesses that are *crime targets* are those located in high-status neighborhoods close to neighborhoods in which high proportions of offenders live. The neighborhoods in which high proportions of offenders *live,* however, tend to be characterized differently. These are areas of higher rates of homicide, assault, residential (as opposed to business) burglary, "highway robbery" (as opposed to business robbery), high proportions of Negroes, more urbanization, and lower social rank.

S. Turner's study (1969) of Philadelphia supports many of Boggs's findings for St. Louis. Turner, too, suggests that a particular type of crime area be distinguished—one in which few criminals reside, but in which a considerable proportion of thefts occur. These "target" areas have a high "effective population"— "effective," that is, for thieves. Many transients move through these target zones which lie close to neighborhoods with high proportions of offenders in the population. When Turner describes the areas high in *resident* offenders, he also finds them characterized by low income and low occupational status, high density, high proportions of Negroes, and high proportions of unrelated individuals living in the household and contributing to its income.

Ecological continuity These many ecological studies tend to confirm each other, with, of course, some variations between cities. What is striking about this kind of research is not merely the parallels in the observations, but also the continuity—the persistence—of the correlations reported. The "things that go together" in neighborhoods tend to cluster in like fashion over the years. Tryon (1967), for example, measured the characteristics of "social areas" in the San Francisco Bay region and found that the dimensions of his homogeneous neighborhoods held up— persisted—over a decade and a half. The neighborhoods may change, but the clusters of social indicators remain fairly constant.

Similarly, Schmid and Schmid, reporting in 1972, found strong similarities in the distribution of the serious offenses recorded since 1945 in the state of Washington and within its major city, Seattle. In like manner, Galle and his colleagues (1972) confirm for Chicago what Shaw and McKay discovered decades before: a *negative* relation between social status and such "social pathologies" as the public-assistance rate, mortality and fertility rates, rate of admission to mental hospitals, and officially recorded juvenile delinquency.

Galle's study is interesting because it has added, for the first time, a *group* of measurements of population density to the usual indices of status and distress. Galle and his colleagues examined the connection between delinquency and other disapproved conditions with four components of density: "(1) the number of persons per room; (2) the number of rooms per housing unit; (3) the number of housing units per structure; and (4) the number of residential structures per acre" (p. 26). Their findings, given in Table 15 show a strong correlation of juvenile delinquency with density and with social class and ethnicity. When the correlation between social class, ethnicity, and delinquency is calculated holding the density measures constant, the relation is reduced to a still significant, but moderate, .57. In Chicago, at least, this kind of crowding is connected with other marks of unfavorable public attention, but the association of lower socioeconomic status with criminality persists.

The ecology of crime around the world With few exceptions, cross-cultural comparisons tend to confirm the North American findings.

English area studies, for example, reveal an inverse association between social class and crime rates. Burt (1944) reports this pattern for London, Bagot (1941) for Liverpool, and Morris (1957) for Croydon. However, Mannheim (1948) did not find this familiar distribution of delinquency in Cambridge, perhaps because of the small size of that borough.

As with the American studies, in the British Isles certain conditions are correlated, so that, within some limits, goods and

Table 15 Social Pathology, Density, Ethnicity, and Social Class

	Social Pathologies				
Parameter	Standard mortality ratio	General fertility rate	Public-assistance rate	Juvenile-delinquency rate	Admissions to mental hospitals
Population densities and social pathology					
Multiple correlation coefficients of the four components of density[a] on each of the social pathologies	.867	.856	.887	.917	.689
Multiple-partial correlation coefficients of each pathology with the four components of density, controlling for ethnicity and social class	.476	.371	.584	.498	.508
Social class, ethnicity, and social pathology					
Multiple correlation coefficient of each pathology with social class and ethnicity	.828	.853	.885	.927	.546
Multiple-partial correlation coefficient of each pathology with ethnicity and social class, controlling for the four components of population density[a]	.143[b]	.351	.574	.574	.086[b]

[a]All measures of density are transformed into natural logarithms.
[b]Not significantly different from zero at $P = .05$.
Source: Reprinted with permission from Galle et al., 1972, table 3.

evils appear bunched together. The familiar pattern is found repeatedly: an ecological association of high rates of crime and delinquency with indicators of physical illness and disability, mental disorders, low standards of hygiene, parental disharmony, and inconsistent, brutal, or lax discipline of children.

A similar picture of the class correlates of crime appears appropriate, with some variations, for Latin American, Middle Eastern, and Eastern cultures. For example, Hayner (1946) has plotted such criminogenic zones for Mexico City. In Bombay, Sheth (1961) found no juvenile offenders at all within the wealthy wards, whereas the highest rates of juvenile offenses were recorded among the immigrant squatter settlements. El-Saaty (1946) also discovered a negative association between status and delinquency in Egypt, although the peculiarities of Cairo required him to distinguish, as did Boggs and Turner, between the slums that produced disproportionate numbers of delinquents and the "attracting areas," the shopping centers, where they committed most of their thefts.

An Individual-case Study: Reiss and Rhodes (1961)   Studies of individuals of various levels of social status tend to confirm the association revealed by ecological research. In one such extensive investigation, Reiss and Rhodes examined the official records of delinquency for 9,238 white boys in Tennessee for the period 1950–1958. They also collected self-reports of delinquency from a subsample of these boys. Both measures were analyzed for their relation with two indices of social status: the occupation of the head of the household and the class status of the residential neighborhood. The major findings of this study may be summarized as follows:

1   There is more frequent and serious delinquency in the lower strata.

2   The persistent delinquent, the "career-oriented" offender, is found only among lower-class boys.

3   The relation between social status and delinquency is not straightforward. It varies with the status structure of the residential community and the extent to which delinquency is

part of a cultural tradition in these residential areas. "The largest proportion of delinquents for any status group comes from the more homogeneous status areas for that group, while the delinquency life-chances of boys in any status group tend to be greatest in the lower status areas and in high delinquency rate areas" (p. 720).

4   There is an interaction between delinquency rate, social status, and intelligence. Holding IQ constant, "the probability of being classified a serious, petty or truancy offender is greater for the blue-collar than white-collar boys" (p. 723). Turning the relation around and holding social status constant, there is also a substantial association between higher IQ and nondelinquency. Table 16 shows the interaction between a boy's social status, his IQ, and levels of delinquency.

A Point of View

If one accepts, with the appropriate caution, the correlation repeatedly found between socioeconomic status and criminality, there remains the matter of how to interpret this correlation. An easy interpretation, as we have seen, is that social class really produces no differences in behavior, but that it does make a difference in one's chances of being arrested and convicted. According to this interpretation, money provides a better legal defense so that, while rich and poor people may be equally criminal, they are not equally liable to conviction. This idea has recently been expressed by Hirschi, who says, "It is of the essence of social class that it can create differences in reward where none exists in talent, that it can impose differences in punishment where none exists in obedience to rules" (1969, p. 82).

Money does provide a better legal defense, but this possibility does not disprove the existence of differences in conduct that are linked to income and culture. It can be true, and probably is true, that both ideas are correct. Within any society types of conduct do vary with wealth; richer people commit the serious predatory offenses at a lower rate than do poorer people. At the same time, money may make a difference in the risk of conviction for commission of any given crime.

Table 16   Rate of Delinquency per 100 White Schoolboys by IQ and Occupational Status of Father

Occupational status of father and type of delinquent offense	IQ						Total[b]	
	Low		Middle		High			
	Number	Rate per 100	Number	Rate per 100	Number	Rate per 100	Number	Rate per 100
White-collar	280	(8.2)	1,263	(6.8)	1,115	(4.6)	3,302	(6.2)
J.C.[a] serious	10	3.6	15	1.2	5	0.4	42	1.3
J.C. petty	8	2.8	25	2.0	15	1.4	67	2.0
Subtotal	(18)	(6.4)	(40)	(3.2)	(20)	(1.8)	(109)	(3.3)
J.C. truant	1	0.4	1	0.1	..	0.0	4	0.1
J.C. traffic	4	1.4	44	3.5	31	2.8	93	2.8
No J.C. record	257	0.0	1,178	0.0	1,064	0.0	3,096	0.0
Blue-collar	926	(10.9)	2,091	(9.4)	672	(5.2)	4,661	(8.8)
J.C. serious	42	4.5	47	2.2	111	1.7	124	2.7
J.C. petty	48	5.2	85	4.1	115	2.2	174	3.7
Subtotal	(90)	(9.7)	(132)	(6.3)	(26)	(3.9)	(298)	(6.4)
J.C. truant	10	1.2	11	0.6	2	0.3	33	0.7
J.C. traffic	..	...	53	2.5	7	1.0	81	1.7
No J.C. record	826	0.0	1,895	0.0	637	0.0	4,249	0.0

[a] J.C. – Juvenile court.
[b] Includes all cases for which IQ information was not obtained.
Source: Adapted with permission from Reiss and Rhodes, 1961, table 1.

Contrary to the allegation that the differential crime rates of the social classes represent *nothing but* prejudice in the justice system, experimental and ethnographic studies confirm the story told by official statistics.

In an interesting series of experiments, the psychologists Hartshorne and May (1928) gave American schoolchildren the "opportunity" to cheat, lie, and steal under a variety of circumstances in which the investigators could check on deceit. They found differences in honesty to be correlated with differences in the economic status of the children's parents. The poorer children tended to be less honest, and the differences between the classes increased with age. Burton (1963) reexamined Hartshorne and May's data to test for the generality of honesty. He affirmed the positive relation between socioeconomic status and honesty, adding the qualification that the higher-status children were more *consistently* honest through the variety of tempting opportunities to deceive.

Ethnographic studies based on observation by participants give similar reports. There *are* differences in styles of life and criminal conduct between persons of high and low social status (Lewis, 1959, 1961; Miller, 1958). These differences are not washed away by charges of injustice traceable to differences in income and ability to pay for defense. Too many of us within the sociological profession have lived "down there" as well as "up here" to believe readily that assault, mayhem, murder, and theft are equally distributed among cultures and classes.

A Preliminary Interpretation

In anticipation of the attempted explanations of these class differentials, it may be noted here that one popular interpretation of the class correlates of crime converts "need" to *relative deprivation* and makes relative deprivation the basis of criminal motivation. Variations on this theme are then employed to explain why some people who "have enough" want more, and why juvenile crimes increase in prosperous times. Versions of the relative-deprivation hypothesis are not very useful, however, in explaining why some people who have little remain honest or why some nonutilitarian crimes against the person are more common among some poor people than among others.

When limited to property offenses only, the deprivation interpretations often reduce to the classic equation: _Temptation + opportunity = theft_. This equation is a valid one as far as it goes. What is left out, and what is supplied by some theories of criminogenesis, is a statement of the factors that define opportunity and condition temptation.

Attention to the factors that define opportunity and build immunity to temptation draws one toward the sociopsychological explanations of differential criminality. These explanations are built from evidence that there are many ways of being rich or poor and that the effects of social class upon behavior are less strong and less direct than popular theorizing assumes. It is questionable to what extent an economic status _causes_ any particular kind of behavior (Brown, 1970-1971).

There are, to be sure, _accompaniments_ of wealth and poverty that are part of the definition of being rich or poor. These correlates of income are the kinds of things money allows one to do, like taking holidays abroad or owning expensive cars, but such things are not the _causes_ of any particular patterns of behavior such as being criminal or lawful, disciplined or dissipated. The common-sense proof of this lies in the long-standing recognition that, just as there are the honest poor and the depraved poor, there are also the productive rich and the filthy rich.

When criminologists examine carefully the relation between measures of delinquency and "social class" _in different kinds of communities_, they tend to agree with the authors of one such study that "class membership _per se_ . . . is a poor predictor of a variety of different and specific kinds of adolescent behavior" (Empey and Lubeck, 1971, p. 33). These authors add that one should not _expect_ social class "to have much predictive efficiency when class is treated as an all-inclusive and global concept, without regard to familial, ethnic, sub-cultural, and other differences within it" (p. 34).

As will be seen, there are other influences, more important than money alone, that affect one's lawful or criminal behavior.

RICH NATIONS, POOR NATIONS; GOOD TIMES AND BAD

If economic "need" is a cloudy motive for the predatory crimes when it is studied in any one society at a particular time, it becomes even more ambiguous when the relationship between wealth and criminality is examined *comparatively* for many countries, and *historically* through time.

It has already been noted that affluence in itself provides no cure for crime. In fact, for industrialized societies in recent times, crime rates and prosperity seem to have moved together. Some criminologists hold that this is so because prosperity means that there are more things to steal and more opportunities for theft. Prosperity also elevates crime statistics, it is said, because affluence is associated with better recording of offenses and because property insurance encourages the reporting of crime. Furthermore, it is maintained that, as long as some people have more than others, theft is both motivated and justified. The justification of offenses against property is allegedly strengthened by the "close affinity between many of the methods, aims, and ethics employed in legitimate business and criminal business" (Smith, 1965, p. 7).

Whether or not one agrees with these explanations and justifications of affluent crime, attempts to link criminality to the business cycle or to unemployment figures have not produced any clear conclusion *except* that the relationship between material "need" and criminal behavior is *not* direct.

Ascertaining the relation between national wealth and criminality is itself complicated. Studies of the effects of business cycles are always tangled with questions about the validity of economic statistics (Morgenstern, 1963), by questions about the time lag to be allowed between changing economic conditions and their presumed effects on behavior, and by the possible impact of different welfare programs in easing the hardships of depressions.

Similarly, when one tries to study the criminogenic effects of unemployment, the meaning of official statistics is again open to question. "Unemployment" is a difficult term to define because in modern countries the condition of "being unemployed" includes persons with various degrees of motivation to work, various dispositions to accept certain kinds of job, and various states of need.

Given these uncertainties, the more than 140 years of research on the impact of business cycles upon crime rates have produced the unsatisfactory "finding" that crime may increase with *both* good times and bad. It therefore seems logical to conclude that *neither* the poverty nor the wealth of nations is a major determinant of the level of criminal conduct. The best that can be said is that the serious crimes are associated *ecologically* (in social and physical space *within* a society) with relative economic deprivation. However, such crimes are not associated *historically* (in time) or *comparatively* (across cultures) with relative impoverishment.

ETHNICITY

The distinctive assumption of a *social science*, and particularly of those studies called sociology and anthropology, is that the interesting aspects of human behavior are learned. When what is learned has some discernible pattern for a number of people, and when such a pattern is distinguishable from that of other groups, the scholar speaks of the style of life as a *"culture."* Although the boundaries of a culture are never mapped exactly, it is assumed that they are roughly discriminable and that cultures are both *products* of human interaction and *generators* of it. Cultures are conceived of as both the causes and the effects of human beings teaching each other how to behave.[1]

Whether one studies cultures professionally or observes them as a peripatetic citizen, it is apparent that *human beings group themselves by categories of learned preferences.* Not only do we group ourselves, but our cultural identity is, in turn, recognized by others. Such "consciousness of kind," acknowledged by insiders and outsiders alike, has been conveniently

---

[1]It is popular in sociology to add that what we teach each other occurs through "symbolic interaction." For example, Hoult's dictionary of sociological terms (1969) defines culture as "acquired by means of symbolic interaction." Unless one stretches the meaning of the word "symbol" beyond definition, this view of how human beings teach each other is needlessly restrictive and false to much of what is known about learning. Some nonsymbolic ways in which patterned social behaviors are learned are described on pages 222–236.

considered a hallmark of *ethnicity*. The word "ethnic" (from the Greek *ethnos,* "the nations") designates aggregates of individuals who share a sense of being alike, who regard themselves as "a people" with a relatively distinct pattern of "doing things." The term "ethnic" points to a subjective reality—to how people think and feel about their affiliations. These feelings of identification are correlated with objective indicators of ethnic difference such as language, race, religion, citizenship, costume, and dietary and artistic preferences. These correlations are not perfect, however. Not all who are of the same race, or who share a citizenship, a language or a religion, regard themselves as being "the same people." Language, particularly *dialect,* is probably the strongest external indicator of ethnic identity. Dialect strengthens an identification, particularly when it is combined with distinctive dress.

Ethnicity is associated, of course, with behaviors other than those that indicate awareness of identity. It is in this association of ethnic identity with a *differing content of lesson learned* that one finds a reason for examining the relation between ethnicity and criminality.

The possible impact of ethnicity upon criminality is usually studied in the context of cultures meeting under the laws of one state. That is, interest in the vulnerability of ethnic groups to arrest is normally a result of there being more than one such group subject to the sovereignty of a government. Where a state is also a nation, homogeneous in its culture, there is little reason to study ethnic differences in criminality. It is where states attempt to govern many "peoples" that ethnicity becomes a significant variable. This is the circumstance that pertains, in differing degree, in the United States, Canada, Israel, Great Britain, India, Spain, the Soviet Union, the Republic of South Africa, and many other states that attempt to govern several nations.

A Sample of Ethnic Differentials in Crime Rates

The variety of amounts and kinds of crime committed by people of diverse cultural heritage in their states of residence is most apparent in a heterogeneous country like the United States, but the same point can be illustrated in the records of other societies.

Israel, for example, in its short history has not only experienced a steady rise in juvenile delinquency, but has also noted differences in crime and delinquency rates among Jews from different lands. For 1957, Shoham reports rates of serious offenses committed by immigrants to Israel as 13 per 1,000 among immigrants from Africa; 10 per 1,000 among those from Asia; and 5 per 1,000 among those from Europe and the Americas (1966, pp. 80–83).

Swedish studies of the differential crime rates of resident ethnic groups also indicate cultural differences in criminal activity. According to Sveri's data (1966), corrected for sex and age distributions, conviction rates for Hungarians and Yugoslavs in Sweden are almost twice that of the host population, and this differential seems particularly associated with a greater propensity among the migrant people to crimes against the person. A different style of offense is reported for the Finns in Sweden, who are susceptible to arrests for violations having to do with drinking (Kaironen, 1966).

Drinking is also associated with the high crime rates reported for Irish migrants to England. The Irish settler tends to be a single, young man cut off from an Irish community; according to Gibbens and Ahrenfeldt, such a person "has two main occupations: work and drink" (1966, p. 141). Irishmen resident in England have had for years a rate of criminal conviction and recidivism higher than that of the majority population (Bottoms, 1967). While their offenses have covered a broad spectrum of crimes *mala in se,* robbery has recently been increasing among them. Toward the end of the 1950s, some 20 percent of convicted robbers in London were Irishmen, although Irishmen constituted only about 12 percent of the single, male population between the ages of 15 and 40 (McClintock and Gibson, 1961).

England has also experienced increases in the rates of violent crimes committed by immigrants from Commonwealth countries in Asia and the West Indies. Such immigrants, while relatively immune to committing offenses against property, have conviction rates for personal attacks that range from 2 to 3 times that of the host population (McClintock, 1963; Wallis and Maliphant, 1967).

Studies of patterns of crime among Italian migrants also indicate ethnic differences. Franchini and Introna (1961) and Introna (1963) found that the migration of rural workers from southern Italy to the "industrial triangle" of northern Italy has been associated with increases in their rates of juvenile delinquency and adult crime. At the same time, the Italian workers who migrated to Switzerland exhibited lower crime rates in the period 1949–1960 than the Swiss nationals (Neumann, 1963). These rates have been increasing, however, and they differ from rates of crime committed by Swiss nationals in that there is among Italian migrants a higher proportion of violent offenses (Ferracuti, 1968).

North America has a long record of ethnic differentials among the peoples who have met in the New World. The native peoples of Canada, for example, are convicted of indictable offenses at rates disproportionate to their representation in the population. Throughout Canada, but in western Canada in particular, Indian, Eskimo, and Metis adults are in jails and prisons in numbers far in excess of their proportions in the general population. Among Canada's four western provinces, the Yukon, and the Northwest Territories in one recent year, the percentages of these native groups who were incarcerated ranged from a *low* of 10 percent of the inmates of one jail on Vancouver Island to *highs* of 100 percent of the inmates of the jails for women at Oakalla, B.C., and The Pas, Manitoba. The *median* native representation among western Canadian correctional institutions was 66 percent (Canadian Corrections Association, 1967).

The United States also records wide differences in the amount and the style of crime committed by its numerous ethnic residents. At the extremes, it is immediately notable that the Oriental and Jewish populations have low rates of arrest and conviction for the serious predatory crimes, while Negroes and Mexican-Americans have high rates. This type of differential persists even where the Orientals constitute a plurality of the population, as in Hawaii. Voss (1963) reports that Hawaiians, who make up about one-fourth of Honolulu's population, account for 40 percent of the delinquency among males and half of the arrests of females. The Japanese and Chinese, who make up about 40 percent of the population, account for less than one-fifth of male delinquency and about 6 percent of violations by females.

Other deviations from the criminal norm are apparent among Dutch, German, and Scandinavian migrants to America, and their children, who have experienced low degrees of contact with the police. The lawful behavior of these people is equalled or bettered by that of ethnic religious enclaves such as the Mennonites and the Amish (Reckless, 1967, pp. 472–475).

Listing these facts is enough to make us question the easy explanation of differences in criminality as due only to racial prejudice and economic disadvantage. On the contrary, *low* crime rates are found among some minorities that are physically visible—"racially" distinguishable, if you will—and that have suffered discrimination and persecution. The Jews have one of the longest histories of any people as objects of hatred and oppression. The Chinese have been victims of lynchings and riots in western American cities. The Japanese are the only Canadian-American ethnic group to have been selected for exclusion and containment in concentration camps (which were euphemistically called "relocation centers").

In addition to the hardships of discrimination, all these groups have also suffered great economic disadvantages. As with most migrants to America, the original settlers tended to be poor people seeking a better way of life, rather than rich wanderers seeking more wealth. As ethnic units, their economic careers have varied, of course. The Jews in particular represent a North American success story.

The experience of Negroes in the New World has been sadly different from that of people who migrated voluntarily. The continuing differentials in crime rates, as in other aspects of social life, are consequences of their awful struggle from slavery to dignity.

Rates of arrest and conviction of black people for serious offenses in the United States differ markedly from that of other ethnic groups. Although Negroes[2] represented about 12 percent of the American population in 1970, they constituted nearly one-third of all persons arrested. This discrepancy has persisted for some years (Wolfgang, 1966, p. 46). At any one time, about one-third of all prisoners in the United States are blacks. Compared with white offenders, a *smaller* proportion of black criminals are *first* offenders (Forslund, 1970). In other words, Negroes have a higher recidivism rate than Caucasians. They are charged with and convicted of more serious crimes, and the population of black offenders is, crime for crime, younger than the population of white offenders (Johnson, 1970).

Toward the end of the 1960s Negroes in the United States accounted for about 60 percent of all arrests for murder (Graham, 1970). A study of criminal homicide in Philadelphia (Wolfgang, 1958) reported that nonwhite men aged 20 to 24 had a conviction rate more than 25 times that of white men of the same age. The ethnic differences in homicide are of such an order, as has been noted, that the murder rates among Negro *women* run 2 to 4 times that of the murder rates among Caucasian *men* (Wolfgang and Ferracuti, 1967, p. 154).

According to the FBI's figures (1971, table 32), Negroes in 1970 accounted for 65 per cent of the arrests for robbery, 64 percent of the arrests for prostitution and commercialized vice, half of the arrests for the illegal possession of weapons, 46 percent of the arrests for aggravated assault, and one-third of the arrests for burglary. The differentials are so great that some criminologists have suggested that the caste-like position of the Negro in American society calls for "constructing a theory of Negro delinquency and criminality which would be quite different from a possible model of criminal behavior among whites" (Savitz, 1967, p. 61).

Differences in crime rate such as have been described do not disappear when comparisons are made holding constant the socioeconomic, sex, and age distributions of white and black

---

[2]In North America, "Negro" is a sociological term. It is associated with "racial" features, but it is not conterminous with the anthropometric idea of "race." The designations "Negro" and "black" probably refer more accurately to ethnicity, as we have defined it, than to biology.

groups (Blue, 1948; Forslund, 1970; Moses, 1970; Stephenson and Scarpitti, 1968). Neither can the differences in arrest be attributed principally to prejudice in law enforcement (Black and Reiss, 1967, 1970; Green, 1970; Kephart, 1957; Terry, 1967).

A Cohort Analysis

The role of ethnic, as well as socioeconomic, factors in the development of delinquency is illustrated by a careful study of the careers of almost 10,000 young men in the United States. Wolfgang, Figlio, and Sellin gathered information on *"all* boys born in 1945 who lived in Philadelphia at least between their tenth and their eighteenth birthdays" (1972, p. 244). This is a "cohort analysis." The term means that the group of subjects to be studied was defined by characteristics *other than those* of interest to the investigators. In this case, the cohort was defined by date of birth and place of residence rather than by criminal conduct.

This study differs in still other ways from much criminological research. The measure of "delinquency" used was not arrest or conviction, but "police contact." The data are the "officially recorded delinquencies" among the 9,945 boys regardless of the disposition of the case by the police. The police can, of course, make a "remedial disposition" of a case rather than an arrest, and they did so, in this study, for some two-thirds of the complaints they received. The authors recognize that using such contacts with the police as the sign of a violation, instead of arrests or convictions, might mean that some innocent boys were included as offenders. They present data (pp. 17–22) to show that this is not likely, however.

This research differs, too, from much previous work in that it made use of the Sellin-Wolfgang (S-W) "delinquency index" to weigh the seriousness of reported offenses. Considering these refinements, the findings of this large-scale study increase in importance. The results may be outlined as follows:

About one-third of all the boys in the cohort experienced at least one "police contact."

28.6 percent of the white boys and 50.2 percent of the

nonwhite boys were classified as "offenders" by the investigators.

26.5 percent of the group characterized as being of "higher" socioeconomic status (SES) were delinquent, compared with 44.8 percent of the boys of "lower" SES.

Race and, to a lesser extent, SES were the variables most strongly related to delinquency.

Repetitive offenders were more likely to be nonwhite boys of low SES. They also have the highest scores for the gravity of their offenses as gauged by the S-W index.

Nonwhite offenders received more severe dispositions from their police contacts than did white boys even when the seriousness of their offense was held constant. The authors acknowledge that they have not studied all the factors that enter into decisions made by the police, but their data suggest bias in the disposition of black delinquents (pp. 220–221).

In summary, this Philadelphia study reports differences in the delinquency rates of black and white boys and suggests that a network of disadvantaging conditions is important to our understanding of the discrepancy. "The nonwhite delinquent boy," these researchers say, "is likely to belong to the lower socioeconomic group, experience a greater number of school and residential moves (that is, be subject to the disrupting forces of intracity mobility more than the nondelinquent) and have the lowest average grade completed, the lowest achievement level, and the lowest I.Q. score" (p. 246). The suggestion in this study of racial discrimination in the *disposition* of boys after a police contact calls for additional investigation of the factors that affect decisions by the police.

Meanwhile, caution is required in the interpretation of differentials in crime rates between whites and nonwhites. In the light of the sad history of racial relations, it is difficult to make comparisons today of the relative importance of the alleged causes of any differences in observed behaviors. Subjective factors, of an unmeasurable sort, may intrude where objective measures reveal no differences of condition or treatment. Enforced segregation, only now ending, and the marks of oppression may make trivial the scientist's attempts to hold constant socio-

economic status or schooling while examining delinquency differentials between the races. The possible operation of such
subjective factors can be acknowledged, although it cannot be
assessed.

None of this denies, however, that *ethnic differences are real
differences*. They have a bearing upon crime rates, and the
explanation of this impact is one of the tasks of theories of
criminogenesis.

In Summary

The research on the differential criminality of ethnic groups can
be summarized cross-culturally by saying that:

Ethnic groups *do* exhibit different patterns of criminal
behavior within the states in which they reside.

These patterns differ both in the kinds of crime committed
and in the relative amounts of specific crimes.

These patterns cannot be explained away as due only to the
length of residence of a minority in a country, its age and sex
distribution, or its socioeconomic position, or to prejudice in the
judicial system.

Migrants tend to exhibit in their adopted lands the kinds of
crime familiar to their homelands.

These ethnic patterns of criminality are, like all else, subject
to change with time.

CULTURE CONTACT AND CRIME

The impact of time upon a culture includes the possibility that a
way of life may disintegrate as well as the happier possibility that
a new culture may grow out of the mixture of old ones. The
metaphor of "the melting pot" is just that—a figure of speech. It
more often expresses hope rather than fact (Glazer and Moynihan, 1963; Novak, 1972).

In the meantime, while old cultures are dying and new ones
are evolving, there is little surprise in finding that the *process* of
"assimilation" may mean the substitution of new styles of crime

for old. After a generation or two in the United States, for example, southern Europeans abandon their traditionally prescribed code of vendetta for the more American property offenses.

It is also not surprising to find that, as an ethnic enclave breaks down, its crime rates, particularly its juvenile-delinquency rates, go up. So-called "ghettoes," areas of ethnic concentration, may be sites of remarkably *low,* as well has high, crime rates. The popular notion of a "ghetto" as necessarily a slum and necessarily crime-ridden is false.

On Ghettoes and Slums

The popular use, and abuse, of the word "ghetto" should not seduce students of sociology into confusing a ghetto with a slum.

Originally a ghetto was an area inside or outside the walls of early medieval European cities, where Jews lived. *The Random House Dictionary* (1966) believes the word may have derived from the Italian *borghetto,* a diminutive of *borgo,* a hamlet outside the town walls.

The first ghettoes were *voluntary* congregations of Jews and only later became areas of legally enforced isolation (Wirth, 1929). Such enacted ghettoes first appeared in Spain and Portugal toward the end of the fourteenth century and were justified as a protection of the "true faith." These compulsory ghettoes were usually closed off by gates, and their residents were subject to curfew restrictions. Within the ghettoes, autonomous institutions operated, such as schools, churches, welfare associations, and courts.

Today the term "ghetto" has been expanded from its original meaning to refer to any area of ethnic concentration. In the cities of Western countries, ghettoes are now less independent of the greater societies in which they are situated. They are, at the same time, more voluntary. The *legally enforced segregation* of cultural identities is now nonexistent in Western European and North American lands. It is debatable, of course, to what extent the law of such states is used to protect or to break down modern ghettoes.

By contrast with a ghetto, a slum need not be a zone of ethnic concentration. The defining characteristics of a slum are vice, dirt, density, and poverty. Fairchild's *Dictionary of Sociology* (1944) calls it "an area of physical and social decadence," while the *Oxford English Dictionary* speaks of "a crowded district . . . inhabited by people of a low class or by the very poor . . . where the houses and the conditions of life are of a squalid and wretched character." "Squalid," in turn, means "foul through neglect or want of cleanliness; repulsively mean and filthy."

It follows that slums and ghettoes are two different things. Some ghettoes may be slums, but some are not. Conversely, some slums may be ghettoes; others are not. It is conceivable that, with time, all slums become ghettoes, while not all ghettoes become slums. What is of interest to sociologists, and to other students who would understand freedom, is the extent to which, in any particular cultural setting and epoch, ghettoes or slums are voluntary. This is meat for debate. In this debate, clarity requires that slums and ghettoes be regarded as distinct.

Ghettoes and Crime

Holding this distinction, it is possible to ask whether ghettoes are more or less criminogenic than "melting pots." Are ghettoes the distinctive locations of high crime rates? Do rates of offenses in ghettoes change with a weakening of their boundaries?

American studies are particularly rich in reporting the effects of the meeting of cultures upon crime rates. These investigations indicate that migrants, and more specifically their children, are relatively immune to the configurations of crime about them as long as a ghetto is intact.

This phenomenon has been well documented, for example, among Oriental residents in the United States and their children (Crook, 1934; Kitano, 1967; Lind, 1930a, 1930b; McGill, 1938; Petersen, 1967). A similar pattern of ethnic protection is reported by Beynon (1935) for Hungarian immigrants to America and by Vislick-Young (1930) for Russian immigrants.

The low delinquency rates among descendants of Chinese

and Japanese immigrants to North America have already been noted. These rates tend to remain low, however, as long as ethnic identity is maintained, but to rise with assimilation to the host culture. For example, Kitano (1967) found some interesting signs of this "contamination" when he compared Japanese-American delinquents and their parents with Japanese-American nondelinquents. The delinquents and their families were considerably *less* "Japanese" than the nondelinquents. Moreover, the delinquent children exhibited their greater identification with the American culture in their speech, dress, hair styles, and patterns of friendship.

Similar observations have been made of the Chinese ghettoes that have defended their children against delinquency in the United States. Sollenberger (1968) lived among the residents of the New York City enclave and, with the help of a Chinese interpreter-interviewer, observed family life and behavior of children in this densely populated ghetto. In this area of near-zero delinquency, Sollenberger found children to be remarkably well behaved—to be able, for example, to go on an all-day outing with "no crying, no scolding, no scuffling or quarreling of any kind" (p. 17). He considered that the sources of this were to be found in family solidarity. There were no divorced or separated parents in this community. Mothers held their husbands in high regard, and authority was shared. The Chinese children spent much time in the company of their parents. Sollenberger reports that, as compared with a sample of Caucasian mothers, the Chinese women were *more strict* in their control of children's aggression, but *more permissive* in regard to weaning, toilet training, and bedtime routines.

This kind of community is, of course, subject to disruption. It is now reported that Chinese ghettoes are feeling the winds of change and that, under the impact of new immigrants, mostly young men, the delinquent warfare reminiscent of other enclaves is being reenacted in some Chinatowns where youths have organized themselves as "Red Guard" and "Wah Ching" gangs (Harvey, 1970; Peterson, 1972).

The experience of the Negro in the Americas has been made different by the fact of his involuntary migration to, and enslavement in, the New World. The lively question, however, is whether, today, his "ghettoization" proceeds differently from that of any other ethnic group and whether, therefore, the consequences may differ.

There is no definitive answer to this question, but informed opinion about it has changed. During the 1940s and 1950s the popular liberal attitude toward this subject was assimilationist. Its ideal was the melting pot. This ideal tended to minimize or to deny cultural differences between blacks and whites and to reduce such alleged differences to class distinctions. The contrary suggestion, that behavior of blacks and whites might differ culturally and not merely as a function of socioeconomic status, was resisted. An illustration of this resistance was the professional response to an anthropologist's study (Herskovits, 1941) demonstrating that it was "a myth of the Negro's past" to believe that *no* cultural elements had been borne by the slaves from West Africa to the Americas. The reviews of this book in professional journals have been characterized as "a furor."

Times change. With the black demand for identity, it now becomes more comfortable for white students to agree that Negroes, like other migrants, brought a culture with them (Jones, 1972; Metzger, 1971). To the extent to which a black culture has been maintained, and to the extent to which it is being revived, it should be expected that the ghetto experience would have the same relationship to delinquency rates among blacks that it has had to delinquency rates among other minorities. The evidence is not at all clear, however. A few attempts have been made to study the effects of ethnic congregation upon crime rates among blacks by examining the variations in known violations as the races live apart or together. The findings vary with the time and place of the investigation.

An early study conducted by the research bureau of the Houston Council of Social Agencies (Hooker, 1945) found that for Houston "the higher the proportion of Negro population, the lower is the rate of Negro delinquency . . . conversely, the higher the proportion of white population, the higher is the rate of Negro delinquency" (p. 23).

A later study in Baltimore reported similar results (Lander,

1954). More recently, Willie and Gershenovitz (1964) tested for this distribution of crime among mixed and separated tracts in Washington, D.C. They too found that ethnic concentration had the effect of reducing crime, with one qualification:

(1) In higher socio-economic areas, there are no differences in juvenile delinquency rates between neighborhoods of homogeneous and heterogeneous racial composition.
(2) In lower socio-economic areas, juvenile delinquency rates tend to be higher in racially heterogeneous than in racially homogeneous neighborhoods [p. 743].

When the effects of the ghetto upon crime rates among Negroes have been tested outside Southern or Border states, however, no such immunization against criminality has been apparent. Chilton (1964) tested for such a "parabolic" association between delinquency and the proportion of nonwhites in Indianapolis census tracts. He reported that the relation is unclear because of the large number of census tracts in Indianapolis that are almost completely white, and he recommends that the curvilinear findings for Houston, Baltimore, and Washington be tested against large bodies of data from other cities. In one such study Bordua (1958–1959) also could find no evidence that delinquency rates in Detroit varied with the proportions of white and nonwhite residents.

The conflicts among these findings have been attributed to differences in police activity and to regional differences in the willingness of victims to call the police. The question remains open whether residential segregation of the races is more or less criminogenic than residential mixing.

An interesting interpretation of the varied findings on this issue holds that the peculiarities of black history in North America do not allow an easy equation of residential segregation with ghetto life, in the classic sense, any more than residential mixing signifies ethnic integration. For example, Molotch (1969) concludes from a study of a changing community that "biracial propinquity," the physical closeness of the races residentially, does not mean "racial integration." In short, when peoples meet, they do not necessarily become one. Ethnic identity is frequently stimulated by ethnic contact, so that the claims of difference and the pleas for a separate life become stronger *after* one has tested assimilation than they were before such an experience. Borhek (1970) found this true of ethnic groups in Canada, and a similar pattern of ethnic cohesion is being demonstrated by the more militant blacks in the United States (Harris, 1972). Research on attitudes of black students, for instance, finds that black students in white colleges are more militant and more separatist than black students in black colleges (Kilson, 1971).

In the process of peoples meeting, then, residential and educational mixing may not mean integration. Conversely, the simple fact of segregation may not be a strong sign of "ghettoization." Some "ghetto effects" may become stronger as ethnic groups meet each other. Research on this issue awaits the development of better measures of ethnic identification and cultural difference than mere patterns of propinquity.

URBANISM

The city has long been considered more vicious than the countryside, and there is a popular explanation available: that the crowding, impersonality, and anonymity of urban relations generate crime.

As with most popular theories, there is truth in this one, but it must be qualified. The truth resides in the fact that the official statistics of North American and European states report a tendency for serious crimes to increase with the size of the city (Clinard, 1942, 1960; Lottier, 1938; Wolf, 1965). Representative figures, for example, are found in the rates of arrests for murder in the United States. Cities of more than 250,000 population had an arrest rate in 1969 of 16.2 per 100,000 people, whereas cities of 100,000 to 250,000 population had a rate about half that, 8.5. These rates decline uniformly by size of city until a low rate of 2.3 is reached for towns with less than 10,000 population (FBI, 1970, table 23). Exceptions to this are the "suburban" rate, 3.7, and the rate for "rural areas," 4.8. Parallel tendencies in rates of arrest among different densities of population have been recorded for forcible rape, robbery, aggravated assault, burglary, larceny, and automobile theft.

There are two important qualifications of the general finding that serious crime increases with increases in numbers of people. First, no one knows whether the underreporting characteristic of all crime is more prevalent in rural areas than urban ones. Some observers of the rural scene argue that many backwoods brawls and even murders ("hunting accidents") are unreported criminal events. This failure to report criminal events may be explained, in part, by the lack of policing in remote areas and in part by the "normality" of some kinds of violent offenses. At present there is no resolution of this question. It is not known whether the underreporting of crime is greater, less, or the same for human aggregations of different sizes.

A second qualification of the assumption that serious crime increases with urbanization is the finding that *some* rural areas and small towns have higher crime rates than larger cities and that cities of the same size within a political territory may have widely varying rates. Radzinowicz (1946) reports this for Poland; and Christie (1960) found some signs of a similar phenomenon in Norway. Wiers (1939) observed that, while urban areas in Michigan had high delinquency rates, there were yet significant differences in rural rates between the logging counties of the north and the agricultural counties of the south, with the northern woodsmen being the more delinquent. French and Swedish rural crime rates are increasingly reported to approximate urban rates (Sutherland and Cressey, 1970, p. 179); and in Israel "the highest rate of delinquency in the whole country was recorded in the rural region of the Jerusalem area, whose population is composed entirely of 'new' immigrants" (Shoham, 1966, p. 82).

This mix of statistics may be interpreted as saying that the effect of population density upon crime rates is not direct. Again, as with the impact of the economy or of occupation upon criminality, those ways of life called "cultural" seem to intercede between the environment, including its human density and its wealth, and the behaviors to be explained.

CULTURE AND CRIME

The explanations of criminality in the following chapters are unanimous in attributing criminogenesis to something in the ordering of relations among people. When these arrangements have some regularity and persistence, they define a "culture." Cultural accounts of criminality are alike in discounting any important contribution to crime rates by such *unlearned* variables as the natural environment or biological differences. This is not to say that these variables have no impact. Some theories of criminogenesis allow for the "triggering effects" of noncultural factors such as the weather and some take into consideration the facts of biological difference. However, today the only persuasive theories of crime causation are theories that look toward some aspects of the social environment as more or less criminogenic. These explanations differ among themselves as to the facets of culture emphasized. They therefore differ in their predictions and in their recommendations.

Chapter 6

Sociological
Explanations
of Criminality:
The Subcultural Variety

In describing the theories with which criminologists explain crime, it bears repeating that the answers that satisfy depend upon the questions that are asked.

WHAT KINDS OF QUESTIONS ARE ASKED ABOUT CRIME?

There are two kinds of questions commonly asked about crime. One is *psychological:* "Why did he do it?" The other is *sociological:* "How come this society has more crime of type X than that one?" Or: "Why have crime rates for our society increased or decreased?"

The psychological question asks for an explanation of individual behavior. The sociological question asks for an explanation of collective behavior. It is true that we expect the answers to these two different "levels" of question to be consistent. It is also true that many explanations of the behavior of groups refer to the motives and intentions of their members. In short, many *sociological* explanations refer to the *psychology* of individuals taken collectively. But this need not be the case. It is possible to explain the actions of aggregates without reference to the actions of their individual components. In human affairs, it remains an open question whether sociological or psychological explanations of the behavior of populations have the greater clarifying power. Explanations which do not refer to individuals do not always satisfy the curious. Intellectual satisfaction depends to a great extent upon what one wants to *do* with his explanation. An explanation that is satisfactory for political and moral purposes is not necessarily satisfactory for purposes of prediction. The advice to students here is to be clear about *what is being explained, how it is being explained*, and what *difference*, if any, the competing explanations might make to action.

In the context of social concerns, the "level" at which questions are asked about crime causation is *sociological*. The public questions are, "Why is there so much crime?" and "Why have the rates of serious offenses increased?"

WHAT KINDS OF ANSWERS MAY BE GIVEN?

To these questions—that is, to questions asked on the sociological level—there have been a variety of answers that overlap each other and that differ, not absolutely, but in what they emphasize. These answers may be grouped by their predominant themes as follows:

1 Sociological explanations
   a The subcultural variety
   b The structural variety
2 Sociopsychological explanations
   a The symbolic-interactionist variety
   b The control variety

In this chapter, the subcultural variety of sociological explanations will be discussed; Chapter 7 will take up the structural variety. The two varieties of sociopsychological explanations will be discussed in Chapters 8 and 9.

The strictly sociological explanations emphasize aspects of societal arrangements that are *external* to the actor and *compelling*. A strictly sociological explanation is concerned with how the *structure* of a society or its *institutional practices* or its *persisting cultural themes* affect the conduct of its members. Individual differences are denied or ignored, and the explanation of collective behavior is sought in the patterning of social arrangements that is considered to be both "outside" the actor and "prior" to him. That is, the social patterns of power or of institutions which are held to be determinative of human action are also seen as having been in existence *before* any particular actor came on the scene. They are "external" to him in the sense that they will persist with or without him. In lay language, *sociological explanations of crime place the blame on something social that is prior to, external to, and compelling of any particular person.*

Sociological explanations do not deny the importance of human motivation. However, they locate the source of motives outside the individual and in the cultural climate in which he lives.

By contrast, sociopsychological explanations of criminality place more of the causal emphasis upon the individual actor, or upon "kinds" of actors, and upon the interaction between persons. These hypotheses, again, do not deny the impact of the cultural environment. They pay more attention, nevertheless, to individual differences and to the ways in which we affect each other. The "control" type of theory, in particular, attends to the societal arrangements that affect learning, interpretation, and motivation among individuals who are *not* assumed to be equally amenable to training.

There is another point of difference between these major types of explanations. There is a strong tendency for these overlapping and yet contrasting styles of explanation to ask different questions. The sociological and the symbolic-interactionist explanations attempt to explain why crime rates vary by asking how, or why, persons become more or less *criminal.* The control theories, on the other hand, tend to explain how people become more or less *lawful.*

It is granted that a description of how criminality is produced ought to tell, by implication at least, how lawfulness is stimulated, and vice versa. The different emphases given by these styles of explanation do not, however, have this symmetrical effect. As these explanations get translated into public policy, there is a tendency to interpret the sociological and symbolic-interactionist theories as saying that people are "really good" unless they are driven to being bad. Attention is directed to the "causes" of badness, while there is silence or presumption about the sources of goodness. This emphasis is, of course, congenial to social reformers.

By contrast, the sociopsychological emphasis upon training in social control holds that people *learn* to be lawful as well as criminal. These sociopsychological theories more readily assume, with Freud, that "being bad" may come as naturally as "being good." They claim that "behaving well" is an acquisition and that the learning requires effort.

Liking the Actor, Approving his Action, and Locating the "Causes" of His Behavior: A Hypothesis

There is experimental evidence to suggest that whether we like or dislike the actor and whether we approve or disapprove of the particular act affect where we locate the "causes" of his behavior (Leifer, 1964; Schiffman and Wynne, 1963).

When a person we like does a good deed, we tend to explain his action by reference to his character or his purpose. When a person we like does a bad deed, we tend to shift the source of his action from dispositions or purposes to causes or accidents.

In reverse, when a person we dislike commits a wrong, it is his character or his purpose that explains his action to us. If the individual we dislike does a good deed, however, it is chance or accident or some causal condition that conventionally explains his behavior to us.

These tendencies are provisional descriptions revealed by limited research which we should like to see extended. The findings are provocative, nonetheless, and they may help to explain our preferences among styles of explanation. It may be assumed that reformers, as opposed to punishers, have more sympathy for the actors whose behavior they would explain and correct. "Liking" the miscreant means, then, that reformers are more apt to refer the offender's misbehavior to "causes," to matters beyond the agent's control that are "not his fault." Good behavior, by contrast, is assumed either to "come naturally" in the absence of evil causes or to be "chosen" under benign circumstances.

The point has never been put better than by the mad, bad Alex, chief delinquent in Anthony Burgess's *A Clockwork Orange* (1962). After a visit from his ineffective probation officer, Alex, who revels in doing the "ultra violent," meditates upon his helper's futile search for the causes of his conduct. Alex comments,

> But, brothers, this biting of their toe-nails over what is the *cause* of badness is what turns me into a fine laughing malchick. They don't go into the cause of *goodness,* so why the other shop? If lewdies are good that's because they like it, and I wouldn't ever interfere with their pleasures, and so of the other shop. And I was patronizing the other shop. . . . I am serious with you, brothers, over this. . . . What I do I do because I like to do [p. 34].

Since the sociological, interactionist, and control explanations are responses to different questions, based upon different assumptions, they give different answers and they make different recommendations. In describing these competing versions of criminogenesis, it should be borne in mind that there is considerable overlap among them, that they need not be all true or all false, and that the pragmatic test of their value is how much they help or hinder people in getting what they want when they act upon them (Nettler, 1970, 1972b).

SOCIOLOGICAL THEORIES OF CRIMINOGENESIS: CULTURE CONFLICT

Sociological theories of crime causation can be said to participate in one general theme: *culture conflict.* This theme locates the source of crime in some division within a society that is associated with differential acceptance of legal norms. It is popular among sociologists to say that the differences in the definitions by which laws are accorded legitimacy or irrelevance are learned. However, social scientists have not paid much attention to this learning process, and at least one variant of the sociological theme—the "reactive" hypotheses—can be interpreted psychodynamically without specification of a learning procedure.

The sociological explanations—all of which, at bottom assume *culture conflict* to be the source of crime—can themselves be subdivided into those that emphasize "subcultures" and those that emphasize "social structures" as criminogenic. Both sorts of explanations rest upon a conflict of norms of conduct as the root of crime, but the two differ in their evaluation of the conflict and, hence, in their prescribed societal responses to crime.

SUBCULTURAL EXPLANATIONS OF CRIME

Political philosophers, sociologists, and anthropologists have long observed that a condition of social life is that not all things are allowed. Standards of behavior are both a *product* of our living together and a *requirement* if social life is to be orderly.[1]

The concept of a *culture* refers to the perceived standards of behavior, observable in both words and deeds, that are learned, transmitted from generation to generation, and, hence, somewhat durable. To call such behavior "cultural" does not necessarily mean that it is "refined," but rather means that it is "cultured"— that is, acquired, cultivated, and persistent. Social scientists have invented the notion of a *subculture* to describe variations, within a society, upon its cultural themes. In such circumstances, it is assumed that some cultural prescriptions are common to all members of society, but that modifications and variations are discernible within the society. Again, it is part of the definition of a subculture, as of a culture, that it is relatively enduring. Its norms are termed a "style," rather than a "fashion," on the grounds that the former has some endurance while the latter is

---

[1] A life of *order* among persons is, in turn, a condition of *happiness* and *freedom*. It only sounds paradoxical to say that freedom requires boundaries to "free action."

evanescent. The quarrel comes, of course, when we try to estimate how "real" a cultural pattern is and how persistent.

The Conflict of Norms of Conduct

The standards by which behavior is to be guided vary among men and over time. It is in this change and variety that norms of conduct may conflict, and it is out of this conflict that *crime* is defined.

An early application of this principle to criminology was given by Sellin (1938), who found the roots of crime in the fact that groups have developed different standards of appropriate behavior and that, in "complex cultures," each individual is subject to competing prescriptions for action. "A conflict of norms is said to exist," Sellin wrote, "when more or less divergent rules of conduct govern the specific life situation in which a person may find himself" (p. 29).

Sellin's description of how crime is caused differs from other explanations of the sociological variety in that it is broader. Sellin is interested in the conflict of *all* norms of conduct, not merely in those that are codified in the criminal law. However, he sees the concern with crime as flowing from the conflict of standards about how we should behave.

Class cultures

Another subcultural explanation of crime grows readily out of the fact that, as we have seen, "social classes" experience different rates of arrest and conviction for serious offenses. When strata within a society are marked off by categories of income, education, and occupational prestige, differences are discovered among them in the amount and style of crime. Further, differences are usually found between these "social classes" in their tastes, interests, and morals. It is easy, then, to describe these class-linked patterns as cultures. Thus the anthropologist Oscar Lewis (1959, 1961) speaks of the "culture of poverty" and the sociologist Walter B. Miller (1958) writes about "lower-class culture."

This version of the subcultural explanation of crime holds that the very fact of learning the lessons of the subculture means that one acquires interests and preferences that place him in greater or lesser risk of breaking the law. Miller, for example, argues that being reared in the lower class means learning a *different culture* from that which creates the criminal laws. The lower-class subculture is said to have its own values, many of which run counter to the majority interests that support the laws against the serious predatory crimes.

Miller's "Focal Concerns" Miller describes these lower-class values as "focal concerns" with "trouble, toughness, smartness, excitement, fate, and autonomy." It is held, then, that the lower class differs from the strata called "middle" and "upper" class in its greater attention to and belief in these focal concerns. The lower-class person believes, with Zorba, that "life *is* trouble," that much in one's life is fated regardless of what one does, and that the proper response to this perception of the world is to be tough, cunning, and independent. It is part of intelligence, too, to be "hastily hedonistic," to enjoy what one can when he can and let tomorrow take care of itself.

According to Miller, some 40 to 60 percent of North Americans may be "directly influenced" by these values, but about 15 percent of our populations are said to be "hard-core lower-class"—that is, people for whom the focal concerns constitute a life style. These hard-core people are also described as being produced by households headed by women, in which "serial monogamy" is practiced—in which, that is, the mother has one "spouse" at a time but more than one in a lifetime.

By contrast with the lower-class culture, middle-class values are usually described as emphasizing ambition, the cultivation of talents and skills, the ability to postpone gratification and to plan for the future, and the acceptance of individual responsibility and social duties (Davis and Havighurst, 1947; Hyman, 1953; Kohn, 1959; Kohn and Schooler, 1969; LeShan, 1952). The middle class tends to control the aggression of its children and to limit their independence. It may, in fact, be a hallmark of having been reared in the middle-class culture that one's mother always knew where one was.

It is also reported that the middle class emphasizes being

rational and reasonable, having good manners, and using leisure healthfully (*to dissipate*, we recall, means "to waste"). The middle class stresses respect for property and the control of violence.

Miller's thesis is that middle-class values are themselves lawful; whereas acquiring lower-class preferences automatically involves one in a greater risk of breaking the laws against the more serious crimes.

Banfield's "Propensity and Incentive" A similar class-oriented thesis is advanced by the political scientist Banfield (1968). He holds that

> crime, like poverty, depends upon two sets of variables. One set relates mainly to class culture and personality (but also to sex and age) and determines an individual's *propensity* to crime. The other relates to situational factors (such as the number of policemen on the scene and the size of the payroll) and determines his *incentive*. The probability that he will commit crimes—his *proneness* to crime—depends upon propensity *and* incentive [p. 159].

Banfield's description of the lower-class "propensity" to crime parallels Miller's description of its focal concerns. Banfield contends that lower-class culture develops a different type of morality, one that he calls "preconventional," in which conduct is guided by what succeeds and what can be gotten away with, and in which the only authority is power.

The propensity to crime is also encouraged, according to Banfield, by the shorter "time horizon" and lesser "ego strength," or ability to control impulses, of the lower class. The lower class is seen as placing a low value on the avoidance of risk. It is less prudent than the middle class and hence more prone to criminality. Furthermore, Banfield, like other reporters, describes the lower class as being encouraged to violence by its training, so that part of its greater propensity to crime lies in its greater willingness to inflict injury.

"The Deprived and the Privileged" in England Similar portraits of subcultural differences have been drawn by Morris

(1957) and Spinley (1964) for English samples. Both these investigators were interested in patterns of child rearing and in the nature of the values found among families of different occupational status. Spinley's intimate observations of working-class and middle-class ways of life in London were supplemented by the use of projective psychological tests.

These English researchers agree with the general description of delinquent subcultures given by Miller and Banfield for Americans. Among the families of unskilled English workingmen, discipline of children is much more haphazard and inconsistently punitive than among middle-class families. Children tend to be ignored or rejected. Punishment is more a function of how the parent feels than of what the child does. Abstract moral lessons are not taught, and life is lived in the present rather than for any future. As a result of such rearing, pangs of guilt and anxiety about shame are noticeably absent.

A caution: On the shifting boundaries of class cultures   In reading these descriptions of class cultures, it should not be assumed that such ways of life are fixed. A "culture" has some stability, but stability is not permanence. Cultures move and mix. The quality of their markers changes and, with that, class boundaries change too. For example, given some social mobility and shifts in income distribution, Bohlke (1961) has suggested that what has been called "middle-class delinquency" may more accurately represent "middle-income" crime rather than "middle-class-culture" crime. Bohlke means by this that the values taught and exhibited by some portion of the middle-*income* stratum are no longer the traditional middle-*class* values of prudence, personal responsibility, restraint, and achievement through disciplined effort.

It need not be expected, then, that merely increasing income will increase whatever *used to be* associated with income. Everything depends on the values that are cultivated as one's standard of living is elevated. An economic determinism is misleading if it assumes that the style of life *presently* associated with different income levels will automatically be generated by changes in income *however* such change is effected. Being given money does not require, or produce, the same culture as earning it does. The subcultural theorist reads with skepticism propositions about

"the economics of delinquency" such as Fleisher advances—
namely, that "the combined effects of a $500 increase in income
would probably be a reduction of about 5.2 arrests per 1,000
population. In areas of high tendencies toward crime, a 10 per
cent rise in incomes might well result in a 20 per cent decline in
delinquency" (p. 117). The subcultural theorist would say that
Fleisher's proposal confuses culture with one of its fluctuating
correlates.

The indicators of class are not descriptions of class   Proponents of subcultural explanations of crime do not define a class
culture by any assortment of the objective indicators of rank,
such as annual income or years of schooling. The subcultural
theorist is interested in *patterned ways of life* which may have
evolved with a division of labor and which, then, are called
"class" cultures. The pattern, however, is not described by
reference to income alone, or by reference to years of schooling
or level of occupational skill. The pattern includes these indicators, but it is not defined by them. The subcultural theorist is
more intent upon the *varieties of human value*, as Morris (1956)
has depicted and measured them. These are preferred ways of
living that are acted upon. In the economist's language, they are
"tastes."

The thesis that is intimated, but not often explicated, by a
subcultural description of behaviors is that single or multiple
signs of social position, such as occupation or education, will
have a different significance for status, and for cultures, with
changes in their distribution. Money and education do not mean
the same things socially as they are more or less equitably
distributed. The change in meaning is not merely a change in the
prestige value of these indices, but also betokens changes in the
boundaries between class cultures.

An unpopular version of this thesis might be termed "the
devaluation of status signs." It proposes a kind of "Gresham's
law of cultures." Just as "bad money drives out good money,"
according to Gresham's law, so it may be that "low culture"
corrupts "high culture."

This allegation is made particularly with respect to the
influence of the mass media upon aesthetic taste, the uses of the

intellect, and even crime rates. Studies of the uses of leisure in the Western world indicate, for example, that the optimistic promise that rising affluence would mean "the maintenance of high standards of diversified excellence among the keepers of high culture combined with a gradual improvement of mass tastes" has been largely unfulfilled (Wilensky, 1964, p. 173).

Wilensky comducted a study of the tastes for leisure activities of a sample of American men who ranged from denizens of Skid Row through the "middle mass" and self-employed merchants to prominent professionals. His research reveals the fragility of exacting standards of *aesthetic* preference, at least. In industrialized countries the mass media, and television in particular, are part of everyone's life—with exceptions so rare as to be almost bizarre. Being schooled or unschooled, monied or not, seems now to make little difference in preferences for the uses of leisure. Wilensky writes:

> High culture has always been precarious, but what *is* new to our time is a thorough interpenetration of cultural levels: the good, the mediocre, and the trashy are becoming fused in one massive middlemush. There is little doubt, from my data as well as others', that educated strata . . . are becoming full participants in mass culture; they spend a reduced fraction of time in exposure to quality print and film . . . The chief culprit, again, is TV" [p. 190].

A similar finding is reported by Mark Abrams (1958) for England. Abrams studied the media habits of a random sample of 13,620 adults over 24 years of age. He found that "the upper one per cent in educational and occupational status reported media habits so similar to those of the mass public, that one is reluctant to use the label 'cultural elite.'"

Whether one believes such tendencies to be good or bad, the point of this lengthy aside is simply that the criteria of "social class" that have been generally employed—criteria like income and schooling—may change meaning with changes in the distribution of these advantages in a population and with the heavy impact of the electronic media. "Class cultures," like national cultures, may break down.

Ethnic Predisposition

A more general subcultural explanation of crime, not necessarily in disagreement with the notion of class cultures, attributes differences in crime rates to differences in eth ic p tterns to be found within a society. Explanations of this sort do not necessarily bear the title "ethnic," although they are so designated here because they partake of the general assumption that there are group differences in learned preferences—in what is rewarded and punished—and that these group differences have a persistence often called a "tradition."

Such explanations are of a piece whether they are advanced as descriptions of regional cultures, generational differences, or national characteristics. Their common theme is the differences in ways of life out of which differences in crime rates seem to flow. Ethnic explanations are proposed under an assortment of labels, but they have in common the fact that they do *not* limit the notion of "subculture" to "class culture." They seem particularly justified where differences in social status are *not* so highly correlated with differences in conduct as are other indicators of cultural difference.

Thus Gastil (1971) argues that in the United States "economic and status positions in the community cannot be shown to account for differences [in homicide rates] between whites and Negroes or between Southerners and Northerners" (p. 414). Gastil then constructs an "index of Southernness" which he finds to be highly correlated with homicide rates in the United States. He claims, therefore, that there is a measurable regional culture that promotes murder.

The Subculture of Violence   In a similar vein, but examining the world as a whole, Wolfgang and Ferracuti (1967) have tried to explain variations in the amounts and kinds of violent behavior by describing the lessons that are transmitted from generation to generation within ethnic groups. Their study brings together an enormous bibliography on the psychology of killing, on the characteristics of aggressors, and on the cultures that facilitate violence. Wolfgang and Ferracuti's thesis, as phrased by one of their reviewers, is this:

Granting all the difficulties of counting behaviors, suppose one observes that persons affiliated with an intimate group, "The Baddies," when compared with their hosts, "The Goodones," more often carry weapons, take umbrage to a wide range of stimuli, and more frequently fight. Suppose, too, that measures of the Baddies' attitudes and values reveal a consensual perception of resort-to-violence as (a) the way life is, (b) the way one had better act in order to maintain a proper identity, get along, survive, and fulfill his ethic, and (c) the way things ought to be.

Assume, last, that these two broad classes of events, *being* violent and *valuing* violence, are causally related, the latter impelling the former [Nettler, 1968].

The question is, of course, "How explanatory is this explanation?" As with other explanations, the adequacy of this one depends upon what one wishes to do with it. If the student wishes only to "understand" variations in violence, his curiosity will be satisfied to the degree to which the "subculture of violence" has been thoroughly described so that its end product, assault and homicide, seems logically related to the description of everything else that is going on within the subculture.

If, on the other hand, one wants to know how to protect himself, he does not need to know what makes violent people as they are in order to know to stay away from them. Furthermore, if one is a reformer and wishes to "cure" the subculture of its violence, he receives no informed instruction from the subcultural explanation. He might as well attack one facet of their culture as another—child-rearing practices or religious beliefs; leisure pursuits or job satisfaction. Insofar as the subculture of violence is a *patterned* way of life, there is no particular lever for reformers to use. This does not make the subcultural explanation untrue; it just makes it unsatisfactory for some purposes.

The hazard of accepting a subcultural explanation *and,* at the same time, wishing to be a doctor to the body politic is that the remedies advocated may as well spread the disease as cure it. Among the prescriptions Wolfgang and Ferracuti provide is "social action" to disperse the representatives of the subculture of violence. Quite apart from the political difficulties of implementing such an enforced dispersion, the proposal assumes more knowledge than we have. We do not know what proportion of the violent people would have to be dispersed in order to break up their culture; and, what is more important, we do not know to what extent the dispersed people would act as "culture-carriers" and contaminate their hosts.

CRITICISM OF SUBCULTURAL EXPLANATIONS OF CRIME

Two major criticisms have been advanced against the subcultural hypotheses. One challenges the description of the differences between people and the alleged roots of differences in culture; the other concerns the possible circularity of subcultural explanations.

Are subcultures cultural?

No quarrels in social science are more heated these days than those that concern the description of differences between people, the sources of the differences (if any are admitted), and their amenability to change. This is particularly true as the debate moves from a description of the different *conditions* under which people live to the possible differences in their conduct which may, or may not, be responsible for these differing conditions. Because there has been pressure from the movement toward egalitarianism, it is today unpopular to recognize differences in conduct among groups. The subcultural explanations of criminality have not escaped this pressure. Thus common responses to the description of criminogenic subcultures are (1) to deny the difference, (2) to deny the durability of the difference, and finally, whether or not these denials seem implausible, (3) to call the difference "rational," "responsive," or in some other way "understandable," if not actually preferable.

An example of this type of criticism, combining all three charges against the subcultural theory of crime, is given by one (among many) critics of Banfield's thesis. Rossi writes:

> There is no "lower class" in Banfield's sense. Indeed, there is little firm evidence that there are many people, black or white, who are

permanently hedonistically present-oriented. The existing evidence is just as supportive of a theory that there are poor people, black and white, whose position in society is such that they might as well be hedonistically present-oriented since acting otherwise does little to improve their position [1971, p. 820].

As this brief passage indicates, the critic of a subcultural hypothesis holds that subcultures are not *that* different, and certainly not *permanently* that different, and that, in any event, poor people *ought* to be hasty hedonists.

A Personal Opinion   If one is interested in "the facts of life" and in reasoned responses to his social concerns, it seems a poor strategy to deny subcultural differences in behavior. These differences have been repeatedly observed and described by both professionals and nonprofessionals.

How durable these differences may be is another matter. No one holds a culture to be "permanent." Nonetheless, it may be highly resistant to change.

How *rational* the differing codes of conduct may be is yet another issue. There has been little, if any, test of the relative efficiency of different ways of life. One reason for this is that such testing always involves the acceptance of matters of taste and of morals. These preferences stand in some relationship to the ways of life being tested. They are either part of the way of life or they are in opposition to it. The professional student of behavior has no special competence for the evaluation of such cultural "objectives." The "technical expert" is no greater *moral* authority than anyone else.

However, when we return to our concern with crime, and when we consider any planned societal engineering in response to this concern, it would seem well advised to reckon with subcultural differences in values.

Are Subcultural Explanations Circular?

A principal criticism of the "subcultural" version of culture-conflict theories is that the idea of a "culture" is sometimes used tautologically. That is, the behaviors to be explained are explained by reference to attitudes and behaviors that are of the substance of that which is to be accounted for. It is as though one were to say that "People are murderous because they live violently," or "People like to fight because they are hostile."

All this may be true, but it seems not to satisfy. There are at least three ways out of the circularity, however: to describe the subculture more completely, to tell how it is learned, and to mix the subcultural explanation with other explanatory devices.

The first way out is to describe the culture that generates the behavior of interest in such breadth that "the whole way of life" is seen as making a particular kind of conduct more probable. This description usually includes a history of how the people "got that way." It becomes more plausible as an explanation when more details on the differences between one group and another are added. These details can be *directly* associated with the behavior to be explained—as when Gastil describes the tradition of carrying weapons as "Southern" and relates such "Southern-ness" to higher homicide rates. On the other hand, the differences may be only *remotely* associated with the behavior in question but nevertheless useful as marks of ethnicity, as are religion and language. When given such a larger picture of a culture, con-sumers of explanations are frequently satisfied. Their curiosity rests.

A second way to escape from circularity in a subcultural account is to add a sociopsychological explanation to it. The sociopsychological explanations, particularly those of the control variety, tell *how* the cultural prescriptions and preferences "get inside" the actors.

The third way out is to combine subcultural explanations with other presumed determinants of criminality. A persistent debate, we have seen, is that between criminologists who hold that ethnic differences reduce to class differences and those who hold that ethnicity has an independent role in the determination of crime rates. The first position is defended by sociologists who emphasize the causal importance of economic power and "the structure of opportunities" within a society. When this position is placed in an ecological context, as Shaw and McKay (1942) have done, it contends that "diverse racial, nativity, and national groups possess relatively similar rates of delinquents in similar social areas" (p. 162).

Some of the critics of such propositions have been cited (pages 119–127). One of the strongest of these critics, Jonassen (1949), has charged advocates of the Shaw-McKay thesis with "ecological determinism"—that is, with assuming that areas *cause* behaviors. To this accusation, Jonassen added the charge that there is a "professional ideology of social pathologists" that confuses democracy with uniformity and that refuses, therefore, to recognize differences in cultures.

A sociological mediator stepped into this debate with an interesting proposal that recognizes the implications for criminality of *both* ethnic values and economic structures. Toby (1950) suggested a resolution of the quarrel by showing how ethnicity and social structures meet to determine risks of delinquency. "Ethnic tradition," Toby argued, "is an intermediate structure between class position and the personality of the individual." Ethnic traditions that foster those attitudes and skills required by legitimate careers within a society reduce culture conflict and crime. On the other hand, those ethnic traditions that are less congruent with the requirements of "a system" are likely to be associated with higher crime rates. In Toby's resolution, ethnic traditions, economic position, and personality traits are intertwined determinants of lawful and delinquent careers. We are back on the general ground of culture conflict. However, a blending of variables, such as Toby proposed, makes the subcultural explanation of crime causation seem less tautological.

While sociologists acknowledge the plausibility of medleys of causes operating to affect crime rates, their attention has been largely diverted to specific kinds of social arrangements that may affect the damage we do each other. Among the sociological explanations of crime, the more prominent hypotheses stress the impact of *social structure* upon behavior. These proposals minimize the facts of subcultural differences and point to the sources of criminal motivation in the patterns of power and privilege within a society. They shift the "blame" for crime from *how* people are to *where* they are. Such explanations may still speak of "subcultures," but when they do, they use the term in a weaker sense than is intended by the subcultural theorist.

Chapter 7

Sociological Explanations of Criminality: The Structural Variety

A powerful and popular sociological explanation of crime finds its sources in the "social order." This explanation looks to the ways in which human wants are generated and satisfied and the ways in which rewards and punishments are handed out by the "social system."[1]

There need be no irreconcilable contradiction between subcultural and structural hypotheses, but their different emphases do produce quarrels about facts as well as about remedies. An essential difference between these explanations is that the "structuralists" assume that all the members of a society want

[1]The phrases "social order" and "social system" are placed in quotation marks here to indicate their vagueness, a vagueness that characterizes much of sociological language (Lachenmeyer, 1971). The lack of clarity of these terms can be verified by reference to dictionaries of sociology such as those edited by Fairchild (1944), Hoult (1969), and Mitchell (1968). The definitions found there justify the philosopher Ortega's comment that "the very name, 'society,' as denoting groups of men who live together, is equivocal and utopian" (1946, p. 24).

more of *the same things* than the "subculturalists" assume they want. In this sense, the structural theses tend to be egalitarian and democratic. With the exception of the version of the structural theory termed "the reactive hypotheses," the major applications of structuralism assume that "people everywhere are pretty much the same" and that there are no significant differences in abilities or desires that might account for lawful and criminal careers. Attention is paid, then, to the organization of social relations that affects the differential exercise of talents and interests which are assumed to be roughly equal for all individuals.

DURKHEIM'S ANOMIE

Modern structural explanations of criminogenesis derive from the ideas of the French sociologist Emile Durkheim (1858–1917). Durkheim viewed the human being as a social animal as well as a physical organism. To say that man is a *social* animal means more than the obvious fact that he lives a long life as a helpless child depending on others for his survival. It means more, too, than that *homo sapiens* is a *herding* animal who tends to live in colonies. For Durkheim, the significantly social aspect of human nature is that human physical survival also depends upon *moral* connections. Moral connections are, of course, social. They represent a bond with, and hence a bondage to, others. "It is not true," Durkheim writes, "that human activity can be released from all restraint" (1951, p. 252). The restraint that is required if social life is to ensue is a restraint necessary also for the psychic health of the human individual.

The notion of *pressure* is implied by Durkheim and his followers. Human beings are depicted as requiring a social environment to keep them sound. The pressure of that environment must be neither too little nor too great. Just as one can be crushed by the excessive demands of others upon his life, so, too, he "falls apart" when he lives without restraint. The metaphor is that of a denizen of the deep sea that requires just so much pressure to survive and explodes when brought to the surface.

Absolute freedom, the escape from all moral bonds, would,

for Durkheim, be a precursor of suicide. The suicide might be the act of a moment—"taking one's own life"—or it might be the piecemeal and prolonged suicide of those bored with life who kill themselves with vice.

Social conditions may strengthen or weaken the moral ties that Durkheim saw as a condition of happiness and healthy survival. Rapid changes in one's possibilities, swings from riches to rags and, just as disturbing, from rags to riches, may constitute, in Durkheim's words, "an impulse to voluntary death" (1951, p. 246). Excessive hopes and unlimited desires are avenues to misery.

Durkheim's conception of the human being is similar to that found among the ancient Greeks: the idea that men and women require a balance, a proportion, between their appetites and their satisfactions, between their wants and their abilities. "No living being," Durkheim tells us, "can be happy or even exist unless his needs are sufficiently proportioned to his means" (1951, p. 246).

Social conditions that allow a "deregulation" of social life Durkheim called states of "anomie." The French word anomie derives from Greek roots meaning "lacking in rule or law." As used by contemporary sociologists, the word anomie and its English equivalent, "anomy," are applied ambiguously, sometimes to the social conditions of relative normlessness and sometimes to the individuals who experience a lack of rule and purpose in their lives. It is recommended that the term be restricted to societal conditions of relative rulelessness (Nettler, 1957, p. 671).

When the concept of anomie is employed by structuralists to explain behavior, attention is directed toward the "strains" produced in the individual by the conflicting, confusing, or impossible demands of his social environment. Writers have described anomie in our "schizoid culture," a culture that is said to present conflicting prescriptions for conduct (Bain, 1958; Henry, 1963). They have also perceived anomie in the tension between recommended goals and available means.

It is this tension between ends and means to which many "social problems" are attributed, including the undesirable conditions of hatred of oneself and hatred of one's social connections. There is truth in Durkheim's vision, and many writers have incorporated it into their political attitudes. The rub comes, however, in deciding whether the gap between desires and abilities is to be narrowed by modifying the desires or changing the world that frustrates their fulfillment. Eastern philosophies and conservative thinkers emphasize the first path; Western philosophies and radical thinkers, the second.

MERTON'S APPLICATION OF THE CONCEPT OF ANOMIE

The American sociologist R. K. Merton (1957) has applied Durkheim's ideas to the explanation of deviant behavior with particular reference to modern Western societies. His hypothesis is that a state of *anomie* is produced whenever there is a discrepancy between the goals of human action and the societally structured legitimate means of achieving them. The hypothesis is, simply, that crime breeds in the gaps between aspirations and possibilities. The emphasis given to this idea by the structuralists is that both the goals and the means are given by the pattern of social arrangements. It is "the structure" of a society, which includes some elements of its culture, that builds desires and assigns opportunities for their satisfaction. This structural explanation sees illegal behavior as resulting from goals, particularly materialistic goals, held to be desirable and possible for all, that motivate behavior in a societal context that provides only limited legal channels of achievement. It is a thesis that has appropriately been named "strain theory" (Hirschi, 1969).

THE OPPORTUNITY-STRUCTURE THEORY: CLOWARD AND OHLIN'S *DELINQUENCY AND OPPORTUNITY*

The most prominent application of Merton's ideas has been to the explanation of juvenile delinquency and, in particular, to that of urban gangs. One formulation is given by Cloward and Ohlin's work, aptly titled *Delinquency and Opportunity* (1960). The central hypothesis is this:

> The disparity between what lower-class youth are led to want and what is actually available to them is the source of a major problem

of adjustment. Adolescents who form delinquent subcultures . . . have internalized an emphasis upon conventional goals. Faced with limitations on legitimate avenues of access to these goals, and unable to revise their aspirations downward, they experience intense frustrations; the exploration of nonconformist alternatives may be the result [p. 86].

This type of explanation sees delinquency as *adaptive,* as instrumental in the achievement of "the same kinds of things" everyone wants. It sees crime, also, as partly *reactive*—generated by a sense of injustice on the part of delinquents at having been deprived of the good life they had been led to expect would be theirs. Finally, this hypothesis, which may with accuracy be described as the social worker's favorite, looks to the satisfaction of desires, rather than the lowering of expectations, as the cure for crime. To be sure, it approaches the satisfaction of desires not directly but indirectly, through the provision of "expanded opportunities" for legitimate achievement.

Since this explanatory schema has been so popular, and since it has provided the theoretical justification of government programs for the reduction of delinquency, its key ideas deserve special note.

It is apparent, first, that, in common with other sociological explanations, this hypothesis is *culturally deterministic*. Cloward and Ohlin's statement does not talk about "what lower-class youths want." It talks about "what lower-class youths *are led* to want." The causal agent is "in the society" that does things to a youth, rather in the youth himself.

Second, it is assumed that the gap between the desires of the lower-class man and his legitimate opportunities is *greater* than the discrepancy between the aspirations of the middle-class man and his legitimate opportunities. This can be believed, but it is not known.

It is argued, third, that gang-running delinquents have "internalized conventional goals," and, fourth, that the legitimate avenues to these goals are structurally limited.

Fifth, the hypothesis holds that lower-class youths do not (and cannot) "revise their aspirations downward." Finally, it is said that the breach between promise and fulfillment generates intense frustration and that the frustration *may* lead to deviant conduct.

While the opportunity-structure thesis as a whole sounds plausible, closer attention to its assumptions lessens confidence in its explanatory power.

Criticisms of the Opportunity-structure Hypothesis

There are four principal charges brought against the opportunity-structure hypothesis. Each criticism has numerous points to it, but the various doubts can be brought together under four questions: (1) "Are the key concepts of the theory clear?" (2) "Is the theory correct about the way gang-running delinquents are?" (3) "Is the theory correct about how they got that way?" (4) "Are the recommendations of the opportunity-structure theory feasible and effective?" The answers to all four questions seem more negative than affirmative.

1 Are the Key Concepts Clear? Two words are central in thinking about crime in terms of the opportunity-structure hypothesis: "aspiration" and "opportunity." Neither concept is clear. Both words are borrowed from lay language, where the denotations of many useful concepts are embedded in emotionalized connotations so that common words, the principal currency of communication, become slippery. Such ambiguity is comforting in politics and journalism where points can be proved by sliding from one respectable meaning of a term to its less reputable meanings. Ambiguity may be a social lubricant in this sense, but it is a defect in a social science that would guide rational social policy.

Like many other explanations of human behavior, the opportunity-structure theory starts with what people want. The engine of action is desire. It is assumed that the desires called "aspirations" have been quite similar for all North Americans, if not for all Westerners, at some time in their careers. However, opportunity-structure theory is silent about the life histories of delinquents and hence takes for granted what needs to be known—the extent to which lawful careers and all they entail *are* preferred or derided.

This neglect is both cause and effect of the structuralist's ready assumption that what people *say* they want out of life is an adequate measure of their "aspiration." Such an easy equation of words with motives leaves out of the definition of "aspiration" that which most dictionaries and common usage include: ambition, drive, yearning. To accept words at face value as indicators of aspiration strips the concept of its motivating power and permits students to confuse daydreaming with the desire that fuels intent. In response to the interviewer with his clipboard and questionnaire, it is easy for any of us to tell "what we'd like"—usually "money and repute." It is another matter, however, to equate this ready verbalization with *aspiration*—with intention, direction, plan.

The likelihood that there is a difference between verbal aspiration and effective motivation is increased by evidence that the values of the more persistent delinquents *are* different from those of lesser offenders. "Values" here refers to what people want as noted in *both* their words and their deeds. The values that energize "aspiration," and give it its proper meaning, *do* differ between committed violators and more lawful people. On this issue, the advocate of the subcultural theory seems to be on firmer ground than the structuralist.

The evidence of such difference is found in a host of studies that draw us a portrait of the more serious offender as a hasty hedonist and jungle cat. The "philosophy" of the persistent miscreant is cynical, hostile, and distrustful. His morality denies the rules of the game. It avoids responsibility for fulfilling obligations to others except under fear of reprisal. It downgrades the victims of his crimes and categorizes them as "punks, chumps, pigeons, or fags" (Schwendinger and Schwendinger, 1967, p. 98). The delinquent's "jungle philosophy" sees friends as fickle and "everybody as just out for himself" (Nettler, 1961). According to the criminal ethic, you should "do unto others as they would do unto you . . . only do it first"; and, "If I don't cop [steal] it . . . somebody else will" (Schwendinger and Schwendinger, 1967, p. 98).

We can declare that the legal philosophy and the criminal philosophy are different without debating the question which philosophy is more correct. The difference in values noted here is not just a difference in words; it is a difference that is acted out. The opportunity-structure hypothesis neglects this difference, apparently as a result of its weak conception of aspiration.

The other term central to this explanation of crime, "opportunity," is equally vague. As dictionaries and most men use the word, it refers to a time or situation favorable to the attainment of a goal; it refers to a "chance." Now the perception of a chance is always a function of the perceiver and where he stands. Its assessment involves some notion, usually tacit, of what a person could have done if he had had the chance, or had seen it. There is, then, a possible difference between *perceived* opportunities and *real* ones, between what was there and what a person perceived was there; between what a person might actually have done and what he, or other observers, believe he might have done if he had acted differently or seen differently. Opportunities, therefore, are by their nature much easier to see after they have passed than before they are grasped.

These many intangibles in the idea of an opportunity mean that sociologists who employ the term "opportunity" come to judge differences in opportunity from differences in result. If people do not end up equally happy, healthy, lawful, or rich, these differences are attributed to differences in "opportunity." This attribution does two questionable things: (1) it assumes that all or most of the causes of a career are encompassed in something called "the chances" or "the breaks," and (2) it performs a semantic cheat by substituting *how one is* for *the chances one had.* This is illegitimate because it first poses a cause of conduct called "opportunity" and then it uses the alleged effects of that "opportunity" as a measure of it. It is as if one were to argue that C causes E, and then prove the causal connection by using E as the measure of C.

For most of us, the proper attribution of a causal relationship requires that whatever is called a "cause" must be a *different set of circumstances* from that which is called its effect. Otherwise we are trapped in a logical circle, an entrapment that may be comfortable for purposes of moral or political debate but that is a hindrance to effective action. The scientific requirement of any hypothesis which proposes that opportunities may be the causes of careers is that the indicators of "opportunity" be defined *before* the signs of outcome are decided upon. The two sets of indicators must then be kept separate if any inference is to be derived as to the causal relation between them.

This research requirement applies with particular force to the opportunity theorists, because going to school has been defined by scholars and laymen alike as one legitimate opportunity. As with any other "chance," some people grasp it while others reject it. Persistent delinquents, we shall see, prefer the latter course when faced with schooling. The difference in career, then, lies less in the *presence* of the opportunity than in its *use*. Both the subcultural and the sociopsychological explanations of crime pay more attention to the determinants of differential perception of opportunities.

2 Does the Opportunity-structure Thesis Accurately Describe Gang-affiliated Delinquents? The fundamental assumption of opportunity-structure theory is equality. Not equality of "opportunity," of course, but equality of aspiration, interest, motivation, application, and ability.

Cloward and Ohlin, for example, attribute juvenile delinquency to the offender's sense of injustice. These authors argue that delinquents see unfairness in "the system," with people of the same ability as themselves, or less ability, getting a bigger slice of the pie. Furthermore, Cloward and Ohlin contend that the delinquents' perception is correct.

The first part of this allegation is hardly news. It has long been common for criminals to argue that "the system" is more crooked than they, that "straight people" are just as dishonest as thieves, and that "it's not what you do, but who you know" that determines one's fate. What is surprising is that social scientists accept this rationalization and, in so doing, confuse a justification of delinquency with the causes of delinquency.

Cloward and Ohlin say:

> It is our impression that a sense of being unjustly deprived of access to opportunities to which one is entitled is common among those who become participants in delinquent subcultures. Delinquents tend to be persons who have been led to expect opportunities *because of their potential ability* to meet the formal, institutionally established criteria of evaluation [p. 117; italics added].

They then support this allegation of equal ability with a footnote stating:

> There is no evidence . . . that members of delinquent subcultures are objectively less capable of meeting formal standards of eligibility than are nondelinquent lower class youngsters. In fact, the available data support the contention that the basic endowments of delinquents, such as intelligence, physical strength, and agility, are the equal of or greater than those of their nondelinquent peers [p. 117, fn. 10].

Unless one is to earn his keep as a professional athlete, the "basic endowments" of physical strength and agility are of slight relevance to occupational achievement. Intelligence, persistence, diligence, reliability, interest, emotional control—these traits are of greater relevance to climbing the class ladder. Contrary to the belief of opportunity-structure theorists, gang-running delinquents do *not* exhibit these abilities in the same proportions as more legitimately successful youths.

Such evidence as we have of how people legitimately climb upward in society indicates that those who successfully use lawful means exhibit differences in interests, motivation, and ability early in adolescence and possibly even before puberty. Furthermore, achievers, when compared with their less successful counterparts, differ in these attributes even when social-class origins are held constant (Jayasuriya, 1960; Straus, 1962). The pattern of difference is quite consistent among industrial countries of otherwise varied cultures.

The legitimately successful tend to be more interested in schoolwork, to score higher on mental tests, and to be more emotionally stable and diligent. They move toward their voca-

tional objectives with greater persistence and defer other gratifications in favor of these longer-range goals. They demonstrate
greater self-confidence and a greater need to achieve. They
function more independently of their parents while yet respecting
their parents more. They are described as being possessed of
greater self-control, responsibility, and intellectual efficiency.
The evidence of these differences is widespread and may be
sampled in the reports of Beilin (1956), Burt (1961), Crockett
(1962), Douvan (1956), Douvan and Edelson (1958), Haan (1964),
Sewell et al. (1969), Sorokin (1959), Srole et al. (1962), Stacey
(1965), Terman and Oden (1947, 1955), Thompson (1971), Warner
(1953), and Warner and Abegglen (1955).

Until recently, at least,[2] going to school has been the major
legitimate ladder by which people have climbed upward in
society. A multiplicity of studies tells us that juvenile offenders,
and particularly the more serious offenders, differ from their less
delinquent counterparts in their greater resistance to schooling.
They hate schoolwork and they hate their teachers. They more
frequently "ditch" school and destroy school buildings and
equipment. They do poorly in academic work, are more frequently retarded in grade, and score low on tests of mental performance. They are perceived by both their teachers and their
classmates as troublemakers and they are, in general, disliked by
both. This dislike is, of course, reciprocated. A partial roster of
the evidence of these differences includes studies by Cooper
(1960), Glueck (1964), Healy and Bronner (1936), Hathaway and
Monachesi (1957), Hewitt and Jenkins (1946), Mannheim (1965),
Paranjape (1970), Peterson et al. (1959), Porteus (1961), Quay et
al. (1960), Rivera and Short (1967), Shulman (1929), Stinchcombe
(1964), Stott (1966), Teele et al. (1966), West (1969), and Williams
(1933).

The hypothesis that delinquents are persons who are the

---

[2]This qualification is required because the higher the proportion of a population that
achieves educational certification, the lower the probable value of that accomplishment as an
instrument of socioeconomic improvement. Subject, of course, to the unknown effects of
future changes in technologies and economies, it may be suggested that there is some limit
beyond which it will be the case that the more people climb the educational ladder, the shorter
that ladder will become as a means of moving upward in class. For discussions of the
oversupply of educated manpower, see Berg (1971), Ginzberg (1972), and Grubb (1971).

same as nondelinquents in ability and motivation, differing from nondelinquents only in the "legitimate opportunities" available to them, fails on its assumption of initial equality. This untenable assumption is but part of a more general descriptive weakness inherent in the opportunity-structure theory. The theory does not accurately portray the talents, preferences, desires, and views of the world that reliably distinguish serious, career offenders from their more lawful counterparts.

This descriptive failure has been attributed to the possibility that the inventors of the opportunity-structure hypothesis are middle-class persons imposing their perceptions upon others, who in fact reject them. However this may be, the hypothesis does slight the fact that tastes differ and that lower-class ways of life may have a rationale and a definition of "how things ought to be" that have their own validity. This structural explanation is blind, therefore, to the *fun* that is involved in being delinquent— fun like skipping school, rolling drunks, snatching purses, being chased by the police, staying out till all hours, going where one wants, and doing what one wants without adult supervision.

3 Does the Opportunity-structure Hypothesis Accurately Describe How Delinquents Are Produced? If there is something deficient in a description of how people are, it is likely that there is something wrong with the related explanation of how they got that way.

The opportunity-structure story holds that the delinquent's response is adaptive, a necessary consequence of a "social structure." The theory is therefore sympathetic to the motives it attributes to a wide category of offenders. It accords "frustration" to the gang-running delinquent and sees the frustration as produced by the correct perception of unjust deprivation.

"Frustration" is another fuzzy word. Sometimes it refers to a blocking, a thwarting, to not getting what one wants. At other times it refers to emotions, to feelings of despair and anger, to a free-floating discontent. The first meaning is *objective.* Observers can watch animals strive for goals and can agree about their success or failure: whether the monkey gets the banana or the runner wins the race. The second meaning is *subjective.* It refers to feelings attributed to the striver who fails. The objective failure that is sometimes called "frustration" is not the same set of events as the angry feelings also called "frustration." The relationship between the two meanings of "frustration" is far from perfect, and it is presumptive to infer one from the other. No one has yet mapped the coordinates of frustration. No one knows which persons under which circumstances feel more or less frustrated by which failure. In fact, the very ideas of "success" and "failure" have not been adequately diagrammed for people of diverse ways of life.

These uncertainties about the meaning of "frustration" and its location leave the opportunity-structure hypothesis untested and perhaps untestable. In the absence of such testing, critics of the hypothesis will rely on more plausible depictions of the process by which serious offenders are produced. They will, for example, continue to stress "structures" as affecting the realization of talent *without* the assumption of equal interests and abilities. They will continue, with the social psychologists, to stress the importance of early family socialization and, with the subcultural theorists, to emphasize the authenticity of ethnic values that may be more or less criminogenic within a given "social structure."

4 Are the Recommendations of Opportunity-structure Theory Feasible and Effective? A fair test of a hypothesis is whether it works. The work of a hypothesis is to prescribe a distinctive course of action that will reliably get one more of what he wants at known and lower costs.

The opportunity-structure explanation of criminogenesis has been interpreted as saying that if young people had more legitimate opportunities to satisfy their aspirations, they would resort less frequently to crime. In the United States several large-scale projects have attempted to expand opportunities and thereby reduce juvenile delinquency. Their record has been one of uniform failure (Hackler, 1966; Hackler and Hagan, 1972; Moynihan, 1969; Weissman, 1969).

Failure itself has many explanations and, when it follows upon kind efforts, many apologists. The failure of programs designed to prevent delinquency and to reform delinquents can always be attributed to insufficient funding or to unforeseen resistance by evil others, rather than to errors in the theories underlying the programs.

Failure may also be attributed to selective attention to what the theory recommends. In fairness to Cloward and Ohlin, they have *not* said in their major work that the cure for crime is simply the expansion of legitimate opportunities. Their emphasis has given this impression, of course. However, Cloward and Ohlin argue that "extending services to delinquent individuals or groups cannot prevent the rise of delinquency among others" (p. 211). They hold that "the major effort . . . should be directed to the reorganization of slum communities" because "the old structures, which provided *social control* and avenues of social ascent, are breaking down" (p. 211, italics added).

"Social control" has been emphasized in this quotation because the opportunity hypothesis finally reverts to an assumption that is common to all sociological and sociopsychological explanations of criminality *mala in se.* All these explanations see serious crime as the result of a weakening of social controls. The explanations differ only in how they believe this deregulation of social life has come about, in what they emphasize as the crucial regulator, and hence in where they specify effort ought to be applied to reduce the harm we do each other.

In Summary

The proposal that differences in the availability of legitimate opportunities affect crime rates is but one version of the structural style of explanation. The weaknesses of this particular hypothesis do not deny the validity of the structural notion in general. There *are* features of the "structure" of a society that seem clearly and directly antecedent to varying crime rates. "Culture conflict" is one such general aspect of a society's structure that seems to promote criminality. Durkheim's *anomie*, the deregulation of social life, may be another such feature, as yet inadequately applied to the explanation of crime. Merton's application of the idea of *anomie* to the production of criminality seems plausible in general, particularly if one avoids translating *anomie* into "opportunity." This more general use of the notion of *anomie* predicts that serious crime rates will be higher in societies whose public codes and mass media simultaneously stimulate consumership and egalitarianism while denying differences and delegitimizing them.

More concretely, the age distributions and sex ratios of societies or of localities can be interpreted as structural features and related to differences in crime rates. Thus it comes as little surprise to learn that situations in which the sex ratio is greatly distorted result in different patterns of sexual offense. Homosexuality, including forcible homosexual rape, increases where men and women are kept apart from the opposite sex, as in prisons. Prostitution flourishes where numbers of men live without women but with the freedom to "get out" on occasion, as from mining camps or military bases.

These more concrete features of the "social structure" seem at once more obvious and less interesting, however, than the "class structure" of a society—the way in which its wealth and prestige are differentially achieved and awarded. It is among these differentials that sociologists and many laymen continue to look for the generators of crime.

The opportunity-structure hypothesis is one way of attending to class differences and attempting to show how they breed crime. It views criminality as *adaptive*, as utilitarian, as the way deprived people can get what everyone wants and has been told he should have.

There is yet another type of explanation that looks upon the pattern of rewards in a society as causing crime. This theory differs from the opportunity-structure theory in its emphasis. It interprets crime as more *reactive* than adaptive to social stratification.

REACTIVE HYPOTHESES

Reactive hypotheses are related to other structural schema in emphasizing the role of the status system of a society in producing crime and delinquency. As one kind of sociological explanation, these formulations also partake of some of the subcultural ideas and may even speak of "delinquent subcultures." The reactive hypotheses, however, describe criminal subcultures as formed in response to status deprivation. They see criminality as less traditional, less ethnic, and more psychodynamically generated. They interpret delinquency as a status-seeking solution to "straight" society's denial of respect. The reactive hypotheses are, then, a type of structural theory that carries a heavy burden of psychological implication.

Crime and Compensation

The "pure" reactive hypothesis claims that the social structure produces a "reaction formation" in those whom its rules disqualify for status. *Reaction formation,* or reversal formation, is a psychoanalytic idea: that we may defend ourselves against forbidden desires by repressing them while expressing their opposites. In such circumstances, the behaviors of which the ego is conscious are psychoanalytically interpreted as an armor against admitting the unconscious urges that have been frustrated. If one is excessively neat, it is because he really wants to be messy but can't. If one is painfully polite, then the psychoanalyst perceives hostility raging beneath the good manners. It is the phenomenon of the sour grapes: "If I can't have it, it must be no good." Thus, it is held, if one can't play the middle-class game, or won't be let into it, he responds by breaking up the play. The denial is proof of the desire. For example, Kobrin (1951, p. 660) says of the young vandal, "The vigor of the rejection of the value system is the measure of its hold upon the person."

Where the subcultural theorists see delinquent behavior as "real" in its own right, as learned and valued by the actor, and where the social psychologists agree but emphasize the training processes that bring this about, the proponents of reactive hypotheses interpret the defiant and contemptuous behavior of many delinquents as a compensation that defends them against the ego-wounding they have received from the status system. Kobrin writes: "The aggressively hostile response of the young male in the delinquency area to his devaluation by representatives of the conventional culture arises entirely from the fact that the criteria of status in the conventional culture have validity for him" (1951, p. 660).

Cohen and Others on Compensatory Crime There are many other students of offensive behavior who believe that hating a social system and doing injury to it are encouraged by status differences. The reactive hypotheses are in agreement with the differential-opportunity theory in regarding denial of status as frustrating and motivating. However, the motivation that results from an invidious lack of status is differently conceived by these two types of structural explanation. The opportunity theorist describes crime as more utilitarian, more rational, and hence as an alternative way of achieving common goals. The reactive hypotheses, by contrast, perceive much crime as nonutilitarian, as expressive rather than instrumental, and as an attack upon the values by which the criminal is himself disqualified.

The reactive hypotheses differ further from the opportunity structure story in accepting the fact that people may not be equally equipped to use the legitimate means of achievement. One of the chief spokesmen for this point of view, Cohen, writes:

> The delinquent subculture, we suggest, is a way of dealing with the problems of adjustment we have described. These problems are chiefly status problems: certain children are denied status in the respectable society *because they cannot meet the criteria of the respectable status system.* The delinquent subculture deals with these problems by providing criteria of status which these children *can* meet [1955, p. 121; italics added in the second sentence].

One can accommodate these differing views by holding that they explain different types of crime or criminals. Certainly the reactive theories are more alert to the gratuitous hostility, the vandalism, and the joy in destruction that characterize some youthful gangs. This explanation recognizes, too, the existence of "uneconomic theft," theft accomplished for the fun of it, with the loot afterward thrown away. The reactive hypotheses are sensitive to the delights of hatred and to the pleasures gained by being shockingly outcast. Thompson, for example, describes the motorcycle gang with whom he ran for a year as "losers—dropouts, failures and malcontents. [The Hell's Angels] are rejects looking for a way to get even with a world in which they are only a problem" (1966, p. 260). "Their lack of education has not only rendered them completely useless in a highly technical economy, but it has also given them the leisure to cultivate a powerful resentment" (p. 258).

The resentment Thompson describes is expressed by "outraging the public decency" (p. 117). The provocation of public outrage becomes for the gang member a measure of his status with his fellow outcasts. "When you walk into a place where people can see you, you want to look as repulsive and repugnant as possible," reports one Angel. "Anything good, we laugh at. We're bastards to the world and they're bastards to us. I think this is what really keeps us going. We fight society and society fights us. It doesn't bother me" (p. 118).

Other students besides Cohen, Kobrin, and Thompson have proposed that some kinds of criminality should be viewed as reactions to status frustration. Schwendinger (1963) has collected one of the world's largest inventories of recorded interviews and moral game-playing with adolescents of varying delinquency. Although he titled his work *The Instrumental Theory of Delinquency*, the motives he attributes to his youthful offenders have to do with status seeking, and the function of much hostile crime is for him what it is for Cohen, Kobrin, and Thompson—an expression of resentment over deprivation of status.

Questions about the Reactive Thesis

The disadvantage of the reactive hypothesis lies in its plausibility. Given the phenomenon of angry young men and women who reject what others accept, it "makes sense" to explain their hostility as a reaction against what has allegedly been denied them. There is also a certain humanity to this interpretation, for it sees the bad actor as just like everyone else, wanting to be as others are but frustrated in his aspirations, kicking back at those who have frustrated him, and destroying what he wants but can't have.

The trouble with this plausible idea is that it may not be

correct. The Italians have a phrase for such convincing but unproved ideas. "It may not be true," they say, "but it's a good story." So here. The assumption that extremely hostile behavior represents a reaction formation cannot be verified. Worse, for scientific purposes, the assumption cannot be falsified. How, for example, could one prove or disprove Kobrin's statement that vandals' "defiance and contempt can be understood as an effort on the part of the delinquents to counteract their own impulses to accept and accede to the superior status of such representatives of the conventional order as school principals" (1951, p. 660)?

Alternatives to Reactive Hypotheses

In scientific work there is a criterion, not rigidly adhered to, which says that the simple explanation is preferable to the complex, that the hypothesis with few assumptions is preferable to the one with many. There are simpler explanations of criminal hostility than the reactive hypotheses. One such theory holds that violence comes naturally and that it will be expressed unless we are trained to control it. Another theory calls envy a universal and independent motive.

Expressing Violence and Learning It   Some social psychologists believe that children will grow up violent if they are not adequately nurtured (Eron et al., 1971). Adequate nurturing includes both *appreciating* the child and *training* him to acknowledge the rights of others. From this theoretical stance, the savagery of the urban gangster represents merely the natural outcome of a failure in child rearing.

Similarly, on a simple level of explanation, many sociologists and anthropologists believe that hostile behavior can be learned as easily as pacific behavior. Once learned, the codes of violence and impatient egoism are their own "positive values." Fighting and hating then become both duties and pleasures, the more so where enemies are defined. For advocates of this sociopsychological point of view, it is not necessary to regard the barbarian whose words and deeds "laugh at goodness" as having the same motives as more lawful persons.

The Autonomy of Envy   Another interpretation of the reactive hypothesis lends it support, but places a different construction upon the resentment described by Cohen, Schwendinger, and Kobrin. This interpretation sees *envy* as a persistent, universal emotion that every society has attempted to control (Schoeck, 1966). According to this view, envy of the superior and hatred of the different are drives lying "at the core of man's life as a social being [which occur] as soon as two individuals become capable of mutual comparison" (Schoeck, 1966, p. 1). Envy is "the consuming desire that no one should have anything [that I do not have]. [It is] the destruction of pleasure in and for others, without deriving any sort of advantage from this" (p. 115).

Although the Freudians believe that envy represents a conflict between the desire to emulate the superior and the desire to reject his difference, as we have seen in Kobrin's construction, there is no need to assume that an individual's resentment is born of his desire to be *like* those whom he resents. One can envy what others *have* without wishing to be as they *are*. One can envy the other person's status—his fame, his success, his wealth and happiness—without wanting to do the things that have secured, or be the person who has won, these advantages. Superiority is its own affront, the more so as its legitimacy is attacked.

Those theorists who acknowledge the normality of envy place less emphasis on the structure of a society as generating resentment and more emphasis upon the cultural themes that justify the expression of it. For these theorists, envy represents a persistent emotion to be controlled through institutionalized beliefs that legitimize differences. They are one with Merton on this point at least—that they accord a determining power to the culture-wide myths and values that raise appetites or control them. For example, the philosopher Ortega (1932) believed that the criminal expression of envy was encouraged by the belief that everyone is as good as anyone and that the fruits of a civilization—the results of discipline, work, effort—are "natural rights" rather than social gains. For Ortega, this ideology, which he called that of the "massman," confuses nature with the social order and denies the legitimacy of difference, particularly that of superiority. The result of this confusion and this denial is violence. Shoeck concurs: "Envious crime—a concept which embraces most juvenile crime and vandalism—will occur chiefly in those societies whose official credo, constantly recited in school, on the political platform and in the pulpit, is universal equality" (p. 114).

SCHOOLS, VOCATIONS, AND DELINQUENCY

The structural theories that have been described thus far all contain some truth. If they are criticized, it is because they sometimes go beyond their cores of veracity and assume too much. The kernel of truth in the structural views of criminogenesis described so far is that young people need apprenticeship to maturity. Human beings who are moving from protected childhood toward independent adulthood need to practice the activities that will be their acceptable ways of life as adults. The best that can be hoped is that adult lives will include vocations which meet their interests and which, therefore, are satisfying. There can be no guaranty of this, of course, and aspirations that are constantly raised are bound to be disappointed. However, structuralists have called attention to some of the grosser deficiencies in the ways in which present social arrangements use youth and produce crime.

Rich societies pay prices for their affluence. One price is the uselessness of many young people. Multitudes of men and women in their teens are presumably not needed by the more successful Western industrial societies. They are, as a consequence, kept in an ambiguous state, half child and half adult. Since these industrialized countries have gained their wealth by employing products of education, science, and technology, it is concluded that more of the same education for everyone will increase the benefits. If academic schooling is good for some, up to some age, it is believed that such academic work is good for everyone for as long as a quarter or even a third of their lives. Under compulsory attendance laws, the schools then become a giant holding operation. They are an "opportunity," of course, for those with academic interests, but they are a jail for those without such interests. For the numerous remainder, who reside somewhere between a modest academic interest and a boredom relieved by social life and sports, the schools are a huge repository.

If this picture of teen-age life in industrial societies seems accurate, no involved psychological assumptions are required to propose that youthful inutility and protracted semi-childhood will generate disturbance, some of it criminal. We need only assume, with Marx and Veblen as with many contemporary psychologists, that human beings are curious animals, makers and doers, who "do best" when they have a vocation that others appreciate and that is rewarding in itself.

Rich societies are hard put to provide such meaningful work for everyone. Many jobs are dull but necessary; and not everyone has the talent for the exciting work of a criminal lawyer or a neurosurgeon. For the sake of domestic peace and psychic health, the societal requirement is to employ the great middle ranges of aptitude and ineptitude (Goode, 1967).

Upon such assumptions several writers have suggested that secondary schools in the Western world are excessively committed to college preparation and insufficiently adjusted to the interests of future workers in trade, industry, and the paraprofessions. It is argued that the pressure to succeed academically and the built-in probability of failure assured by lack of interest and ability produce hostility (McDonald, 1969). If to this cauldron of discontent one adds poor teaching, resentment is brought to a boil.

The hostility is further stimulated by the meaninglessness of academic work for what many young people want to do, and see themselves doing, as adults. Such a way of life for juveniles is a way of "growing up absurd," Paul Goodman says (1956). Similarly, the sociologist Stinchcombe (1964) sees a source of rebellion in the disjunction between school life and the adult life toward which many young people, the boys in particular, are moving. The thesis advanced by Goodman, Stinchcombe, and many other critics of Western education is that compulsory schooling is itself criminogenic for those youngsters who find no immediate gratification in the academic work and who can see, correctly, no future reward from their present training.

Stinchcombe argues that schools in Western nations

"threaten the self-respect of those who don't achieve" academically and that the reaction to such wounding is violent. The
violent reaction to failure in school is accompanied by the
substitution of "ascriptive symbols" of personal worth for
the achieved marks of academic success. These ascriptive symbols are signs of adulthood and a denial of the adolescent and
submissive role in which schools place young people. Things like
smoking, drinking, owning a car, freer dating, and financial
independence are status symbols that take the place of the school
symbols. By their very adoption, they challenge the legitimacy
and authority of the school. They are more than mere challenges,
however; they are also indicators of an alienation from the
honors that schools value and can give.

Goodman's description of "growing up absurd" is in accord
with Stinchcombe's, but Goodman's interpretation proposes a
more radical rejection of industrialized Western societies. Goodman believes that there is not enough "man's work" in
North America and that our absurd societies are "lacking in the
opportunity [for young men] to be useful," that they "thwart
aptitude and create stupidity," that they "corrupt the fine arts
... shackle science ... and dampen animal ardor" (p. 12). Goodman believes that delinquent behavior "speaks clearly enough. It
asks for manly opportunities to work, make a little money, and
have self-esteem; to have some space to bang around in, that is
not always somebody's property; to have better schools to open
for them horizons of interest; to have more and better sex
without fear or shame; to share somehow in the symbolic goods
(like the cars) that are made so much of; to have a community and
a country to be loyal to; to claim attention and to have a voice"
(pp. 50–51).

The extremity of Goodman's position is likely to obscure
the validity of what he, Stinchcombe, and other authors have
pointed out—that Western schooling does not provide an adequate apprenticeship in adulthood for a sufficient number of
young people and that this inadequacy may be criminogenic. The
schools are changing, however, and some educators are experi-
menting with broader avenues on which adolescents may move as
they grow up. There is criticism of compulsory schooling of the
same kind for every youth. There is experimentation with "elec-

tronic self-teaching." There is awareness among educators that, beyond establishing some minimum of literacy and calculating competence, schools may not be the best providers of vocational initiation.

Such experimentation is not assisted, however, by the stimulating comments Goodman offers. Goodman is essentially an anarchist. His vision is utopian and, consequently, disillusioning. The high ideals are in accord with neither present reality nor future possibility, and they do not generate useful recommendations. As always, it is one thing to decry the world we live in; it is quite another matter to know how to change it without making it worse.

It is, for example, debatable whether there is "not enough manly work" in our societies. Much depends upon who is defining "manly." It is even more debatable whether the pastoral life Goodman proposes is an adequate substitute for the jobs, the organization, the "system" which Goodman despises but which, nevertheless, produce the wealth that makes possible his disaffection. Goodman's recommendation is for something no one can give and no group can create. No one can produce the "symbolic goods (like the cars)" without *organizing* the work. Some of that work will be dirty work, and calling it "unmanly" will not help us appreciate it. Similarly, in a world growing more crowded, space will always be allocated, whether it be "somebody's property" or the state's. As for the "more and better sex" that Goodman recommends "without fear or shame," delinquents are certainly less deprived in this regard than more conventional young people (Kinsey et al., 1948), and it is difficult to see how this remedy might be implemented or how it might reduce the rates of serious crimes, with the exception, perhaps, of forcible rape.

A Gloomy Conclusion

It needs no radical vision to agree with Goodman, Stinchcombe, McDonald, and others that the school systems of Western societies presently provide poor apprenticeship in adulthood for many adolescents. A poor apprenticeship for being grown up is criminogenic.

In this sense, the "structure" of modern countries encourages delinquency, for that structure lacks institutional proce-dures for moving people smoothly from protected childhood to autonomous adulthood. During adolescence, many youths in affluent societies are neither well guided by their parents nor happily engaged by their teachers. They are adult in body, but children in responsibility and in their contribution to others. Placed in such a no-man's-land between irresponsible depen-dence and accountable independence, they are compelled to attend schools that do not thoroughly stimulate the interests of all of them and that, in too many cases, provide the uninterested child with the experience of failure and the mirror of denigra-tion.

Educators are wrestling with remedies. However, in demo-cratic societies, they are torn between conflicting prescriptions. On the one hand, the democratic ethic is interpreted as demand-ing that everyone be given the same education with at least some minimum of equal result—such as an "adequate" competence in reading, writing, and arithmetic. On the other hand, beyond this undefined minimum level of literacy and basic skills, the reformer acknowledges that different schools or different curricula must be provided for children of varied talents and interests. This open-ness in the apprenticing institutions would not produce uniform results in academic skills, in knowledge, in know-how, or—what hurts most—in status. This is the dilemma of the democratic educator. He wants equality *and* individuality, objectives that thus far in history have eluded societal engineers. Meanwhile, the metropolitan schools of industrialized nations make a probable, but unmeasurable, contribution to delinquency.

RATIONAL CRIME

Some crimes are rational. In such cases, the criminal way appears to be the more efficient way of satisfying one's wants.

When crime is regarded as rational, it can be given either a structural or a sociopsychological explanation. The explanation is structural when it emphasizes the *conditions* that make crime rational. It becomes a sociopsychological explanation when it emphasizes the *interpretations* of the conditions that make crime rational, or when it stresses the *training* that legitimizes illegal activities. No one emphasis need be more correct—more useful—than another. Conduct, lawful and criminal, always occurs within some structure of possibilities and is, among "normal people," justified by an interpretation of that structure. Both the interpretation of and the adaptation to a structure of possibilities are largely learned. It is only for convenience, then, that we will discuss the idea that crime may be rational as one of the structural, rather than one of the sociopsychological, explanations.

The most obvious way in which a "social structure" produces crime is by providing chances to make money illegally. Whether or not a structure elevates desires, it generates crime by bringing "needs" into the view of opportunities.

This kind of explanation does not say that people behave criminally because they have been "denied" legitimate opportunities, as does the theory of Cloward and Ohlin. It says that people break the criminal law, particularly those laws concerning the definition of property, because this is a rational thing to do. The idea of "rational crime" is in accord with the common-sense assumption that most people will take money if they can do so without penalty. It is an idea that was well phrased over two hundred years ago by the Scottish philosopher David Hume, who wrote: "A man who at noon leaves his purse full of gold on the pavement at Charing Cross may as well expect that it will fly away like a feather as that he will find it untouched an hour after" (1758, p. 101).

Obviously there are differences in personality that raise or lower resistance to temptation. These differences are the concern of those sociopsychological explanations that emphasize the "controlling" functions of character. However, without attending to these personal variables, it is notable that the common human proclivity to improve and maintain status will produce offenses against property when these tendencies meet the "appropriate" situation. These situations have been studied by criminologists in four major contexts. There are, first, the many situations in civil life in which supplies, services, and money are available for theft. Theft is widespread in such situations. It ranges from taking what isn't nailed down in public settings to stealing factory tools and store inventories to cheating on expense accounts to embezzlement. Second, there are circumstances in which legitimate work makes it economical to break the criminal law. Third, there are "able criminals," individuals who have chosen theft as an occupation and who have made a success of it. These expert thieves are sometimes affiliated with "musclemen" and organizers in a fourth context of rational crime, the context in which crime becomes an economic enterprise fulfilling the demands of a market.

A Note on Rationality

The criminal response in contexts such as these has been called "rational" because the criminal behavior is an efficient way of satisfying the actor's desires. Since the word "rational" has good connotations, since it is generally considered better to be rational than nonrational or irrational, it ought to be pointed out that calling crime "rational" does not constitute approval of it. "Being rational" and "being moral" are two different things.

The idea of "being rational" signifies employing one's "reason" to select the most appropriate means for the attainment of one's empirical ends (Cousineau, 1967). All the terms in this definition are important.

This definition states, first, that a rational act is a purposive act. It is done consciously for the reason of obtaining an objective. Purely expressive behavior, behavior that is its own end, is not rational in this sense. Dancing for joy, for example, is an expressive act, not a rational one.

Second, the definition limits the objectives of a rational act to those that are empirical, to those that can be experienced. One can ascertain whether the objectives of "rational actions" have been achieved. Good goals whose attainment can never be experienced, like getting to heaven or achieving "the greatest good for the greatest number," are not rational goals.

Finally, a rational act is one based upon a reasoned (informed) choice of the most economical means for the actor.

This idea of rationality, it is noted, says nothing about the goodness of the ends toward which the agent is using his reason efficiently. It says nothing, too, about the goodness of his means. The definition of *moral* behavior is quite another matter. It has its own difficulties. The point here is simply that many categories of crime, however they may be judged morally, are nonetheless rational.

Crime as a Way of Increasing Reward

Economists seem more ready than sociologists to perceive crime as rational. This is a result of the economist's practice of regarding human behavior as channeled by the actor's tastes and by the actor's perception of costs and benefits. This economic model of man is more easily applied to rational action than to purely expressive behavior, for it is as one acts rationally that he gives consideration to price and value.

This point of view agrees with Hume's belief that, if the costs of taking the other man's gold are low, theft is likely. The social psychologist prefers to throw into this equation the variable of personal predisposition, including strength of desire (how much do you want the gold?) and resistance to temptation (how much "conscience" do you have?). These are significant variables, and their genesis will be discussed in Chapter 9. However, in looking at crime on the sociological level, on the level of the behavior of large numbers of people in roughly similar situations, the differences in personal predisposition may be ignored. The sociologist can estimate how much theft is to be expected within a particular social setting over some limited period. On the simple assumption that the easy chance to steal makes a difference, it is possible to calculate how much of this theft might be reduced through the obstruction of the opportunity for it.

The rule of thumb that follows from a number of studies testing public honesty is that "getting something for nothing" is a common frailty. For example, Merritt and Fowler (1948) measured "the pecuniary honesty of the public at large" by dropping stamped, addressed postcards, letters, and letters bearing a lead coin simulating a 50¢ piece on the streets of a number of American cities. While 72 percent of the postcards and 85 percent of the letters were placed in mailboxes, only 54 percent of the letters containing the "coins" were mailed.

In other studies "lie detector" (polygraph) tests have been conducted among employees of chain stores and banks. McEvoy (1941) reports that about three-fourths of the workers had taken money or merchandise from his sample of chain stores. Among the banks surveyed, about one-fifth of the employees were reported to have "increased their salaries" by stealing money or property.

The President's Commission on Law Enforcement and the Administration of Justice (1967b) estimates that shoplifting and larceny by employees take some $1.33 *billion* annually from retail stores in the United States. The loss by theft from wholesale businesses and industries can only be guessed at, but it must represent at least as large a sum. American banks estimate their losses from embezzlement at about $16 million a year, and this kind of theft from all American businesses is estimated at about $200 million a year. Income tax fraud is common in Western nations and almost institutionalized in Latin American countries. It is difficult to separate honest errors from conscious evasions in the reporting of income, but the United States government believes that unreported income by its citizens runs as high as $40 *billion* a year.

On a pettier level, thefts from libraries are now so great that libraries from Harvard University to San Quentin prison are employing costly "sensing" devices (*Time,* 1964); and from Mexico to Canada things left unguarded on the public streets— "roller skates, bicycles, baby carriages, appliances, garbage cans, tools, lawn mowers, and the like—disappear as if by magic" (Lundberg, 1954). *The Wall Street Journal* verified this picture from its own experience when Dow Jones and Company, which publishes the paper, moved into new offices while the building was still under construction. A spokesman for Dow Jones reports:

> "They stole us blind. As much as $10,000 worth of office equipment and furnishing was taken, despite the presence of uniformed guards on each floor."

Among the items taken:

—A 15-by-20 foot piece of carpet ("It was glued to the floor and they peeled it right up," the spokesman says).

—A 20-foot long walnut counter-top ("I don't know what anyone wanted with the Payroll Department's counter—maybe someone needed a bar").

—At least 30 chairs, worth about $200 each ("We had the guards sitting in them").

In addition, so many telephones were stolen, the spokesman says, that "the phone company threatened to stop installing them. Not because they're so expensive but because they were running out of phones" [1972, p. 12].

This sample of measures of public honesty could be expanded, of course. It is sufficient, however, to illustrate the point that much theft occurs when the stealing carries a low risk of penalty.

Crime as "Required" by Legitimate Work

There is no clear division between the crime that is rational because the loot is there, ready to be taken at low probable cost, and the crime that is impelled by the work one does. Motivation of the crime that seems to be "required" by legitimate life overlaps that of the crime which is stimulated by the "gold left on the pavement at Charing Cross." The crimes encouraged by the "necessities" of legitimate work differ only in the social settings—the structures—in which they are bred.

Work-stimulated crimes range from those in which the businessman or the employee "needs" more money and takes it illegally in the course of his work to the grand frauds of big business to the less larcenous, but still dangerous, cheats in which the normal operation of a legitimate business puts pressure on officers and employees to break the criminal law.

One of the earliest illustrations of business-generated crime derives from a survey conducted by *Reader's Digest* (Riis, 1941a,b,c). A man and woman were employed by this magazine to tour garages and radio and watch repair shops in the United States. The automobiles, radios, and watches that they submitted for repairs had been deliberately "jimmied" to make them appear to be out of order, and the test employed was to observe how many shops made charges for unnecessary repairs. In this survey two-thirds of the garage mechanics and radio repairmen and about half of the watchmakers were dishonest.

A variation of this kind of crime is seen among entrepreneurial blue-collar employees. Mayer (1972a) provides this description:

> Richie is an electrician, working on a high-rise office building now under construction. In an average week he takes home about $250; in a good week, with overtime, up to $400.
>
> But it isn't always enough. "I don't have to tell you how tough it is to make ends meet," says the 42-year-old father of five. To support his family (two of his sons are in college), meet the mortgage on his Staten Island house and make payments on his two cars, Richie supplements his income on weekends: He wires basements for homeowners trying to beat the high cost of regular contractors.
>
> It's a booming business. Right now, Richie is booked up for the next 2 1/2 months. "They call me because I can do the work a lot cheaper than a regular electrician," he explains.
>
> The secret of Richie's low prices: "I don't have to pay for materials or tools. I just take what I need from the site I'm working on."

Richie's justification is the common one: "You steal it, instead of letting them steal it."

This kind of entrepreneurial theft by the small businessman and the blue-collar worker is more than matched by some of the frauds perpetrated under the pressures of business competition in a risky market. The outstanding example is "the incredible electrical conspiracy," a price-fixing fraud among some of the world's largest manufacturers of electrical equipment. In this case (the trial was held in the United States), 45 executives of 29 corporations were indicted for conspiracy to violate the Sherman Antitrust Act by preestablishing prices, "rigging" bids, and thus dividing more securely and less hazardously a market valued at close to $2 *billion* dollars a year. This crime, or series of crimes, was also *rational,* and the testimony of the defendants indicates their confusing what seemed rationally required with what was criminal. As Smith (1961), who reported the trial, points out, "There was . . . a failure to connect ordinary morals and business morals; the men involved apparently figured there was a difference."

There are other work-inspired pressures to break the criminal law which are less larcenous than misrepresentation, theft, and fraud, but which have dangerous consequences. These are the many circumstances in industry where the demands of production quotas and quality-control standards encourage faking. Such cheats occur in both communist and capitalist economies (Bensman and Gerver, 1963; Berliner, 1961; Connor, 1972; Moore, 1954; Vandivier, 1972). These "crimes in the factory," like frauds in sales and service, result from the plurality of objectives existing in any large organization and from the ever-present conflict between efficient means, moral codes, and empirical ends.

The urgency to get the job done makes such criminal activity rational in the short run. Its long-run rationality (how much does one "get away with" for how long?) is not always known. Its morality, we have seen, is another matter.

Crime as a Preferred Livelihood

The conception of some kinds of crime as rational responses to "structures" indicates that in the struggle to stay alive and in the desire to improve one's material condition lie the seeds of many crimes. Some robbery, but more burglary; some "snitching," but more "boosting" (Cameron, 1964); some automobile theft by juveniles, but more automobile "transfers" by adults represent a consciously adopted way of making a living. All "organized crime" represents such a preference. The organization of large-scale theft adopts new technologies and new modes of operation to keep pace with increases in the wealth of Western nations and changes in security measures. Such businesslike crime has been changing from "craft crime" to "project crime" (McIntosh, 1971) involving bigger risks, bigger takes, and more criminal ingenuity.

Conversations with successful criminals, those who use intelligence to plan lucrative thefts, indicate considerable satisfaction with their work. There is pride in one's craft and pride in one's nerve. There is enjoyment of leisure between jobs. There is expressed delight in being one's own boss, free of any compelling routine. The carefree life, the irresponsible life, is appreciated and contrasted with the drab existence of more lawful citizens.

Mack (1972) has studied such "able criminals" in Scotland and finds that these successful thieves come from the same social background as less adept thieves, "the textbook criminals." They differ from these inept offenders, however, in their greater freedom from emotional disturbance, in their higher IQs, and, of course, in their greater ability to stay out of jail. Mack's able criminals had spent, on the average, only about one-fifth as much time in jail as the "textbook crooks." Mack describes these successful criminals as making much more money than they would in such law-abiding occupations as are open to them, and he reports that their expenditures and style of life are "very high by ordinary standards."

Given the low risk of penalty and the high probability of reward, given the absence of pangs of guilt and the presence of hedonistic preferences, crime is a rational occupational choice for such individuals.

On a level of lesser skill, many inhabitants of metropolitan slums are in situations that make criminal activity a rational enterprise. Young men in particular who show little interest in school, but great distaste for the authority of a boss and the imprisonment of a menial job, are likely candidates for the rackets. Compared with "work," the rackets combine more freedom, more money, and higher status at a relatively low cost. In some organized crimes, like running the numbers, the risk of arrest is low. The rationality of the choice of these rackets is therefore that much higher for youths with the requisite tastes.

Even for those who get caught, the rationality of crime may still seem clear to the actor himself. For example, Hassan (1972), a several-time loser, tells us:

Wrong was my only salvation . . . Don't be telling me what is right . . . There ain't no such thing as right or wrong in my world. Can you dig? Right or wrong is what a chump chooses to tell himself. And I chose to tell myself that stealing is right. I had a choice: to be a poor-ass, raggedy-ass mathafukker all my life or to go out into the streets and steal me some money . . . I ain't ashamed of what I did or who I am [pp. 21–22].

"Hustling" is a generalized term for "doing wrong" and living better for it. The hustler justifies his occupation by saying that "everyone has his hustle; everyone is on the take." It does not require a dispute about the validity of this justification to comprehend that, for some rational people, crime may be as reasoned a choice as becoming an accountant.

Crime as a Market

Some criminal activity involving offenses against both person and property is an enterprise engaged in to fulfil the demands of a market. There are always people ready to make their living supplying any public "needs" that are made illegal. Whenever a relatively inelastic demand, like that for gambling, sex, and the habituating chemicals, meets a short supply, the price of the service goes up and, with it, the opportunity to make money illegally. Some of the largest incomes ever gained have been made by criminal merchants supplying the public with illegal merchandise. Thus the gangster Al Capone is reported to have earned the highest gross income ever achieved by a private citizen in a single year, something in the order of $105 million for 1927 (McWhirter and McWhirter, 1966, p. 230). This money came principally from the illegal manufacture and marketing of liquor, but also from gambling, prostitution, extortion, and some legitimate businesses. In his time, Capone had some popularity. If he and his henchmen killed their rivals, it was only assassin murdering assassin, and good riddance. Meanwhile, a public "need" was being met. As Capone himself said, "Public service is my motto. I've always regarded it as a public benefaction if people were given decent liquor and square games" (Kobler, 1972 , p. 210).

Governments are forever torn between attempting to control the vices through police power and encouraging their illegal satisfaction by making them criminal. From the experience of recent times, it would seem that vice is durable and that, short of control of slim minorities by heavy majorities through the application of severe sanctions, "black markets" and their criminal suppliers will persist (Schelling, 1967).

IN SUMMARY

The structuralist emphasis on the criminogenic features of a stratified society is both popular and persuasive. The employment of this type of explanation becomes political. If the *anomie* that generates crime lies in the gap between desires and their gratification, criminologists can urge that desires be modified, that gratifications be increased, or that some compromise be reached between what people expect and what they are likely to get.

The various political positions prescribe different remedies for our social difficulties. Radical thinkers use the schema of *anomie* to strengthen their argument for a classless or, at least, a less stratified society. Conservative thinkers use this schema to demonstrate the dangers of an egalitarian philosophy. At one political pole, the recommendation is to change the structure of power so as to reduce the pressure toward criminality. At the other pole, the prescription is to change the public's perception of life.

Criminologists are themselves caught up in this debate. The major tradition in social psychology, as it has been developed among sociologists,[3] emphasizes the ways in which perceptions and beliefs "cause" behaviors. Between how things are ("the structure") and how one responds to this world, the social psychologist places "attitude," "belief," and "definition of the situation." The crucial question, then, becomes one of assessing how much of any action is simply a response to a *structure* of the social world, and how much of any action is moved by differing

[3]The psychologists in social psychology tend to agree with the sociologists on the general formula that places *belief* between "the world out there" and our response to it. However, the more psychological of the social psychologists have also attended to the processes of *learning* and *training* that affect our conduct. See Chapter 9.

interpretations of that reality. Social psychologists of the symbolic-interactionist persuasion, and particularly those who have advanced the popular "labeling hypothesis," attempt to build a bridge between the structures of social relations and our interpretations of them and, in this manner, to describe how crime is produced.

Chapter 8

Sociopsychological Explanations: The Symbolic- Interactionist Variety

Social psychology is the study of human behavior based on the assumption that significant portions of conduct are the result, directly or indirectly, of what other human beings have done to us and for us. Social psychology is concerned with the alterations in behavior that seem to be influenced by both enduring and short-term relations with others. The others may be physically present or only symbolically so. Social psychology is interested in the behavioral effects of "immediately present" others, but it also includes as a "social effect" the influence of past human interactions such as may be represented by a printed page, a work of art, or a folktale.

With so wide a definition of its interest, social psychology becomes coterminous with the study of conduct. Its distinctive perspective, however, is *interactional*. It accepts the possibility that it may be difficult, if not impossible, to divide the sources of behavior between those "inside" the organism and those external to it. It assumes that human behavior, particularly the "significant" behaviors to which moral approval is attached or denied, are the result of some reciprocal connection between an organism and its environment. According to a popular sociopsychological saying, in the production of human behavior "there is no evironment without a heredity, and no heredity without an environment."

The interactionist perspective is carried beyond the study of heredities and environments and is applied also to the study of the effects of different styles of relationship between individuals. The assumption, again, is that John's behavior toward Mary is influenced by Mary's conduct toward John, and by John's memory of previous experiences with other Marys.

This assumption perceives less continuity in the behavior of individuals or groups than does a cultural or a statistical explanation of behavior. In contrast with these ways of describing action, the sociopsychological premise is more optimistic as regards the possibility of "engineering" behavioral changes. It looks for the ways in which behavior is conditioned by the social environment and it is hopeful, then, that knowledge of the "laws" of such influence will permit the beneficent control of behavior.

VARIETIES OF SOCIOPSYCHOLOGICAL ATTENTION

The interactionist assumption on which social psychology is based does not, and could not, function as an explanation without specifying particular variables to be attended to. It is easy to agree with the general idea that people somehow influence each other. The question is "How?" In attempting to answer this question, social psychologists have looked at different portions of reality. For example, many scholars have attended to the patterns of rewards and punishments by which behaviors seem to be shaped. Others have studied the kinds of models and associates with whom the developing human is reared. Such investigators tend to emphasize the necessity of "control" if crime is to be reduced.

There are other social psychologists, however, who are less concerned with training in self-control as one kind of interpersonal relationship. These students pay more attention to what they regard as a distinctively human product of interpersonal influence: *thought.*

Since thinking is believed to depend heavily upon the manipulation of symbols,[1] the sociopsychological school that emphasizes the guiding function of thought has become known as *symbolic interactionism.*

THE SYMBOLIC-INTERACTIONIST PERSPECTIVE

The fact that human beings symbolize their worlds means that we regard some parts of our environment as stable, as being "out there," and as capable of being known. As a corollary of this assumption, the recognition of a world "out there" is associated with awareness of a "self" which can be distinguished from other objects and which, however vaguely, may become the object of its own thought.

It is assumed that awareness of "self" is developed in a process that is characterized, largely but not entirely, by the development of symbols and their interpersonal exchange. It is believed also that this process teaches each individual to take the role of the other person, that is, to imagine one's "self" in the other person's situation. This empathy, this ability to generalize from one's self-awareness to that of others, is both a social bond and a means by which we continue to instruct each other. The descriptions and the explanations that are given by art, drama, poetry, and even psychology and sociology gain much of their plausibility through their appeal to empathy (Nettler, 1970, chap. 3).

The interactionist's attention to symbolic activity has meant that this kind of social psychology is cognitive psychology. It looks for the explanations of social behavior in *learned disposi-*

---

[1]The fact that thinking depends heavily upon manipulation of symbols does not mean that thinking is *nothing but* symbolic activity. Most psychologists distinguish between *thinking,* "any activity . . . which demonstrates . . . intelligence" (Furth, 1966, p. 23); a *symbol,* which is a conventionalized sign of some object or event; and *language,* which is a system of symbols. Symbolic activity is one indicator of thinking, but thinking is more than just symbolic activity. Thinking is neither restricted to human beings nor "neatly separated from other human activities" (Furth, *ibid.*). On this matter, see also Langer (1967) and Premack and Premack (1972).

tions identified through their expression in symbols. These dispositions are variously called "attitudes," "beliefs," "meanings," "perceptions," "expectations," "values," and "definitions of the situation."[2] Such concepts refer to assumed "internal states of the organism," located largely in the frontal lobes of the cerebral cortex.[3] These internal states are defined as "symbol-containing." The symbols are conceived of as "images" that represent our worlds and that are subject to such manipulations as *reasoning* (internal symbolic exchange), *translation* (transfer from one system of vocabulary to another), and *communication* (interpersonal symbolic exchange). It is assumed that the presence of these symbol-containing states can be reliably inferred from certain classes of behavior like speech, gesture, and perception.

The distinctive professional task of social psychologists of the interactionist school has been to describe and measure these cognitive conditions, to assess how they vary with circumstance, and to determine how they affect feeling and action. The last point is crucial. Symbolic interactionism locates the *causes* of our behaviors in *what* we believe and *how* we interpret the reality around us.

APPLICATIONS OF SYMBOLIC-INTERACTIONIST THEORY TO CRIMINOLOGY

There have been two major applications of symbolic-interactionist assumptions to the explanation of crime. The earlier representation is that advanced by the late E. H. Sutherland and his students under the title "differential-association theory." A more recent version of symbolic interactionism in criminology is known as the "labeling" hypothesis. Both types of explanation are more American than European or Asian.

Before describing these interpretations, it is worth repeating

[2]These concepts are often used as synonyms. They should not be. Rose (1962, p. 5), for example, distinguished between the *meaning* of a symbol and the *value* associated with that meaning. The best recent clarification of parts of this conceptual tangle is that offered by Fishbein and Ajzen (1972).

[3]"Attitudes," "meanings," "beliefs," and "definitions of the situation" have been held to be "internal states of the organism." The neural characteristics of these internal states are not specified by the symbolic-interactionist theory. It is assumed, however, that changes in neural switching are associated with the learning of these dispositions.

that these explanations of criminality need not be contradictory to other hypotheses, that there is overlapping among various accounts, and that some of the differences in what is emphasized as causal remain important, however, as the emphases are translated into policies.

The Differential-Association Hypothesis

This explanation attempts to spell out in some detail the rather common-sense idea that people are apt to behave criminally when they do not respect the law. The core assumptions of the differential-association hypothesis are that criminal behavior is learned behavior (rather than the release of some inherited predisposition); that learning such behavior includes learning both the techniques of committing the crime and the motives for committing it; and that, as Sutherland and Cressey have said, the "specific direction of motives and drives is learned from definitions of the legal codes as favorable or unfavorable" (1970, p. 75). A person becomes delinquent, Sutherland and Cressey believe, "because of an excess of definitions favorable to violation of law over definitions unfavorable to violation of law" (*ibid.*).

The differential-association hypothesis proposes that most members of complex societies are subject to a continuing balance, a competition, among definitions of situations which justify breaking a particular law and definitions which legitimize that law in the actor's mind and thereby immunize him against the propensity to break it. This is what is meant by "differential association." Contrary to what the term suggests, this hypothesis is not just a statement about *the kind of people* with whom one associates, or even a statement about *the kind of behaviors* with which one is familiar. The "differential association" refers to a differing balance, a changing balance, within each actor among *the definitions* he has learned to associate with categories of conduct defined by law as legal or criminal. These "definitions" are attitudes. They are evaluations. As such, they are presumed to be motivating.

Proponents of this schema acknowledge that the definitions of actions as justified or not justified vary in the intensity with which they have been learned, in the time at which they have been acquired, in the frequency with which the definition is repeated for the learner, and in the span of time over which the lesson is reinforced or challenged. It is assumed, without detailed specification, that some lessons are taught more authoritatively and have a greater emotional charge attached to them, and that, therefore, lessons may vary in the intensity with which they are impressed upon one. It is also assumed, without elaboration, that lessons learned early in life and repeated often and over a long span of one's life have a greater impact than those acquired later and "associated" less frequently and more briefly with one's actions.

While the differential-association schema does not emphasize culture conflict, the assumption of conflict underlies it. The existence of changing ratios between the criminogenic and lawful definitions of situations requires, at bottom, culture conflict. Competing attitudes toward the law constitute a principal indicator of the conflict of norms of conduct. The differential-association hypothesis is thus similar to other interpretations of criminality in considering criminality a consequence of breaches in the moral bond. *Despite their different foci of attention, all explanations of crime that locate its source in the social web reduce to a description of conditions that weaken moral community.* In this, such theories accord with the moral beliefs of the great religions. They thus say little that is new *except* as they specify processes characteristic of alienation among men. It is the *description* of these processes that lends substance and authority to theories of criminogenesis. It is *what* such theories specify as eroding moral unity that makes them interesting and of political importance. It is on this point that the differential-association theory has been called "both true and trivial," for it does not describe in detail the learning process it assumes to be central to the manufacture of criminality.[4] This deficiency has led critics to regard the differential-association theory as plausible, probable,

---

[4]Although the originators of differential association theory have not described the process by which differential definitions are acquired, other investigators may do so. Burgess and Akers (1966), for example, have strengthened the differential association notion by adding "reinforcement theory" to it.

and logical (DeFleur and Quinney, 1966), but at the same time irrefutable and uninformative (Gibbons, 1968, p. 204; Jeffery, 1959).

Specific criticisms are that differential-association theory (1) neglects individual differences, (2) neglects variations in opportunity, and (3) neglects passionate or impulsive crime. A more serious criticism is that the theory (4) is so general and so loosely phrased as to be impossible to disprove. A further consequence of this generality is that the formulation (5) provides no sure guide for action. Each of these criticisms deserves attention.

Criticisms of the Differential-Association Hypothesis: An Assessment

1 The differential-association hypothesis neglects individual differences The neglect of individual differences is common to all sociological explanations of criminality. Such neglect may not be a disadvantage if one is interested only in comparative crime rates between aggregates of people or in changes in crime rates within a population over time. However, the neglect of differences in human interests and abilities makes it difficult for the differential-association schema to account for the nondelinquent boy who lives in a highly criminal neighborhood or the "bad actor" reared in a "good" environment. The request for such explanation is addressed to sociopsychological explanations of criminality where one might not ask it of the strictly sociological explanations.

2 The differential-association hypothesis regards opportunity as a constant Common-sense ideas about crime assume that the opportunity to commit an offense has something to do with the probability that it will be committed. Temptations are strong or weak, close or distant. Although it is agreed that grasping an opportunity may be a function of the actor's definition of his chances, structuralists and others assume also that degrees of opportunity exist. The gold at Charing Cross was, or was not, left unguarded. The gangster did, or did not, offer the policeman a bribe. The emphasis in differential-association theory upon beliefs and attitudes obscures the role of situations in the production of crime. This means, in turn, that impulsive crimes are less well explained.

3 The differential-association hypothesis seems inapplicable to the explanation of passionate crimes The law agrees with most observers of the social scene in distinguishing between premeditation and impulse, and between plan and accident. The distinctions sometimes become blurred and open to debate. For example, psychoanalysts see "unconscious motivation" and even plan where others see accident. Nevertheless, the proposals of the differential-association theory seem to fit better those behaviors that are routine, characteristic, and patterned. It is more comfortable to think of *beliefs* as affecting *decisions,* rather than *accidents,* and it is easier for us to perceive choice where there is a consistency of both belief and action. It becomes more difficult for most observers to perceive "definitions of the situation" operating where the behavior is unusual, out of character, impulsive, and, hence, less easily linked to "a choice."

As an illustration, many homicides are impulsive crimes. The killing occurs in the heat of an argument between spouses, lovers, friends, or acquaintances. There is often a history of squabbling, and the arguments are frequently assisted toward their fatal end by alcohol in both the killer and his victim (Pokorny, 1965; Wolfgang, 1958). A sociopsychological observer may wish to interpret such passionate outbursts as reflecting changes in "definitions of the situation," but it is not clear what this adds to our understanding of such crime, much less our ability to predict it. Referring such kinds of crime to some balance of attitudes in the actor does less to help us comprehend the acts than does a detailed description of them.

4 The differential-association hypothesis is impossible to falsify An explanatory account that holds true no matter what happens is ordinarily considered unsatisfactory by scientists, although it may satisfy other consumers of explanations. The proposals of differential-association theory, like many other explanations of human behavior, locate the causes of conduct in dispositions inside the actor which are to be inferred by his observers. Such inference is not necessarily false. It is built upon empathy, upon a projection of our own thoughts and feelings in similar situations, and it is thereby useful in developing an understanding of the other person, particularly when he is similar

to us. The difficulty with explaining behavior by inferring dispositions is that an inference can always be constructed after the fact
to fit every act. Dispositions, like instincts, can be multiplied
endlessly. "The ratio of definitions of the situation favorable and
unfavorable to the law" can be moved about at will by the
explicator to suit every crime. The risk of using dispositions as an
explanation, then, is that one may construct a circular explanation in which the acts are said to be caused by the dispositions
(beliefs, attitudes) and the dispositions are said to be known from
the acts. Such circularities may be comfortable and may allay
curiosity. They may not, however, point the way to defenses
against crime.

   **5   The advice to be gained from the differential-association
hypothesis is poor**   The major deficiency of the differential-
association theory, and of the symbolic-interactionist account of
human behavior from which it derives, is that it artificially
separates one element of action and calls it "cause." There would
be nothing intellectually wrong in doing this if the separated
element—in this case, "attitudes" or "beliefs"—actually had the
causal power imputed to it. However, what is at issue in the
criticism of the differential-association hypothesis is whether it is
justifiable to separate thoughts from actions and to assume that
"definitions of the situation" have *that much* independent impact
upon behavior.

   A contrary view holds that, as we became what we are, our
beliefs and behaviors were intertwined; it holds that, in being
what we are, both are measures of our "selves." We often do not
know what we believe until we see how we behave. There is no
good reason, except that of some intellectual convention, for
separating behavior and belief and placing one before the other as
its cause. There are good reasons for *not* making this separation;
the major reason is that attending to talk alone is not the best way
of knowing the other person. It is not the best way of knowing his
beliefs, or of predicting his behavior, or of changing his conduct.[5]

---

   [5]Evidence for these allegations is to be found in studies of clinical prediction and in
the weak (even negative) contribution made by the "talking therapies" in the cure of
unwanted behaviors. The literature is large, but it may be sampled in the writings of Eysenck
(1966a), Fancher (1966, 1967), Levitt (1957), and Meehl (1954).

These considerations underlie public disappointment with the differential-association hypothesis. From the viewpoint of the nonprofessional consumer of explanations of crime, the differential-association hypothesis does not explain much. In fact, it leaves unexplained precisely what most people would like to have explained. That is: "How do crimes get motivated?" "What conditions foster increases or decreases in the rates of serious crimes?" "What can we do about increases in crime rates?"

Everyone assumes that beliefs are part of acts; that the way a person thinks is part, but only part, of his "character"; and that "character," in turn, both describes and accounts for an individual's lawfulness or criminality. Differential-association theory pulls one strand from this web of being, believing, and acting, and locates causation along it. This emphasis satisfies some scholars. It lends order to their worlds. However, it leaves others dissatisfied with both the logic of this explanation and its practical impotence.

Calling attention to "definitions of the situation" as "causing" behaviors leaves the behaviors unexplained *because the sources of these differing definitions are left unspecified.* It is these sources of behavior and belief which concern most laymen and to which social psychologists of the "control" school address themselves.

The common-sense reluctance to accept the differential association of attitudes and beliefs as an adequate explanation of criminality gains support from the related suspicion that trying to change these definitions of the situation may not be the most effective way of preventing or reducing crime. Changing conduct through preaching or, as it is sometimes called, "education," is an uneconomical procedure. Worse, attending to beliefs as the sole motors of actions may, in fact, obscure the conditions under which crime rates increase or decrease.

An Illustration: The Prevention of Embezzlement An illustration is provided in the recommendations made for the control of embezzlement by a prominent exponent of the differential-association hypothesis. Cressey (1953, 1971) has studied hundreds of embezzlers and has interpreted their careers in the light of the symbolic-interactionist theory. Cressey reports on the well-known tendency of many embezzlers to rationalize their crimes by saying that they had just been "borrowing" the money and had intended to return it when their affairs were straightened out. For the symbolic-interactionist, it is this justification that indicates the actor's "construction of reality" and that constitutes the criminal motive.

Cressey holds that "the process of verbalization is the crux of the individual embezzlement problem. This means that the *words* that the potential embezzler used in his conversation with himself actually are the most important elements in the process which gets him into trouble, or keeps him out of trouble. The rationalization is his *motive*" (1964, pp. 19 and 22).

One can agree that justification may become part of the motor of action; however, it need not be the "source motive." Other social psychologists would say that talking to oneself helps or hinders that which has been otherwise generated. Most rationalization of deliberated crime comes rather late in the causal process, and there are, of course, offenders who do not rationalize their crimes at all except as the official helper asks them, "Why did you do it?"

This debate gains importance as Cressey's hypothesis is translated into recommendations for those who need to defend themselves against embezzlement. Cressey's prescription is two-fold: (1) that companies start programs designed to reduce those "unshared problems" that Cressey believes create breaches of the employer's trust, and (2) that companies institute "education programs emphasizing the nature of the verbalizations commonly used by trust violators." We must, advises Cressey, "make it increasingly difficult for trusted employees to . . . think of themselves as 'borrowers' rather than as 'thieves' when they take the boss's money" (1964, pp. 25–26).

It need not be held that these measures might not "do some good." They are, however, not good enough. Other explanations of human action lead to different recommendations. For example, detectives, bondsmen, and accountants think of embezzlement as produced when desire meets opportunity. They perceive desire as constantly subject to inflation. When they look upon the trusted employee or professional man who violates the financial confidence placed in him, detectives and auditors tend to think of desire as particularly subject to inflammation under the stimulus of vice—"the other woman," gambling, drinking.[6] Given desire, opportunity provides the spark.

The recommendation that follows from this interpretation is that the symbolic-interactionist prescriptions should *not* take the place of alertness to vice, to the trusted officer's living beyond his means, and, most important, to rigorous audit.

In contrast to the suggestion that criminogenic "definitions of the situation" be attacked through lectures to employees about "borrowing is stealing," the bondsman and the auditor suggest that opportunities for theft be reduced through accounting controls. While there is no perfect insurance against the hazards of crime, this sort of protection seems sounder than attempts to change the beliefs of adults.

In Summary   Social behavior is guided by belief, but behavior and belief are acquired together. There is as good (or better) reason for assuming that altered actions change beliefs as for assuming that altered beliefs change actions. If a "societal engineer" set out to design a society in which people were to behave differently, he would attend to the educational process by which conduct *and* its justification were channeled.

To protect ourselves against the world as it is, we must first reduce the causes of and opportunities for damaging actions. Then, after these defenses have been set up, we may have the time to quarrel with the offender's definition of the situation that gives him his reasons, but not necessarily his motives, for hurting us.[7]

[6]The detective's theory has been termed the theory of the "3 B's—babes, booze, and bets." The detective, the bondsman, and the auditor all see embezzlement as becoming more probable under the stimulus of such temptations. Given the kinds of occupational position that permit embezzlement, there are good reasons for making this assumption.

On this point, it is illuminating to read the account provided by Maxwell (1972) of one of North America's largest one-man embezzlements. This story of the "proper theft" of an estimated $4.7 *million* should be compared with the symbolic-interactionist explanation of embezzlement as a test of the soundness of advice given by the competing explanations.

[7]"Reason," "motive," and "cause" are terms that are sometimes used interchangeably and sometimes used distinctively. Our discussion illustrates good reasons for keeping the concepts separate. The reasons for an action may not be the motive for it; and the motive, as it is commonly understood, may not be operating as the cause of the action.

The "Labeling" Hypothesis

The most popular new set of ideas employed by sociologists to explain crime is a bundle of assumptions known as the "labeling" hypothesis. This hypothesis depends heavily upon the belief that social relations are "constructed," that reality is defined and interpreted before it becomes meaningful. This is a way of saying that we act in terms of the *meanings* attributed to events rather than to objective events. Conditions, it is said, are *defined* before they are reacted to. How we respond to each other is a function of the way we have categorized each other and of the significance we have assigned to our interactions.

From this point of view, "crime" is a word, not an act. Crime is socially defined and criminals are socially "produced" in a process which allows majorities to apply labels to minorities and which, in many cases, permits majorities to enforce the consequences of this labeling. As a result, the "labeled" person—the stigmatized person—may be unable to act in any way different from the role ascribed to him.

The Transcendence of Roles over Behaviors   Labeling theory emphasizes the processes of human interaction that result in the attribution and acceptance of *roles*. The emphasis upon role construction calls attention to the way behavior may be shaped by the expectations of those with whom one is interacting and to the way our perceptions of each other are reinforced by the early assignment of labels to samples of our acts. Once roles are defined, clusters of attributes are inferred. Such inference stimulates a selective perception that permits a linking together of diverse acts under some meaningful label (Turner, 1972, p. 310).

The emphasis upon role formation means that less attention is paid to how people behave than to how they categorize each other on the basis of small segments of behavior. The tendency of the labeling theorist, then, is to deny or ignore differences in the ways in which people act and to stress the utility and the consequences of having the power to categorize. Throughout the literature, the prevailing sentiment is to deny differences and to cast doubt upon the validity and the justice of popular images of minorities.

Translating "Criminality" into "Deviance"   Given this attitude toward difference, the labeling theorists find it more convenient to talk about "deviance" than about "criminality." This translation directs attention to the fact that majorities are reacting to minorities and that it is being different in the sense of being powerless because of small numbers that permits arrest, censure, and punishment to be attached to a difference.

Such a viewpoint is, obviously, sympathetic to minorities. The labeling school has, consequently, been termed an "underdog philosophy." Its spokesmen ask, "Whose side are we on?" (Becker, 1967).

The philosophy of the underdog turns the tables on conventional thought. Instead of assuming that it is the deviant's difference which needs explanation, it asks why the majority responds to *this* difference as it does. This shift of the question reverses the normal conception of causation; the labeling school suggests that the other person's peculiarity has not caused us to regard him as different so much as our labeling has caused his peculiarity. This reversal, among other characteristics of the labeling hypothesis, has made the theory interesting and has contributed to its popularity (Davis, 1971).

Proponents of the labeling hypothesis distinguish between "primary deviance," that is, some offensive act, and "secondary deviance" (Lemert, 1951), that is, the process by which the reaction of society to an initial difference may confirm the deviant in the stigmatized behavior. Being cast out means being an outcast and makes it comfortable for stigmatized persons to band together in defense of their egos and in justification of their "peculiar" interests.

The labeling theorist deemphasizes the difference in the deviant. He holds that "initially" everyone deviates somewhat from some standards some of the time. What confirms the difference is some official attachment of a label to the apprehended deviant. The labeling theorist is concerned, then, to study how much deviance is produced by the very correctional agencies that are supposed to reduce difference. How much delinquency do reform schools manufacture? How much crime do prisons create? How much psychosis is perpetuated by mental hospitals?

What is to be explained is not so much the deviant as the people who have the power to attach the scarlet letter and thus to confirm the deviation. The labeling theorist sees the judicial response to crime as "the dramatization of evil" (Tannenbaum, 1938).

Implications for Methodology   The research method advocated by the labeling theorist is intensive observation of labelers and their victims. Field work is preferred to the collection of statistics. The result of such study is a description of how the labeler comes to recognize and define the deviant and of how the deviant reacts to and interprets his own world. The test of the adequacy of such a description is understanding and insight rather than prediction and control.

As compared with statistical and experimental studies, the reportorial field work recommended by the labeling theorist is more fun for students. It is good sport to engage in "participant observation," particularly among people who are "different." To this element of pleasure, labeling theory has added the advocacy of the "rights" of minorities. Its appreciative methodology and its political stance have combined to make it a fashionable way of thinking about undesirable behaviors and "social problems." The fashion has spread from its application to crime and has been extended, with variations, to attempts to understand blindness (Scott, 1969), stuttering (Lemert, 1967), illness (Lorber, 1967), civil disturbances (R. H. Turner, 1969), "welfarism" (Beck, 1967), paranoia (Lemert, 1962), death and dying (Sudnow, 1966), mental retardation (Mercer, 1965), and neurosis and psychosis (Braginsky et al., 1969; Plog and Edgerton, 1969; Scheff, 1966). An evaluation of this popular mode of explanation must recognize both its advantages and its liabilities.

The Advantages of the Labeling Hypothesis   The value of the labeling hypothesis lies in its attention to the possibilities that (1) people may respond more to their definitions of others than to the behaviors of others and (2) stigmatizing definitions may produce the bad behaviors they condemn.

1   The labeling hypothesis asks "society" whether it is reacting to the deviant's behavior or to its own definition of the deviance   The idea that deviance is produced in some process of interaction that results in our pinning tags on each other calls attention to the possible inaccuracy of the names we apply. To say that "deviance" is created by labeling is to suggest that the labels may be inappropriate, and to raise the question whether we are responding more to what the other person did or more to the image of the other person that is called up by the name we have given him.

This is a valuable question, and it deserves a scientific answer. Thus far, the answer has been assumed by the labeling theorists rather than tested. This assumption partakes of a tradition in social psychology that has itself applied a label to the common-sense categories which most of us use to order our social worlds. The label applied by social psychologists to such popular concepts is "stereotype." Calling a popular image a "stereotype" assumes, without adequate evidence, that the ordinary citizen's notions about the "different" kinds of people around him are mostly wrong. However, the sociopsychological assumption itself seems more false than true. The few studies that have attempted to test the accuracy of popular images have shown that "stereotypes" are more accurate than inaccurate. This has been found true of popular perceptions of occupations (Rice, 1928) and of ethnic groups (Mackie, 1971, 1973). No adequate research has yet been completed on the validity of popular images of various kinds of criminals, although one such study is under way (Solhaug, 1972). Until some research on this matter has been completed, we can appreciate the point made by the labeling theorists without subscribing to it.

2   The labeling hypothesis alerts us to the possibility that official reactions to some disapproved behaviors may do more harm than good   The chief value of the labeling hypothesis has been to call attention to the possibility that official reactions to some kinds of disapproved behaviors may confirm the actors in their deviant ways. It is suggested, for example, that some "sick behaviors" improve more rapidly when they are untreated and that some cures are worse than the diseases they treat.

The labeling theorist emphasizes how minor events in the stream of life may become major events through official reaction. The careers of some different kinds of people are made even more different by the fact that some portion of their lives must be spent in dodging the consequences of the official response to their deviance. The model here is that of the marijuana user,[8] whose life may be changed by the criminalization of his preference.

Labeling theory gains credence as it develops biographies showing that being "officially handled" increases the chances of future official attention. There is evidence that some part of this risk is incurred by the discrimination associated with a criminal label. *There is no way of knowing, however, how much of repeated offense is so caused.*

The labeling hypothesis could prove more useful if its ideas were associated with a taxonomy of offenders in such a way that we might know who could be best "saved" from future criminality by ignoring his present offense. This is not an easy question.[9] It is, however, part of what probation is about.

The labeling hypothesis is politically important because it challenges the *status quo.* This is congenial to revolutionaries, of course, whose ideology translates the label "convict" as "political prisoner." Less radically, the labeling hypothesis stimulates thinking about the costs of applying the criminal law to certain categories of disapproved behaviors. It suggests that there may be limits to the efficacy of the legal sanction (Packer, 1968) and urges assessment of the relative costs and benefits of the criminalization or decriminalization of immoral, peculiar, or unhealthful conduct.

The Liabilities of the Labeling Perspective   (1) Labeling theory has been criticized for ignoring the differences in behavior

---

[8]The labeling theorist's point can be made by substituting for marijuana the criminalization of any other chemical, like tobacco or alcohol, that many people habitually use.

[9]The answer to this question is made difficult by the possible antagonism among the various goals of justice. The antagonism is the desire to rehabilitate some apprehended offenders, the need to deter others, and the need to express, through the symbolism of punishment, society's rejection of criminal conduct.

described by labels. The labeling schema draws attention from deeds to the public definitions of those deeds. Such diversion means that (2) labeling theory does not increase, and may well decrease, our ability to predict individual behavior. Its low predictive power is a result not only of its neglect of individual differences but also of the fact that (3) it contains a defective model of causation. This in turn means that (4) its relevance to social policy is lessened. Each of these points will be amplified.

1 Labeling theory does not explain the behaviors that lead to the application of labels The labeling theorists argue as if popular and legal categories were devoid of content, as if they were never "well earned." The labeling explanation pays little or no attention to the fact that people do *not* behave similarly. It slights the possibility that a label may *correctly* identify consistent differences in conduct, and it pays little attention to the reasons why "society" continues to apply a label once it has been used.

Labeling theory denies, therefore, the causal importance and explanatory value of personality variables. In fact, labeling theorists regard as futile the search for personality differences that might distinguish categories of more or less criminal persons. The labeling hypothesis prefers a political interpretation to such a psychological one. It prefers to believe that deviants are minorities lacking power to challenge the rules by which a majority has labeled them. The theory denies, then, that a label may be properly applied to describe personality differences which may underlie real behavioral differences. This denial has unfortunate consequences for the prediction of individual behavior.

It has unfortunate consequences, too, for the development of public policy. The prescription that follows from the labeling hypothesis is to change the attitudes of majorities toward misbehaving minorities. In reply, majorities tell us that they are not yet convinced that a more compassionate attitude toward the robber or the burglar will change the offender's behavior and reduce the pain he gives.

2 When applied to the understanding of individual behavior, the labeling hypothesis has low predictive power The low predictive power of labeling theory results from its denial of personality differences. The interactional bias of the labeling theorist encourages such optimistic but risky beliefs as these:

> He will be honest if I trust him.
> She will be reasonable if you are.
> He will be pacific if we are.
> Her psychosis is not "in her," but "in her situation." When the mirrors in which she sees herself are changed, she will change.

On the contrary, there *are* personality differences that are reliably associated with behavioral differences and that are remarkably persistent. These persistent ways of feeling and acting are not readily changeable with changes in the labels attached to them. Regardless of what we have been called, *most of us continue to be what we have been a long time becoming.*

The research literature on this subject is vast. It may be sampled in the works of Honzik (1966), Kelly (1963), Mischel (1969), Robins and O'Neal (1958), Roff (1961), Schaefer and Bayley (1960), Thomas et al. (1970), Witkin (1965), and Zax et al. (1968). The point is made in the autobiography of the playwright S.N. Behrman (1972) who, after years of failure and impoverished struggle, wrote a play that was a hit. Behrman comments, "With the production of a successful play, . . . you acquire overnight a new identity—a public label. But this label is pasted on you. It doesn't obliterate what you are and have always been—doesn't erase the stigmata of temperament" (p. 37).

The statement that there are persistent temperamental and cognitive differences underlying our behaviors can be qualified by adding that such personality variables have more of an impact upon behavior as circumstances are equalized. Nevertheless, most of us can tell the difference between behavior—our own and others'—that is only situationally reactive and behavior that is characteristic. All of us operate, implicitly or explicitly, with the idea of *character*—the idea that there *are* enduring personal predispositions relevant to moral behavior. This means that, unless there are tremendous changes in environments, people are likely to continue to behave as they have behaved. Against the optimistic recommendations of the interactionist, it seems more sensible to believe that:

The embezzler may need to be arrested, and stigmatized, before he "turns honest."

Being reasonable with a fanatic is futile.

A soft answer turns away the wrath of some men, but not of others, and there is no point in pleading for your life with a Charles Manson.

The cures of psychoses are exceptional. Most people who are "peculiar" are not disordered in all ways, all the time. Misbehavior may be episodic; but ordinarily, safety lies in the assumption of behavioral continuity.

3 The model of causation implicit in the labeling hypothesis is questionable Every explanation of human behavior makes assumptions about its causes. The labeling theory locates the causes of adult behavior in an unusual place—in the people who respond to it. It shifts the "responsibility" for my action from me to you. It stresses how much of what I do is a result of what you have done to me, and for me. My "self," it is said, is reflected to me by the social mirrors available to me. My "self" is the presumed agent of my actions, but my "self" is itself largely constructed by the responses of "significant others" to my initial efforts.

This is a shorthand statement of the hypothesis of "socialization." In its general formulation, there is no quarrel with such a hypothesis. All theories that would explain human behavior, including popular theories, assume that our behavior has been shaped by the actions of others. The sociopsychological hypotheses of the "control" variety pay particular attention to the "how" of this socialization process.

It is not denied, then, that how people respond to us when we misbehave may affect our subsequent conduct. The lively questions are, however, at what periods of our development, and to what degree, others mould us. What is at issue is *how much* of the adult behavior to be explained varies with the response of others to it.

It is our ignorance that permits the continuing quarrel, for no one knows which kinds of behaviors, in which kinds of personalities, at which "stage" of life, are affected how much, by which kinds of response, from which others, in which situations. Some generalization about this is part of our popular wisdom, but much of that is truistic. We expect more than truisms from criminological theories.

The valuable contributions of the labeling hypothesis have tended to obscure its deficiencies. It is one thing to study the way in which a defining process affects our response to the behavior of others. It is another matter to study the causes of the events we are defining. Studying how we respond to deviant others may suggest to us a more economical (more rational) mode of reacting. This suggestion should not be confused, however, with information about the causes of the crimes that concern us.

Such confusion is created when spokesmen of the labeling theory tell us, for example, that *"social groups create deviance by making the rules whose infraction constitutes deviance,* and by applying those rules to particular people and labeling them as outsiders" (Becker, 1963, p. 9). Some readers will translate statements like this as saying that "social groups create crime by making the laws whose infraction constitutes crime." This translation is slippery: it slides between the truth that social groups create the *definition* of "crime" and the falsehood that the *injuries* condemned by these definitions would disappear (or would not have been "created") if the definition had not been formulated. To the layman, it sounds as though the labeling theorist believed that people would not wish to defend themselves against burglary or murder if they had not learned a rule defining these acts as crimes. It sounds, also, as though the labeling theorist believed that there would be less "burglary" if we did not use that term. The nonprofessional consumer of criminological explanations recognizes this for the semantic trick that it is—the trick of saying, "If a crime is a breach of a rule, you won't have the crime if you don't have the rule." The ordinary reaction to this semantic sleight of hand is to say, "A mugging by any other name hurts just as much."

Applied to "real life," the labeling hypothesis functions as another of the "power of positive thinking" philosophies: "If disease is an error of thought, positive thinking will cure it." "If crime resides in our definitions of deviance, redefining it will change it."

Our question has to do with the location of causation. When the causation implied by the labeling hypothesis is tested, it fails. The causes specified by this schema do not account for the production of the behaviors that disturb us. "Mental hospitals" do not cause "mental illness" (Gove, 1970), nor do the agencies of social control, or the labels they apply, account for crime (Ward, 1971).

The assumption of labeling theory is that those who become "criminal" are mostly those who, while behaving much like everyone else, just happened to get tagged, or that those labeled "criminals" were more liable to the tagging because they fit some public's prejudiced stereotype of the criminal. Contrary to these assumptions, however, studies of the operation of the system of justice show that it works like a sieve: as we have seen, the people who end up caught in the sieve tend to be the more serious and persistent lawbreakers (Black and Reiss, 1970; Bordua, 1967; Terry, 1967).

In summary, the labeling theorist does not think about causes and effects, about antecedents and consequents; he prefers to think about interactions. This preference does not eliminate the idea of causation; it only obscures it by shifting the locus of causes from actors to their judges. This shift has some moral and political value in the fight between outsiders and insiders. It justifies a challenge of the police and the courts, or any other mechanism of social control, that would condemn the conduct of minorities. When the labeling hypothesis is applied to the explanation of the serious crimes, however, its model of causation reduces its value for public policy.

4 On the level of social concerns, the labeling hypothesis does not answer the perennial questions about crime We are reminded that explanatory theories are only as good as the questions they answer. The answers provided by the labeling theorists are not addressed to the questions about crime that are asked by most people. These questions are, again, "What causes crime?" "What accounts for increases or decreases in crime rates?" "How can crime be reduced?"

To these questions, the labeling theorists give no good reply. The policy recommendation of the labeling hypothesis comes down to "Avoid unnecessary labelling" (Schur, 1971, p. 171). This may be helpful in decriminalizing some activities. It is a recommendation that is already being followed in some areas, as in the euphemistic use of language that substitutes kind words for harsh ones—"sanitary engineer" for "garbage collector" and "special child" for "imbecile." Such translations bespeak a change in attitude, yet the categories persist. Categorizing is an inevitable part of our response to the world. We should wish our categories to be clean, accurate, and useful, as social psychologists have urged. It is doubtful, however, whether attention to our vocabularies will tell citizens and public officials how better to reduce robbery and rape.

IN SUMMARY

Symbolic-interactionist explanations of conduct, criminal and lawful, locate the causes of action in thought. These explanations start from the teachings of the great sociologist W. I. Thomas, who held that "If men define a circumstance as real, it is for practical purposes real" (1923). This means that beliefs are important, that if you believe the shadow is a ghost, you will respond to it as if it were a ghost.

The proposition is true enough; but the interesting questions are, "What can one do with it?" and "Where might it mislead us?"

As one attempts to answer the first question, it becomes apparent that it is difficult to ascertain how others define their situations. It is difficult to know what others believe.

Belief is usually recognized by what people say *and* do. When belief is thus recognized, the doing that is part of the believing is also the doing that was to have been explained by the believing. One is trapped, again, in circularity. I know that you "really believe" X when you *act* as though X were true. However, acting *that* way is what we set out to explain.

In trying to get out of this trap, the symbolic-interactionist turns his attention from the acting to the saying as a measure of the belief. As Lindesmith and Strauss put it, "In order to explain why people do what they do we must know how they think. The chief source of information about how people think is what they say" (1956, p. 9).

This reliance upon talk as the best measure of thought entangles the inquirer in the deficiencies of words as indicators of motives. People do *not* always act as they *say* they want to or should or intend.

In such a bind, the attitudinal psychologist is hard put to know which is the more valid index of a person's "definition of the situation"—his words or his deeds.

A Personal Opinion

The symbolic-interactionist chooses words as the more valid marks of beliefs. My own advice is to attend to that which best answers your question. Thus, if you are more interested in predicting behavior than in understanding it—and the two satisfactions are not the same—then you should never divert your attention from what people do. What people do *includes* what they say, but it does not *reduce* to that.

It would be foolish to deny the importance of belief in guiding human action. The important issue is how to determine the weight of belief in the total package that is behavior; or, even, whether a scholar ought to bother doing this.

For example, let us observe a person with a syndrome that we have denominated, for communicative convenience, "paranoia." Our subject differs in degree from the rest of us by:

Being more nervous, tense, and excitable.

Being exquisitely sensitive and alert to interpersonal cues.

Acting and talking *self-referentially,* by which we mean that more acts of others are seen by our subject as directed toward him than you and I can perceive.

Being suspicious and jealous.

Demanding much of loved ones at the same time that he is critical of them for their obvious lack of appreciation of him.

Talking with hate and behaving aggressively.

Saying that he is rejected unfairly.

Believing that people and the fates are against him.

Talking more dirty sex than is "normal" and seeing more perversion in others.

Being unreasonable.

And, of course, talking and acting as though the social world were a jungle. (There is much of the jungle in our social lives, but the world is not *just* that.)

Now, in looking at this package of actions—and we must bear in mind that talk is a form of action—we may, if we wish, isolate those actions to be called "attitudes" or "beliefs." We can even measure those characteristic behaviors of our subject that we might wish to call his "definitions of the situation." Having done this, two questions remain: First, are the beliefs we have isolated causal or only correlative? A test of the answer to this question may be derived from the answer to the second question: If our subject's physician works on his paranoid beliefs, will he change the subject's other behaviors?

There are other versions of the sociopsychological explanation of behavior that acknowledge the importance of defining our worlds *without* calling the definitions causal. These schools of social psychology attend to the ways in which beliefs and other actions are acquired together. They do not assume that there is a "real attitude," a "real definition of the situation," that is indicated more validly by utterances than by other actions. These versions do not assume the causal priority of believing as opposed to being. On the contrary, they view human action more as a closely woven fabric out of which the thread of "what we believe" can be pulled for inspection. However, the color and texture of the whole cloth will be only imperfectly known from looking at this thread.

The alternative formulations of sociopsychological explanation have received the unfortunate title of "control" theories because they emphasize the ways in which behavior has been channeled. Changing the label, however, would not change the substance of these formulations, which are taken up in the next chapter.

Chapter 9

Sociopsychological
Explanations:
The Control Variety

Some crime, we have seen, is rational. There have always been "good reasons" for people to commit some of the serious offenses. It is to one person's advantage to take what the other person has—if this can be done without penalty. There is advantage, too, at times, in seeing the other person dead. The fact that killing and stealing have these rational justifications means that, for some people, some of the time, they *are* justified. It is this fact with which moralists have wrestled for centuries and from which ordinary men and philosophers have developed the tragic sense of life.

For centuries, too, there has been agreement that this tragic fact can only be countered, to some degree, by training the human organism *not* to do "what comes naturally"—*not* to take, grab, kick, bite, and walk over the other person if he gets in the way. When those who must live together lack this training, the only remaining defense is force. If we will not control ourselves "internally," out of conscience, we shall attempt to control each other "externally," through force. If we are not regulated by our "will," we shall be controlled against our will.

Pacific human association requires this moderation of appetite. This requirement contends constantly with self-interest and with the aspiration for freedom. A major issue in political philosophy is how to reconcile the need for social order with the struggle to be free. The best answers to this question recognize the seeming paradox that freedom requires order, which means that freedom in a social web does not include doing whatever one likes at the prompting of an impulse. Civil life is a controlled life. Civilization is bought at the cost of "repression," Freud told us (1958). Civilization requires that not every desire be appeased or every feeling expressed. The prohibition of license is a price paid for civility. In exchange, civil life constitutes the condition of freedom and makes it possible for us to be creative and to be different while living among strangers.

The tradition in political thought that has produced this compromise between order and freedom has been carried into social psychology by investigators who acknowledge that "aggression is as original as sin" (Rieff, 1959, p. 274). These students, like the Church before them, see no great difficulty in explaining why men injure each other. Self-interest is "original." It is part of how we are. In response to how we are, law has evolved. Law is one of the many efforts to control "what comes naturally." Some anthropologists and some psychologists assume that the "crimes forbidden by law are crimes which many men have a natural propensity to commit" (Rieff, 1959, p. 225).

THE BASIC ASSUMPTION OF CONTROL THEORY

What needs to be explained, then, is not so much why we behave badly as how we can be induced to behave well. The socio-psychological accounts that try to answer this question are called "control theories." They start from the assumption that the higher organisms require training if they are to behave socially. The psychologists Margaret and Harry Harlow say that "one of the most important functions of social learning in primates—and perhaps in all mammals and many other classes of animals as well—is the development of social patterns that will restrain and check potentially asocial behavior. These positive, learned social social patterns must be established *before* negative, unlearned patterns emerge" (1967, p. 47; italics added).

So too with man. *Homo sapiens* is born only *potentially* human. If the potentiality is to be realized, if the infant is to develop into a recognizable human being, nurturing must take place. Without nurturing, the human animal grows up wild. It behaves violently. It destroys what it has not been trained to appreciate. It does not understand "right and wrong" except as greater and lesser might. As a consequence, what offends the conscience of socialized persons cannot offend the conscience of the unsocialized. There is nothing to offend.

To speak of the "originality" of theft and assault is not to deny that these kinds of behavior may also be learned, channeled by a culture, and justified by its philosophy. To say that feral man *expresses* violence does not deny that nurtured man may *learn* it. There *are* patterned urges toward larceny and aggression as well as unlearned sources of such self-interest. The subcultural and structural theories of criminogenesis attend to the patterning of these antisocial behaviors; the control theories attend to their expression in the absence of discipline.

There is general agreement among students of human behavior as to the validity of the basic assumption of control theory: that *social* behavior requires socialization. The assumption is neither new nor novel. It says, with Pope, that "just as the twig is bent, the tree's inclined" (1731). Disagreement arises only in describing how human beings become socialized and in assigning weights to the various influences that mould us.

TWO VERSIONS OF CONTROL THEORY

Among the attempts to apply this assumption about socialization to the explanation of criminality, two stand out as systematic efforts. One point of view has been proposed by the American criminologist Reckless (1967) and his associates under the title of "containment theory." Another application has been advanced by the British psychologists Eysenck (1964) and Trasler (1962), working independently of each other. Since Eysenck and Trasler present so similar an explanation of crime, their theses may be combined as the "Eysenck-Trasler formulation." In describing the Eysenck-Trasler hypothesis, some additional learning modes will be incorporated within their model. These additional ways of learning were not considered by Eysenck and Trasler in their original work, but they are used here to supplement the explanation.

Containment Theory

Containment theory recognizes that not everyone in the same environment catches the same disease. There are differences in immunity. So, too, with criminality. Individuals are differentially immunized against the temptation to be criminal. Reckless and his colleagues conceive of the immunity to contagion by criminality as a matter of control, of one's being "contained," or restrained, against the allure of crime. The controls that "contain" a person are, in turn, considered to be of two orders: "outer" and "inner."

Outer Containment or Social Pressure   This source of restraint consists of social pressures to obey the norms of one's group. The pressures are exerted through training in roles, through affiliation with a community and a tradition, and hence through the development of a sense of "identity and belonging." The exercise of these external pressures may be seen in such relatively crime-free groups as the Hutterites of Alberta and Manitoba and the Mennonites of Pennsylvania and Ohio. The pressures to conform to community expectations constitute a defense against crime as long as the religious community remains segregated from the host society. The point is that there *are* community standards condemning antisocial conduct and there *is* training in obedience to those standards.

Inner Containment or Self-control   No community can depend completely upon the constant control of individuals through social pressure. All socialization aims implicitly, if not explicitly, at the development of self-control. The agent of such control is commonly called "conscience." In Reckless's schema this inner control is the result of a moral training that produces five indicators of its presence: (1) a healthy self-concept, (2) goal-directedness, (3) a realistic level of aspiration, (4) the ability to tolerate frustration, and (5) an identification with lawful norms.

1 Self-concept Reckless and his colleagues conducted a number of studies that demonstrate the generally poorer self-concept of young boys who get into trouble with the law. At an early age, boys from the same neighborhood and economic background show differences in how they feel about themselves, their families, their fate, and figures in positions of authority. The more delinquent boys are more likely to believe that they will break the law and go to jail, and that their friends will too. They are more likely to believe that they will not finish school, that their families are "no good," and that teachers, clergymen, judges, and policemen are not worthy of respect (Dinitz et al., 1962; Rothstein, 1961).

2 Goal-directedness An element of the controlling self-image, according to Reckless, is orientation to goals. It is claimed that individuals who commit themselves to long-range, legitimate goals are thereby insulated against criminality. Critics see some circularity here since *a commitment to a legitimate career* is, by definition, a defense against crime and therefore part of what theories of criminogenesis seek to explain. However, Reckless and his colleagues use signs of such commitment as *indicators* of self-control rather than as the causes of it.

3 Realistic objectives A related sign of the presence of effective inner control, according to the containment theorist, is the "realism" of a person's goals. As is true of Durkheim's model of man, Reckless sees some goals of young people as extravagant. Such unrealistic aspiration, such striving beyond one's means, indicates to Reckless the possibility of a "collapse" of inner containment.

4 Tolerance of frustration Living *is* frustrating. We call a grown person a "baby" when he has not yet accommodated himself to this fact. An indicator of the self-control that is expected of adults is tolerance of frustration. Delinquents have less of it than nondelinquents.

Tolerance of frustration is, of course, related to having realistic goals and to being oriented toward a future. A person whose goals are out of reach is bound to be frustrated, and one who is easily frustrated is not apt to pursue long-range objectives. Conversely, when one has a dedication to some distant and achievable goal, present obstacles are *less* frustrating than they are to the person who lives for nothing but the present.

In support of Reckless's hypothesis on this point, there is evidence that urban delinquents are more hedonistic, impulsive, and impatient than nondelinquents. Time seems *longer* to them. That is, when you ask youngsters to "guess a minute"—to tell you when a minute has passed—the delinquent guesses *sooner*. This impatience is compounded by the delinquent's less rich fantasy life; it is recognized that fantasy is one of our mechanisms (an "inner resource") for "filling up time." Being impatient and being deficient in imaginative self-stimulation mean being easily bored. The evidence of such differences between delinquents and their more lawful neighbors may be found in Barndt and Johnson (1955), Bixenstine and Buterbaugh (1967), Mischel (1961), Siegman (1966), and Stein et al. (1968).

5 Identification with lawfulness   A fifth aspect of the "self" which, according to containment theory, immunizes a person against criminality is attitudinal. It is a set of beliefs in support of the law and its agents. The beliefs acknowledge the legitimacy of the criminal law and "identify" the actor with lawful standards of conduct. Again, there is abundant evidence that this feature of the "self," this attitude toward the law, does distinguish more lawful people from the more serious lawbreakers. The distinction is discernible *before* a criminal career is developed; although, as labeling theory argues, official handling of the offender in response to his crime may confirm him in his hostility toward the law.

It is no surprise to learn that people who break the law dislike the law. A host of studies report that convicted offenders have more unfavorable conceptions of the law, the court system, and the police than do nonoffenders who live in the same environment. Toro-Calder and his colleagues (1968) found this to be true in Puerto Rico, and similar findings have been reported in Ohio, Ontario, Quebec, Rome, Athens, West Pakistan, and South Korea (Cho, 1967; Mylonas and Reckless, 1963; Toro-Calder, 1968).

In Summary Containment theory, like the differential-association hypothesis, is true. At the same time, it is quite "general." It points to a set of interlocking conditions that move people toward or away from criminal careers. For some critics, the theory is too broad to inform public policy. For other critics, this generality is "good enough" to illuminate the roots of crime. What is omitted, however, from this sociological version of control theory is a statement of *how* the organism is socialized. This is better specified by psychologists' contributions to control theories of crime causation as exemplified by the work of Eysenck and Trasler.

Eysenck and Trasler's Formulation, with Some Additions

The explanation advanced by both Eysenck and Trasler assumes that criminal behavior results from *defective social training* in lawful standards of conduct. Social training, which the sociologist calls "socialization," involves two distinct, but overlapping, processes: *teaching* and *training*.

"Teaching" refers to the transmission of techniques that may be used in solving problems. The techniques include having information, having mechanical and research skills, being able to use a language, and having knowledge.

"Teaching" may be distinguished from another process by which we learn, namely, "training." "Training" describes the events through which values, purposes, preferences, and moral codes are instilled. Training differs from teaching in how it works and what it is used for. Training is more likely to proceed by manipulations of the environment of which the trained organism is unaware. Teaching, on the other hand, is more "intellectual," more cognitive. Where the learner in a teaching situation knows that a teacher is teaching, the learner in a training situation is less apt to know what is happening to him. This is a matter of degree, of course, but of a degree that makes a difference. It is also a matter of timing, so that a learning process that begins with training may end with teaching.

The Training Repertoire The training of mice and men is accomplished by rewarding desired behaviors, punishing unwanted behaviors, and setting models of behavior for the organisms to imitate. This is the repertoire of techniques by which moral desires are instilled. This is how one learns what is forbidden. It is also how one learns his moral preferences.

One result of training is channeled behavior. Another result is reflected in conscience—the feelings of duty and responsibility, of shame and guilt, of the *need* to do "the right thing" and anxiety lest one do the wrong thing. It is because the training process is so subtle, and so much less cognitive than teaching, that moral people do not necessarily know "where their morality comes from." This is why we recognize that we have touched the other person's morality when, despite all reasons and against all arguments, the moral man says, with Luther, "I cannot do otherwise."

The training repertoire is not limited to one kind of learning. There is an assortment of training tools available. Each human being has experienced these training techniques to some extent, but for each person the blend, consistency, timing, and content are unique. The inventory of training tools includes at least (1) *classical conditioning,* (2) *operant conditioning,* and (3) *modeling.* A deficiency of the Eysenck-Trasler formulation is that it emphasizes the first of these training methods to the exclusion of the other two processes (Hamilton, 1965). The addition of these procedures here is intended to amplify the Eysenck-Trasler theory and to describe more fully how we have come to be as we are.

1 Classical, or respondent, conditioning In this form of associational learning, a stimulus, previously inadequate to produce a response, becomes adequate through simultaneous or nearly simultaneous association with an adequate stimulus. Pavlov's dogs are a famous example: they were trained to salivate to the sound of a bell rung, repeatedly, just before the hungry animals received their meat. In this sort of training situation, the experimenter looks for stimuli that "unconditionally" produce a response. For example, a strong light directed into the eye will produce a pupillary contraction. Any other stimulus, such as a sound, that is presented about the same time as the flash of light will, with repetition, become adequate to cause a pupillary contraction. Such an associated cue is called the *"conditioned"* or *"conditional"* stimulus.

There are humanists who deny that human beings are "conditionable." This is nonsense, as a large research literature demonstrates (Franks, 1961; Greenspoon, 1962; Staats, 1968). We have all been "classically conditioned," although we cannot easily ascertain for ourselves how much or to what. The important psychological questions concern the conditions under which respondent conditioning occurs, the degree to which a conditional response is similar to an unconditional response, the permanence of the conditional "lesson" learned, and how much of our conditioning has been planned and how much has been accidental or incidental.

Present purposes do not require answers to these questions. It is enough to acknowledge that one way in which we have become as we are is through such associational training. A sign that we have been thus trained is our preference for the familiar (Johnson et al., 1960). The process by which associational training can occur has been described in numerous studies, both observational and experimental. For example, Staats and Staats (1957), gave emotional significance to nonsense syllables by presenting these meaningless letters in association with pleasant and unpleasant words. In this manner, what began as nonsense ended with emotional meaning.

2 Operant, or instrumental, conditioning This is one of the most powerful ways of guiding behavior. It differs from classical conditioning in that the organism is changed by the consequences of its acts. Whereas in classical conditioning a new stimulus is "hooked up" to an adequate stimulus *before* the organism responds, in operant conditioning the organism is trained by what *follows* upon its action.

Apart from the varying heredities with which we begin life, probably no discernible influence has a greater effect upon our individual destinies than the immediate consequences of our acts. *What happens when we act determines how we act.*

The consequences of our conduct are usually classified as "rewards" and "punishments," although this classification is not always neat. We may express the hypothesis of operant conditioning, then, by saying that conduct is moulded by the pattern of reward and punishment it has elicited. The pattern can be studied in terms of the *styles* of punishment and reward experienced, in terms of their *balance,* and in terms of their *intensity, timing,* and *consistency.* Furthermore, psychologists have studied the varying effects of *giving* a reward as opposed to *withdrawing* it and of *giving* punishment as opposed to *relieving* it (Campbell and Church, 1969).

It is not necessary here to review comprehensively the many investigations of the effects of punishment and reward. The inventory of research is large. It allows generalizations about the shaping of behavior that are sufficient for the purpose of specifying crime-producing conditions. A sample of these research findings will give their flavor and show us how "densely packed" are the many kinds of consequences that flow from our actions.

Reinforcement contingencies: A sample of effects We know, first, that neither a reward nor a punishment has a uniform effect. A pain, or a pleasure, is "an event in a temporal and spatial flow of stimulation and behavior, and its effects will be produced by its temporal and spatial point of insertion in that flow" (Solomon, 1964, p. 242). Thus, if a dog or cat is given an electric shock *while* it is eating, it will become fearful and avoid the feeding dish even to the point of starvation (Lichtenstein, 1950; Masserman, 1943). On the other hand, if the pain *precedes* the reward, if the animal is first shocked and then fed, the punishment becomes a cue that food is available and the learner feeds without disturbance (Holz and Azrin, 1962).

As a training tool, punishment varies in its effectiveness with its frequency, its intensity, and its timing. It also varies in its effects depending upon who administers the punishment and upon the trainee's personality, his previous experience with punishment, and the "schedule" of pleasures and pains administered to him. "A punishment is not just a punishment," Solomon tells us. "The effects of punishment are partly determined by those events that directly precede it and those that directly follow it" (1964, p. 242).

Punishment is more effective as a training technique when it is administered to the acts that are *premonitory* of forbidden behavior than when it follows the undesirable behavior. Furthermore, the longer the delay in punishment *after* the bad act, the less effective is the pain. Punishment "when Dad gets home" and punishment in prison have little power to change conduct. They are too remote in time from the anticipatory cues that mark the start of a disapproved act. On the other hand, intense pain administered *early* in the series of acts leading to the undesirable behavior readily conditions the organism (Aronfreed and Reber, 1965; Solomon, 1964; Walters and Demkow, 1963). Moderate punishment administered later in the series of acts preceding an unwanted behavior, but given consistently and in a supportive environment, has an enduring effect in shaping behavior (Walters, 1967). If pain is attached to what a person *does* as opposed to *how he has been,* its controlling effect is greater (Church, 1963). Under some conditions, even observing the punishment of others can inhibit behavior (Walters et al., 1965), just as observing the aggression of others can stimulate it (Bandura et al., 1961; Geen and Berkowitz, 1967; Lovaas, 1961; Walters et al., 1962).

Operant conditioning and criminal careers This brief summary is sufficient to indicate the variety of circumstances that determine the efficacy of punishment as either a conditional stimulus or an operant. What is of significance in producing more and less lawful persons is the childhood diet of reward and punishment. A balanced diet is, of course, recommended, with the balance inclined toward the child's being nurtured, appreciated, and guided by a rewarding model, rather than toward his being only "disciplined." For the appreciated child, the very withdrawal of approval becomes a penalizing consequence and a substitute for the physical pain otherwise used as an operant. By contrast, it is notable that juvenile delinquents and their parents consistently speak of having punished each other, physically and verbally, and observation of their behaviors confirms their memories (Glueck and Glueck, 1962; Shulman, 1959). The point is that punishment by parents who reject their children is likely to be erratic and hostile. Its efficacy as an operant is reduced by its being inappropriately scheduled and imposed in the absence of nurturing—that is, in an environment in which the organism is more frequently punished than rewarded for his acts. A relationship between parent and child that is loaded with penalties and devoid of reward is not an efficient system of guidance toward moral conduct. It tells the child what *not* to do, but it does not tell the child *what to do.* In psychological language, the operants for preferred behavior are lacking.

   3   Modeling and "social learning"   The terms "modeling" and "social learning" refer to the age-old observation that human beings and a host of other animals learn by imitation. In many languages, the verb "to teach" is synonymous with the verb "to show" (Reichard, 1938). Much of what we have been taught or, better, trained to be is a result of what we have been shown.

   In their theory of criminogenesis, Eysenck and Trasler do not stress the role of modeling. However, the impact of social learning should not be neglected. There is a convincing body of research that shows how large segments of behavior are acquired by watching others perform. This is most striking at youthful ages, of course, and it is now well substantiated that even behaviors unusual for a species can be "imprinted" if a deviant model is presented exclusively to the organism at certain critical periods in its development (Cairns, 1966; Gray, 1958; Hess, 1959, 1972; Sluckin, 1965).

   The role of a model in training a child has been most thoroughly documented in the imitation of aggression (Bandura and Walters, 1959). However, there is also experimental evidence showing that dependent behavior, sexual conduct, and fearful reactions can be transmitted from models to children (Bandura, 1972; Bandura and Walters, 1963).

   The training given by models interacts with that acquired by conditioning. The effect of a model varies, so that models who have been rewarding to us are more likely to be imitated. Similarly, those models who are deemed to be competent or prestigious—who, in short, have high status in our eyes—are more likely to be copied. For example, in a simple but effective experiment, Lefkowitz and his colleagues (1955) employed a rich-looking person and a poor-looking person to act as models of illegal behavior. They had these models walk against a traffic light and observed how many pedestrian bystanders followed them in their lawbreaking. More people imitated the rich model.

Bandura and Walters (1963, p. 107) point out that what happens to the model also influences imitation. Models who are rewarded for their aggression, for example, are more readily copied. Similarly, aggressive models who are *not* punished, who are seen to "get away with" being violent, are more likely to be imitated by children (Soares and Soares, 1969).

The tendency to imitate varies not only with what happens to the model, but also with certain personality characteristics of the observer. Soares and Soares present evidence that children who have had a history of failure more readily copy violent models. So, too, children who are comparatively incompetent in social relations and who exhibit low self-regard and dependent behavior are more likely to imitate aggressive models.

Additional factors that affect imitative behavior include the individual's experience in having been rewarded or punished for copying the model; his mood; and his perceived similarity to the model (Rosekrans, 1967). All these bonds between personality traits and imitative tendencies are strengthened in emotionally charged situations (Soares and Soares, 1970).

Given the abundant evidence of modeling effects, it is not surprising to learn that dramatic crimes are contagious. This seems true of the assassination of public figures (Berkowitz and Macaulay, 1971) and also of skyjacking, campus vandalism, and urban guerrilla warfare (Moss, 1972). The "communications revolution" that brings televised images of distant violence into almost every European and American house may in this sense be regarded as criminogenic.

The effects of televised models In rich nations, generations are now being reared before the television tube. In the United States and urban Canada, and in the metropolises of Europe and Latin America, almost all homes have one or more television sets. In the United States, at least 96 percent of all homes have television, and the sets are running an average of six hours a day. North American children are now normally television viewers by age 3 and their attention to television remains high until about age 12. The impact of television's violent models upon children's aggressive behavior has been demonstrated in limited circumstances. The issue of how great this impact is, however, continues to be debated (Surgeon General's Committee, 1972).

Most research on the effects of televised violence tests the short-run results of aggressive modeling. For example, Liebert and Baron (1972) exposed boys and girls of two age groups, 5 to 6 years and 8 to 9 years, to portions of actual television programs that were rated "aggressive" and nonaggressive." The children were then given a chance to act aggressively toward a playmate and were also observed in play situations. Liebert and Baron report:

> Children exposed to the aggressive program engaged in longer attacks against an ostensible child victim than subjects exposed to the nonaggressive program. The aggressive program also elicited a higher level of aggressive play than the nonaggressive one, particularly among the younger boys [p. 469].

Bailyn (1959) also tested the possible effects of exposure to violence on television by gathering data on the social characteristics of children's families, the children's viewing preferences, their "psychological adjustment" as measured by a variety of standard tests, and reports of their aggressive behavior. Bailyn found that there was a correlation in the range of .50 between viewing habits and violent acts, but that this correlation was limited to a small proportion of the child subjects, that proportion (about 3 percent) that had already exhibited signs of emotional disturbance.

Kaplan and Singer (1972) reviewed a host of experiments assessing the effects of television on aggressive behavior. They conclude that "the majority of the experimental studies showed that witnessing violence can instigate 'aggressive' behavior. These experiments, however, most frequently gained their effectiveness through the intentional arousal of subjects and the use of dependent measures that removed ordinary sanctions against aggression. Instigation effects were rarely found in studies or experimental conditions in which the subjects were not aroused intentionally. When the measure of aggression has been some naturally occurring behavior, it has been shown that television violence either has no effect (Feshbach and Singer, 1971; Siegel, 1956), or only affects children who were initially highly aggressive (Stein et al., 1971)."

Such immediate effects of dramatic modeling might be expected, particularly among those predisposed in the direction of the model; but the long-range consequences of a taste for televised violence are of more interest, though they are more difficult to establish. Eron and his colleagues attempted to isolate such long-range effects by following a group of youngsters over ten years. They studied 875 children in the third grade and found that, at that age, "children who preferred violent television programs were more aggressive in school as rated by peers than children who preferred less violent programs" (1972, p. 262).

Of these youngsters, 427 were studied again ten years after the original observations. This group was almost equally divided between boys and girls. *For the boys only,* a continuing correlation was discovered between early television habits and aggressive behavior as teen-agers. Since the correlation between teen-agers' viewing habits and measures of their "violence" (.31) is slightly higher than the correlation that was obtained when these boys were 8 and 9 years old (.21), the investigators conclude that television viewing had an *enduring, independent causal impact* upon adolescent aggressive behavior. This effect appears both when adolescents are rated for aggression by their peers and when they are scored for "aggression" on a standard psychometric, the MMPI. The television effect was said to "explain a larger portion of the variance than does any single factor which we studied, including IQ, social status, mobility aspirations, religious practice, ethnicity, and parental disharmony" (p. 623).

The conclusion of this longitudinal study—that television viewing has an *independent causal* significance for the development of violent behavior—ought not to be accepted too readily. Such an interpretation may be regarded as suggestive, but not as conclusive, because controls were lacking for possible causal factors *common to both aggressive behavior and taste* in television viewing. Whenever a correlation of this sort is reported for behaviors that may be assumed to be generated in a dense causal web, the student must consider whether his correlation is unidirectionally causal or, rather, a common product of many causes that produce the associated behaviors.

It must be concluded, then, that the long-range effects of televised models have yet to be ascertained. In the short run, a modeling influence of a qualified nature has been demonstrated. These research findings may be used to support the modeling thesis. However, no proponent of social learning theory maintains that imitation is the exclusive agent shaping behavior or that it is all-powerful. It is recognized, as we have seen, that situational variables affect the copying of a model. In addition, personality differences influence how we learn.

Individual Differences in Training The effects of conditioning and modeling vary with personality. Human beings do not respond equally to seemingly similar portions of reward and punishment. A piercing pain to one person may be quite tolerable to another (Petrie, 1967).

In contrast to many other theories of criminogenesis, the Eysenck-Trasler formulation acknowledges individual differences, recognizing that some of us need more training than others. It has long been noted that this is true of the "lower" species, but we have been reluctant to admit that it is true of man. Different breeds of dogs, for example, are more or less easy to train (Lorenz, 1952). Sheep dogs condition readily, while Basenjis are relatively difficult to teach (Freedman, 1958). Similarly, human beings may be differently "wired" and may require differing balances of support, pleasure, and pain if they are to develop conscience and resistance to temptation.

Eysenck and his colleagues emphasize the introversion-extraversion dimension as affecting the way in which we learn. There are data showing that introverts condition more readily than extraverts. Franks (1956) reports that both the eyeblink and psychogalvanic reflexes can be conditioned to an auditory stimulus "significantly more easily" for introverts than for extraverts. Furthermore, the loss of these conditional responses, their "extinction," is reported to be considerably greater for extraverts than for introverts.

The Eysenck-Trasler hypothesis assumes, then, that extraverts need more training than introverts. They may also require a different style of training. Praise and blame seem to affect them differently (Thompson and Hunnicutt, 1944). "While praise motivates introverted children," Eysenck writes, "blame motivates extraverted children" (1966b, p. 23). Of interest to this point is Kennedy and Willcutt's report that, while praise *generally improves* the performance of schoolchildren, it *lowers* the performance of "underachievers" (1964).

There are other aspects of personality than introversion-extraversion that seem related to how people learn. One's "need to be nurtured" is another such dimension. Epstein (1964) finds that children who need much approval are easier to condition than those who are less oriented to approval. In addition, the child who needs more nurturing is more sensitive to the *hostile* content of stimuli and conditions more readily to it.

It is a well-established fact that individuals respond to sensations differently. Styles of perception vary among us and are enduring features of our personalities (Witkin et al., 1962; Witkin, 1965). In a series of clever experiments, Petrie (1967) and others have demonstrated that people can be ranked along a continuum in the way in which they "handle sensation." While some people are fairly accurate in their perceptions, others markedly "reduce" what they perceive and others "increase" what they perceive. Petrie had subjects estimate the width of blocks of wood felt with the thumb and forefinger of one hand by running the fingers of the other hand along a tapered block until the subject felt he was at a place on the tapered bar that was the same width as the measuring block. She found that some people consistently overestimated the width of the measuring block, in some cases by as much as 50 percent. These persons are "augmenters." Others consistently underestimated the size of the stimulus, and to as great a degree. They are "reducers."

Whatever may have caused these differences in the handling

of sensation, they are there, and they affect how we learn. Compared with the augmenter, the reducer needs more stimulation before he "gets the message." Whether male or female, this type of person is less responsive to pain (Ryan and Foster, 1967; Ryan and Kovacic, 1966). Among males, the reducer tends to be more "athletic" (mesomorphic) in body build (Wertheimer, 1955) and to prefer contact sports. He has a quicker reaction time and, like the persistent delinquent, estimates moments of time to be longer than they are (Ryan and Foster, 1967). The reducer cannot stand isolation, silence, or monotony as well as the augmenter can. He needs "to do things" and to have things happen. In the poet Wordsworth's terms, the extreme reducer has "a raging thirst for outrageous stimulation."

It is notable that serious juvenile offenders, male and female, disproportionately perceive their worlds as reducers do (Petrie, Chapter Five). Petrie believes that, as reducers, such delinquents have a greater immunity to pain which explains, in part, their inability to sympathize with the pain of others. This might underlie the reducer's greater involvement in accidents, his noisiness, and even the preference among both male and female reducers for tattooing, an ornamentation rather painful to acquire. Petrie suggests that the often-remarked more frequent bedwetting among delinquents (Michaels, 1955) may result from the reducer's lesser responsiveness to internal cues.

Petrie's findings, along with those of the Gluecks (1950, 1956), Eysenck, Trasler, Sheldon (1949), and others, tell us that some individuals need greater stimulation before they can be trained. These findings fit in with the repeated descriptions of serious offenders as bored with school, conscience-free, adventurous, and difficult to condition (Franks, 1961).

There is evidence that introversion-extraversion and perceptual style have constitutional and, probably, genetic roots (Rosenthal, 1970; Sontag, 1963). Assuming this to be so, the facts that there are personality differences which affect the way individuals respond to reward and punishment and that the more persistent offenders score differently on these traits do *not* mean that criminality is inborn. They mean only that, in learning to conduct ourselves, some of us need more lessons than others.

Consequences of Training An organism that has been trained through some history of classical conditioning, operant conditioning, and modeling is a different organism from an untrained one. What has been learned is not merely stored in some nonphysical space called "the mind." The learning is in the physiology: the trained organism's neurochemical response system has been changed. This is why we commonly say things like, "I know I shouldn't be afraid of the snake. It's harmless, but I can't help myself." In a case like this, involuntary alarms are going off in the "internal environment" of the organism. Such alarms are largely a result of training, and they *literally* affect us in gut and gland and heart (DiCara, 1970; Gaito and Zavala, 1964; Miller, 1969).

Eysenck and Trasler hold that, in the morally conditioned person, these internal alarms constitute an anxiety triggered by the cues preceding a "bad deed" and that the anxiety is inhibiting. There is evidence that such inhibition of the forbidden act in the well-trained organism results from a different pattern of conditioning than that which produces guilt.

Resisting temptation versus feeling guilty Punishment administered *early* in a response sequence leading to an unwanted act is more likely to produce immunity to temptation; punishment given *late* in the sequence is more likely to generate "self-punitive" behavior (Aronfreed, 1963).

Puppies punished as they approach tempting food learn to resist it with little emotionality. Puppies punished while they are eating the forbidden food show little resistance to temptation, but more "emotional behavior" (Black et al., 1960).

As with puppies, so with children (Allinsmith, 1960; Burton et al., 1961; Whiting and Child, 1953). Resistance to temptation is learned by a different process from that which teaches guilt. Bandura and Walters (1963, p. 203) believe that resistance to temptation is learned largely by classical conditioning, while the self-punitive habit (guilt) is learned through operant conditioning. However this may be, the important point is that the person who has been trained to resist temptation need feel no guilt; the person trained to feel guilty need have little resistance to temptation. Both resistance and guilt, however, are acquired by human beings

who have been *reared.* These activities do not come "naturally"—that is, they do not come without training.

   Conscience as a motivator "Conscience," measurable
either as immunity to temptation or as vulnerability to guilt, is
built by means of conditioning and modeling. The result of this
training is not merely inhibition, as our examples may have
suggested. Another result is the *development of new drives.*

   An "honest" person is not merely one who *refrains* from
stealing under opportunity. The honest person also *does* things
that are honest. The story of Abe Lincoln walking many miles to
return his customer's forgotten change is a paradigm.

   Similarly, the moral aversion to cruelty or to sexual license
is *not* inborn, yet the person who has been trained in these values
will engage in prolonged behavior to defend them.

   Training does not only change physiology. It also builds
motivation. Once constructed, the acquired motives operate
without memory of their origins. They are autonomous.

   Three Determinants of How We Are How we are today,
then, is a result of three classes of causes. These determinants lie
in our neurophysiological constitutions, in *how* we were reared,
and in *what* we were taught.

   In assessing the career of one person or in explaining the
varieties of conduct within a group, behavioral scientists do not
have measuring instruments that allow a definitive assignment of
relative importance to these three determinants. An impact of
each of these sets of causes can be separately ascertained; but the
interaction of these causes cannot be accurately gauged, because
the causal web in which they achieve their effects is dense. Each
set of determinants has variations within it and the numerous
causes are closely intertwined. These determinants of our lives
can be assumed, and they can be observed, but they cannot be
accurately weighed.

   In considering the first determinant we acknowledge that
there are individual differences in amenability to training, including persistent differences in temperament, tempo, and cognitive
capacity. It need not be debated here how much of our different
neural "wiring" and chemical construction is genetic, how much

is constitutional, and how much has been affected by the environment. The fact of difference in learning ability and ways of becoming conditioned is indisputable. But the question *how malleable* we are remains open. An inherited constitution is not a fixed one.

The second set of determinants has to do with how we were brought up. *The quality of training* we have received has been studied in terms of at least these dimensions of learning:

1 Respondent (classical) conditioning
2 Operant (instrumental) conditioning
3 Modeling ("social learning")

Each of these dimensions is itself a variable, as we have seen. For example, operant-conditioning theory holds that a principal determinant of how we are is what has happened when we have acted. What happened when we acted may, in turn, be analyzed in terms of "reward" and "punishment," although these nouns are themselves without clear boundaries. However, the effects of "reward and punishment" are known to vary with at least their:

Intensity
Frequency
Consistency
Balance
Temporality (their placement in time)
Setting (which includes who gave the reward or punishment and in what "social context")

The third determinant of how we are is what we were taught. The *content of the lessons* we have learned can be assessed as:

Rules, preferences, tastes, values
Skills (which may range from solitary manual performances to interpersonal abilities)
Information and belief

In considering this third determinant we recognize that the same quality of training can impart different lesson content. "Good" training can teach "bad" lessons. It is possible for wicked lessons to be well taught and for good lessons to be poorly taught. If we can learn to be lawful, we can learn to be criminal. If we can learn how to earn money, we can learn how to take it.

Among these three sets of the causes of our careers, sociologists tend to ignore the first, to slight the second, and to emphasize the third. Subcultural, rational, and symbolic-interactionist explanations of crime attend to *what* has been learned. It is only the "control" variety of sociopsychological explanation that stresses *how* we were trained. Both sets of determinants are important, however.

CHILD REARING AND THE CORRELATES OF CRIMINALITY

There is a neat fit between the Eysenck-Trasler thesis and the social location of serious crime. This is particularly so as one adds to Eysenck and Trasler's emphasis on classical conditioning the possibilities of other modes of learning such as operant conditioning and modeling.

Both the ethnic and the class correlates of the graver offenses fit with what is known about the training routines, the content of the socializing lessons, and the nature of the models available for children reared in different status and ethnic situations. The sociopsychological attention to individual differences in training susceptibility is a way of allowing for variations in the effects of these social climates upon individual behavior. At the same time, the sociopsychological attention to *patterns* of child rearing bring this schema into harmony with subcultural explanations of criminality. Both modes of explanation have emphasized the impact of human nurturing upon human development.

Modeling Deficiency and Delinquency

The control hypothesis holds that serious juvenile offenders have been defectively reared. In particular, it is claimed that such persons have lacked adequate models of lawful conduct. This fact can be documented in two ways. One procedure is to observe children from different nurturing environments and to record how they grow up. Another procedure is to compare the childhood backgrounds of serious offenders with those of less criminal people from a comparable environment. The two methods of study yield similar conclusions.

Developmental Studies Observations of children in orphanages, hospitals, foster homes, and intact families uniformly indicate that there is some physical, mental, and social damage to the child who lacks nurturing (Spitz, 1946). The damage to physical functioning is least; that to cognitive functioning is most serious; and that to social conduct is midway between these extremities (Bowlby, 1952). Children who have been reared in institutions or concentration camps tend to be more aggressive and to have difficulties in interpersonal relations, including difficulty in behaving honestly (Freud and Dann, 1951; Goldfarb, 1943b; Trasler, 1960).

Longitudinal research confirms these findings. Goldfarb (1943a, b, c; 1944a, b; 1945a, b) reports a series of studies of adolescents who had spent the first three years of their lives in institutions. In addition to the learning deficits frequently associated with such rearing, Goldfarb found the institutionalized children to have trouble controlling their impulses. Either they were overcontrolled, rigid, and submissive or they were aggressive. Furthermore, the children who were aggressive did not exhibit normal anxiety about, or guilt reactions to, their aggressiveness.

An earlier follow-up study by Theis (1924) yields similar results. Theis studied over 200 adults who had been orphaned in infancy and compared the careers of those who had been institutionalized for at least five years with those who had lived in foster homes. The proportion of institutionalized children with records of persistent criminality was *3 times* that of the foster children, and there were corresponding, but smaller, differences in their records of less serious misconduct.

Rohrer, Edmonson, and a team of behavioral scientists (1960) observed Negroes in the southern United States *20 years after* these same individuals had been described by other investigators (Davis and Dollard, 1941). Rohrer and Edmonson's research is a clinically oriented study concerned with the development of individual careers. Although this longitudinal research did not use a control group for comparison, it confirmed the image of the male gang-running criminal as a person who denies the legitimacy of religion, schools, law, and morals, and who considers occupational striving worthless. The descriptions of each career are well drawn and illustrate a central theme of control theory, namely, the harmful impact of fatherless households upon the emotional development of boys. In the authors' words:

> Our data reaffirm, often dramatically, the great importance of significant adults to the shaping of the individual's personality. The presence or absence of such figures and the nature of the model they present are intimately linked to the individual's development of ego ideals: vague or vivid images of what he would like to become [pp. 299–300].

A cross-cultural study   A similar conclusion was reached by Bacon and her colleagues (1963) who brought together ethnographic data from 48 societies and examined them for the correlates of crime. These societies, most of them preliterate, were distributed across Africa, Asia, Oceania, and North and South America. They represent a range of family settings, child-rearing practices, degrees of social stratification, and levels of political integration.

The investigators concluded that "the frequency of both Theft and Personal Crime increases as the opportunity for contact with the father decreases" (p. 294). Crimes against the person, in particular, were found to be significantly associated with a mother-child household in which there was "inadequate opportunity in early life for identification with the father," in which the sleeping arrangements for the mother and child fostered "a strong dependent relationship between the child and the mother," and in which the training for independence was abrupt and punishing (p. 298).

The authors of this study incline toward a psychoanalytic interpretation of their findings. In the present context, however, this cross-cultural analysis corroborates the repeatedly reported relationship between hostility and dishonesty in males and the lack of a loving and lawful father-figure with whom to identify.

Comparative studies Comparing the early training of criminals and more lawful persons is made difficult by the obstacles to direct observation of familial practices. The usual research procedure involves asking parents how they treated their children, and asking parents, peers, and teachers how the children behave. Investigators have a problem in coding these reports, but, in addition, the defects of memory, the inaccuracies in parental observation of themselves and their children, and the defensiveness of parents in responding to interviewers have guaranteed that there can only be a slight relation between how parents *say* they trained their children and what actually went on (Yarrow et al., 1968). Furthermore, training is subtle. It is composed of many lessons taught and learned of which both teacher and learner may be unaware. Parents, even highly schooled ones, are not necessarily accurate recorders of their own behavior toward their children.

Sociologists have tried to compensate for these obstacles to observation by analyzing the effects of broad categories of childhood environment, such as illegitimacy and broken homes. In addition, self-report instruments have been used to compare the ratings of family climates given by delinquents, nondelinquents, and their parents.

Illegitimacy and delinquency One measure of the quality of model available to youngsters is an indirect gauge of the presence or absence of a parent. Illegitimate birth rates have been used as such an index with which to correlate crime rates.

"Illegitimacy," like the "broken home," is a crude category, however. It is crude because the social meaning of "illegitimacy" varies with the culture. There are societies in which being born out of wedlock carries less stigma and betokens less lack of fathering than it does in the Western industrialized states (Goode, 1960). For example, "consensual unions" in South American

countries often constitute stable marriages, so that the illegitimacy rates of 50 percent reported for some of the shantytowns in
Latin America (Germani, 1961) and of 65 to 75 percent reported
for some of the West Indies (United Nations, 1970), need not
indicate the same degree of deficient fatherhood as it does in
European or North American locations.

Among cultures in which illegitimacy is more accepted,
accommodations are often made so that a substitute may serve as
the model for the child if he loses his father. Such father-
surrogates are largely lacking, however, in the urban centers of
Western nations, many of which have experienced an increase in
both the numbers and the rates of illegitimate births since World
War II (United Nations, 1970). For the United States, the overall
illegitimacy rate is estimated to have risen from about 4 percent in
1940 to nearly 5 percent in 1960 (Goode, 1966, p. 490). During the
1960s, both Canada and the United States experienced increases
in rates of illegitimate births, while the rate in Mexico declined
somewhat. The United Nations reports a steady increase in
illegitimate births in the United States from 6.3 percent in 1963 to
9.7 percent in 1968 (1970, p. 415). Canada's illegitimacy rate also
rose year by year from 5.3 percent in 1963 to 8.3 percent in 1967.

In cities of the Western nations, illegitimacy now occurs at a
disturbing rate. Copenhagen, Denmark, reports a rate of about 1
illegitimate child for every 7 live births. The rate is 1 in 4 in
Washington, D.C., Dallas, and Houston, and close to 1 in 3 in
Chicago (U.S. Department of Health, Education, and Welfare,
1963). In central Harlem, New York, the illegitimacy rate among
nonwhites for 1963 was reported at 43.4 percent of all live births
(Moynihan, 1965, p. 8).

The control theorist argues that, *in these urban settings,*
being illegitimate means being functionally fatherless. This lack
of a father shows itself in deficits in almost every measurable
aspect of socially important behavior (Jenkins, 1958). Functionally fatherless children, according to Goode, "are more likely to
die at birth or in the first year, to do poorly in school, to become
juvenile delinquents, and to land eventually in unskilled jobs"
(1966, p. 491).

For individual children, the damage of illegitimacy in such

settings may be lessened by early adoption and the compensatory training given by parental substitutes. However, on the ecological level, the social location of high rates of illegitimacy overlaps the social classes and the ethnic groups that yield higher crime rates. To this extent, the control hypothesis receives support. Similar indirect "proof" of the control hypothesis has been attempted, with dubious results, from the many studies of broken homes and their behavioral effects.

Broken homes and delinquency The trouble with attempting to test control hypotheses, or any other explanations of criminality, by looking at "broken homes" is that the concept of the broken home is not a clear one. As regards effects on child rearing, there may be as many styles of "broken homes" as there are of "intact" ones. There is, in fact, evidence that some ruptured families may be healthier nurturing environments than some whole ones (Burchinal, 1964; Goode, 1956; Nye, 1957). Much depends on how the home was broken, when in the child's life the break occurred, and what kind of modeling relationship succeeded the disruption of the household. A household broken by divorce after years of wrangling provides a different psychic climate from one disrupted by sudden death; and a family that changes early in an infant's life has a different impact from one that is broken during a child's middle years. There are differences in effect, too, dependent upon the sex, as well as the age, of the child, and upon the sex of the parent with whom the child remains. For example, Toby (1957) presents data showing that the "broken home" has a different effect upon girls and preadolescent boys from that which it has upon older boys. The impact is greater (worse) for girls and for the younger boys.

Despite these weaknesses in the notion of the "broken home" as a measure of a child's nurturing, research on delinquency has produced a mass of indigestible data on the comparative incidence of broken families among more and less lawful youth.

An early study by Shaw and McKay (1931) compared 1,675 black and white delinquent males 10 to 17 years of age in Cook County, Illinois, with a sample of 7,278 less delinquent schoolboys of like age. Shaw and McKay reported that 42.5 percent of their offenders came from broken homes, as compared with 36.1 percent of the nonoffenders, and this small spread is interpreted as insignificant.

Other students have quarreled with this finding and, as might be expected, have challenged the kinds of controls employed, the lack of females in the sample, the lumping together of all styles of disrupted households as "broken" ones, and even the interpretation of the statistical spread.

Maller (1932), for example, argued that, given the shape of the distributions of delinquency among broken and intact families, a difference of 6.4 percent between them *is* statistically significant. Hodgkiss (1933) conducted a replication of Shaw and McKay's investigation in Cook County using *female* subjects. Here a wide discrepancy was found between delinquents and lesser offenders in the experience of broken homes. Of the delinquent girls, 67 percent came from broken homes as compared with just under 45 percent of the nondelinquent sample.

Investigations in England and the United States tend toward findings that juvenile offenders are the products of broken homes from $1^{1}/_{2}$ times to 2 times more frequently than nonoffenders. An illustrative result derives from the Gluecks' research (1950), which compared the familial experiences of 500 delinquent boys with a matched control group of 500 nondelinquents. More than 60 percent of the delinquents were from broken homes as compared with 32.4 percent of the nondelinquents. Merrill (1947) found comparable differences in a study of 300 consecutive arraignments in juvenile courts in the United States in which the offenders were matched by age, sex, and ethnicity with a sample of nondelinquents. Some 50 percent of these delinquents were from disrupted families as compared with 26.7 percent of the control group.

Monahan (1957) studied all delinquency charges brought over a six-year period in Philadelphia. He analyzed the family status of over 44,000 cases, holding constant the sex and race of the offenders. His findings are in essential agreement with those of Merrill and the Gluecks, with the additional observation that the broken home had a more harmful effect upon the girls and the blacks in his sample than upon the boys and the whites. The proportions of delinquent girls and blacks from broken homes exceeded that found for delinquent boys and whites. In addition, Monahan reports that repetitive offenders were disproportionately from broken homes and that the highest recidivism rate was among children who had been reared in institutions.

A more recent replication of this type of research yields parallel conclusions. Chilton and Markle (1972) compared the family situations of 5,376 delinquent children in Florida with the family situations of children in the general United States population. As expected, they observed that children from disrupted families were more likely to be charged with delinquency and that this association was closer for the more serious offenses.

Studies conducted in England produce comparable findings. Burt's early research (1925) contrasted the domestic experience of young delinquents and nondelinquents, holding constant their cultural background, social class, age, and place of residence and school attendance. Burt reports that 61.3 percent of the delinquents came from broken homes as compared with 25.1 percent of the nondelinquents.

These, and similar investigations, are retrospective studies. They look backward from the age of delinquency to ascertain whether the youth's family was disrupted. As noted, these studies seldom control for *when* the family was broken, or for *how much* decay the family experienced before its rupture, or for the *quality of control* exercised after the break. Longitudinal studies that begin *before* the domestic breach or *before* the commission of a crime are rare. In one such investigation, however, Gregory (1965) followed the career of boys who had lost parents during childhood and found that the children of divorced and separated parents were disproportionately represented among delinquents. Boys who had lost parents through death were slightly more likely to be involved in delinquencies than boys from intact families, but their rates of offense did not approach those of the boys from the homes disrupted by divorce and separation.

A summary conception and a caution A common summary of this kind of research claims, as do Peterson and Becker, that "the gross relationship is well established—the families of delinquents have been disrupted by death, desertion, divorce, separation, or prolonged parental absence much more frequently than the families of nondelinquents" (1965, p. 68).

It must be cautioned, however, that the research on the association of "broken homes" with criminality provides a weak test of the control hypothesis. The test is poor for all the reasons mentioned, reasons that can themselves be summarized by saying that a "broken home" is not the only kind of broken family. Families can be divided, and are divided, while they continue to share a legal status and domicile. For a measure of the possible extent of such riven households among prominent Americans, read the report by Cuber and Harroff (1966).

It is the *quality of training* and the *content of the lessons* taught that are the important determinants of lawful behavior, according to control theory. Neither of these dimensions of nurturing is well described by statistics on divorce, although they may be better described by the figures on desertion.

Meanwhile, times change. Divorce is now the expectation of about one-fourth of all people who marry in North American societies, and remarriage is the expectation of about one-fifth of all who marry. With these and other changes in the nature of the family, it is probable that family ties may loosen so that "intact" homes in various social settings, may come to have no more modeling effect upon their youngsters than some kinds of single-parent households.

These changes may be expected, too, with changes in socioeconomic stratification, with a blurring of differences in child-rearing practices among families of high and low occupational status, with a decline of neighborhoods and neighborhood schools, and with the intrusion of other models of behavior for youngsters as replacements for defaulting parents. The independent role of television viewing has already been mentioned (pages 227–230).

Memories of childhood and portraits of the present Another way of comparing the backgrounds of more and less lawful people is to analyze their perceptions of their childhoods and of their present family relations.

Research on this matter uniformly finds that "bad actors" say their rearing was unpleasant. Persistent lawbreakers disproportionately reject the parental models that are normal for most children in most cultures (Medinnus, 1965).

For example, delinquents tend to deny that "My mother was a good woman" (Hathaway and Monachesi, 1957). Compared with their more lawful counterparts, young criminals believe that "My parents were too strict with me when I was a child" and that "I was often punished unfairly." The offender also believes that his parents "never really understood" him and that his home life was miserable (Gough and Peterson, 1952). For all these perceptions, there is independent evidence that the delinquent is probably correct (Barker, 1940; Burt, 1925; Glueck and Glueck, 1950; Healy and Bronner, 1936).

Such findings confirm those reported by the developmental studies. These pictures of the making of the less lawful person have a cross-cultural validity, a validity that lends credence to the control hypothesis.

A recent study of a cross-cultural nature that adds to these findings was conducted by Rosenquist and Megargee (1969). These investigators and their aides compared delinquent and nondelinquent samples from similar socioeconomic levels among three cultures: lower-class "Anglos" in San Antonio, Texas, and "Latins" living in the same city; and Mexicans living in Monterrey, Nuevo Leon. Extensive testing of physical and intellectual abilities was pursued, along with an assortment of psychological probes concerning personal values, self-perception, and attitudes toward parents. The major observations of importance for control theory are these:

[1] The delinquents in all three [ethnic groups] expressed significantly more deviant behavior and attitudes and less family cohesiveness. The Latin and Mexican delinquents were much more likely to express disrespect of the father, criticism of the mother, and disrespect of elders [pp. 305–306].

[2] Marital stability was evaluated in a number of ways, and it was found that significantly more of the delinquents in each sample came from unstable or broken homes [p. 457].

[3] In every sample the Card Sort responses indicated that more delinquents wanted to leave home, that more delinquents felt rejected, and that fewer delinquents confided in their parents.

Moreover, the Card Sort data indicated that within the delinquents' families there was less communication and more quarreling and dissension [p. 457].

[4] In all three cultures more delinquents depicted one or both of the parents as using threats of punishment when confronted with undesirable behavior, while more nondelinquents indicated the parents would reason with their sons [p. 459].

[5] Delinquents' parents were less likely to be aware of their sons' whereabouts or behavior [p. 459].

Rosenquist and Megargee conclude:

The same basic factors differentiated the delinquents from the nondelinquents in all [ethnic groups]. This means that delinquency cannot be ascribed to fundamentally different factors in the different cultures sampled. Mexican, Latin, and Southwestern Anglo delinquency are basically the same. It is not valid to ascribe the Latins' delinquency to culture conflict, for example, or the Mexicans' to poverty. . . . the patterns found in one ethnic group are for the most part generalizable to other ethnic groups, which suggests that theoretical explanations derived in one sample could well apply to others [p. 461].

IN SUMMARY

Both developmental and comparative studies yield the same description of what makes us the way we are. If we grow up "naturally," without cultivation, like weeds, we grow up like weeds—rank. If our nurturing is defective—unappreciative, inconsistent, lax, harsh, and careless—we grow up hostile, and the hostility seems as much turned inward as turned outward. The nurturing environments that produce this denigration of self and others are the same ones that breed criminality.

Control theories have an advantage over the more strictly sociological explanations of crime causation in that they allow for individual differences in reaction to an environment. It is not assumed that "culture" or "class" or "the family" is a huge stamping mill producing stereotyped images upon the human material. The material varies. Some is tough alloy; some is more malleable. Furthermore, the production process itself varies. Being taught and being trained are not just one kind of procedure. *The Oxford English Dictionary* tells us that education is "the process of 'bringing up' [young people]." The "bringing up" is not accomplished on only one escalator. We have been brought up, in some part, by parents, if we had them, or by substitutes for parents. We have been trained, too, by everything that happened when we acted; and this means that we have learned from friends and strangers, lovers and enemies, and even from the jumbled lessons available in books and paintings, in newspapers and on film. This means, further, that we are still learning, that there are lessons in adulthood as in childhood, and that, therefore, even a "well brought up" child may be moved by his later lessons into rational or impetuous crime.

For a theory of criminogenesis, it is not necessary to give exact weights to the many determinants of our destinies. It is particularly unnecessary if we are interested in the sociological questions. To answer these questions it is enough to know the kinds of causes that make a difference, so that the consequences of broad changes in any of them may be estimated.

Although no one has polled social scientists on this matter, it seems likely that the public at large may accept the propositions of control theory more readily than do sociologists at large. Polls of how citizens assign "blame" for crime place the source of criminality where control hypotheses place it—in the nurturing process (*Newsweek,* 1971). Insofar as some sociologists may be reluctant to accept the control formulation, their reluctance seems attributable to the fact that the control propositions, like those of the subcultural hypothesis, do not point to easy or popular political solutions. From the point of view of these hypotheses, the usual welfare recommendations, commendable as they may be in their own right, do not address themselves directly to reducing crime. It cannot be said that guaranteeing everyone a minimum income or redistributing wealth will reduce crime. Better housing, better health care, and "better education," (the last usually undefined)—all these comforting proposals, however ethical in themselves, have little relevance to the diminution of crime if the control formulation is correct.

The requirement of both the subcultural and the control

theories is that young people be nurtured, taken care of, so that they grow up as adults whose lives are explicable and purposeful. The requirement is that as adults we should live in some pattern of accord with others, an accord that allows us individuality bounded by the legally defined rights of those with whom we live and limited by the reasonably probable possibilities open to each of us.

The theme of this theory is that the human being may be a domestic animal, but he needs domestication. The human being may be a civic organism, but he needs civilization; and this means a steeping in a culture.

Chapter 10

Criminogenic
Conditions

A review of the explanations of criminality reminds one of the fable about the blind philosophers confronting for the first time that marvelous beast, the elephant. The blind man who felt the elephant's ear thought the animal resembled the leaf of the banana plant. The philosopher who grasped his tail described the elephant as like a rope. The one who felt the elephant's flank thought the animal was like a mud wall. And the one who felt his leg believed the elephant to be like the trunk of a tree. All the descriptions are partly true—as are the explanations of crime rates.

The structural theories stress *where we are.* The symbolic-interactionist theories emphasize *where we believe we are, what we think we want,* and *how we believe others to be.* The subcultural thesis and, more strongly, the control propositions describe *how we came to be where we are, wanting and believing and behaving as we do.*

For the various consumers of explanations, how satisfactory the different theories are is only in small part a function of how logical and factual they are. The study of criminal conduct, and of society's responses to it, is approached out of concern. This concern has moral roots. The moral conceptions, in turn, affect policies and politics. The morality that determines what one would like to see done politically influences his choice of an explanation of crime.

Causes as Comforts The motivation to believe those explanations that best accord with our moral urges makes it difficult to present a dispassionate statement about criminogenic conditions. One of the comforts of thinking about the "causes" of crime is that the notion of causation carries with it the promise that correcting causes provides cures. This assumption moves us, then, to attend only to those causes that we should wish to change. "Good" causes of crime ought to be left alone; "bad" causes ought to be corrected. One's selection of *"the* causes" of crime is thus biased by his preference for one moral prescription rather than another and for this course of public action rather than that.

Against this tendency, the student who would look clearly at criminogenic conditions is constrained to discipline his moral preferences and to do without the comforting delusion that undesirable behaviors must have only evil causes. On the contrary, the behavior of aggregates, like the behavior of individuals, is probably generated in a *dense* system of causes, a system in which the roots of action are numerous, intertwined, and not uniformly entangled. Some roots are more closely bound to each other; some are stronger than others. It may be impossible, however, to disentangle one source of action from all others. In dense causal systems there are ramifications. Touching the system here affects it there, and there, and there. The despair of would-be societal engineers is this fact, that in the social web one cannot "do just one thing." One cannot change a law, enforce it, ignore it, or enact any reform of our collective enterprise without starting a chain of effects, many of which are bound to be unforeseen and some of which are bound to be undesirable.

Values and Prices   This preamble to a statement of criminogenic conditions is required as part of our understanding that
the *specification* of a probable crime-making condition does not
constitute an *evaluation* of it. Description need be neither com-
mendation nor condemnation.

This qualification recognizes the fact that values have
prices. The social arrangements we prefer carry a cost. Crime
may be one such cost. It is its own pain. It may be a consequence,
nonetheless, of some of the circumstances, and some of the
movements, that are otherwise preferred.

This is said as a caution against zealotry. Images of how
people ought to be and, more to the point, images of how to get
people from where they are to where they ought to be—both
these images are encouraged by the *denial* of their costs, by the
disclaimer that such good intentions and good ends might involve
pains as discomforting as the social "dis-eases" they are designed
to cure.

In brief, and to repeat, a description of some of the roots of
crime does not signify that all these causes ought to be removed.
Some kinds of crime, under some circumstances, may constitute
a price paid for other things we value—like freedom.

The Key to Criminogenesis: Culture   The governor of
crime, as well as its generator, is culture. Every "factor" that is
selected for attention as possibly criminogenic is embedded in a
culture and reflects that culture. Every current explanation of
crime looks at some facet of culture as central.

"Culture" refers to a way of life of a people with a sense of
identity and, usually, with a demarcated territory. Culture is, in
Eliot's phrase, "a peculiar way of thinking, feeling, and behaving" (1948, p. 57). It is a patterning of our way of living together.
The pattern is discernible in its partial manifestations—in the art
of a people, in their diet, dress, and customs, in their religion and
values, in the structure of their society, and in their language.
These dimensions can be, and have been, measured.

Calling culture the key to crime emphasizes the point that
each factor listed as criminogenic makes its impact in terms of the
total way of life of which it is a part. That way of life probably

*over*determines many behaviors, including some criminal careers. Culture means a *reinforcement* of the way we are, as well as a *rearing* in how we are.

If this perception is correct, it implies that, for some people lawful or criminal conduct is more than "just caused." It is "overcaused" so that amelioration of cause 1 leaves alive causes 2, 3, 4, and 5—any one of which may be sufficient to produce the behavior under attention.

To the extent to which this is so, attempts to treat crime by acting upon any singular factor or any small set of factors—like housing, schools, incomes, or families—will be only as successful as the culture allows. This is to say that, just as social reform can seldom "do just one thing," so too does social reform require "doing more than just one thing."

Culture means regulated conduct. This includes the regulation of criminal conduct. A culture includes the training that controls crime. At the same time it defines the occasions on which crime is rational and, even, required. The code of *vendetta* requires murder in defense of honor. The same honor, however, that moves the vengeful man to murder makes it difficult for him to lie or to steal from "his own." Culture limits crime, and channels crime where it calls for it. The circumstances that destroy a culture are, therefore, the circumstances that induce crime.

Cultures live and die. Patterns of behavior and belief fluctuate. They receive more and less allegiance. Innovators are ever-present to question customs; barbarians are ever-present to destroy them. Technologies change, and with them the economic arrangements that underwrite a culture. Information changes, too, and with it the beliefs that were our morals.

These are some of the forces that change cultures. As they change cultures, they weaken them. The debility is seen in the failure of institutions—schools that become "irrelevant," laws that become unjust, families that become unnecessary. The failure of institutions is a cause, a sign, and an accompaniment of the loss of community, and it is with this loss that the serious crimes are generated. *Whatever destroys community fosters an increase in the predatory crimes.*

There is nothing novel in this proposition. It is an idea embedded in the moral teachings of every major religion. It is an idea reflected in each of the propositions to follow.

A ROSTER OF CRIMINOGENIC CONDITIONS

Outlines of "the causes of crime" are always artificial. They can never do more than point to conditions whose impact is subject to "everything else that is happening." Since "everything else that happens" occurs uniquely in each historical instance, it becomes impossible to assign weights to each of the criminogenic conditions. These conditions can be listed, but they cannot be ranked in importance. This is why each proposition in an inventory of criminogenic conditions requires the deadening qualification "other things being equal."

On "Other Things Being Equal" Any set of statements about the causes of crime ought to carry the defensive *caeteris paribus* clause, the qualification that the proposition holds true insofar as "other things remain equal." This defense is an admission that the student is looking at factors one at a time when, in actuality, they never operate that way. The fact that variables do not function "one at a time" is a justification of speaking of patterned variables, of culture, as central to the understanding of criminogenesis. However, it is part of Western thinking to attend to the kinds of things that make crime more or less probable. As we have seen, this style of thought is congenial to the reformer's assumption that if he knows causes, he can treat them and cure "social diseases." To treat causes requires their isolation. It is the desire to isolate causes that has led to the naming of criminal conditions. If we go along with this intellectual custom, it is only with the proviso that each criminogenic condition be considered, *not* as "its own thing" with strongly independent effects, but as one among a shifting complex of causes that affects crime rates.

1 The Movement of People Cultures require transmission, indoctrination, and room in which to operate. The flow of carriers of diverse cultures weakens the process by which a culture is nurtured. When people of diverse cultures meet in large numbers and attempt to live together in some accommodating way, each culture is threatened. *The physical relocation of large masses of people is a criminogenic condition.*

   a   This statement is more true as the meeting of culture carriers occurs under conditions of "freedom," that is, under conditions in which there is no etiquette that governs the relations between them.

   b   Proposition 1 refers to the *process* of peoples' meeting. It is this process that is criminogenic, and it is during the time of seeking a settlement that crime rates may be expected to increase. Once separate settlements are established, a stable accommodation may develop, accompanied by lower rates of the serious offenses.

   c   States that attempt to make one nation out of many will have higher crime rates than states of similar development that allow voluntary separation.

   d   Multi-nation states that regionalize their nationalities, as the Soviet Union and Switzerland have done, will have lower crime rates than states of similar development that do not regionalize.

   2   Crowding   Beyond some ill-defined threshold, the more crowded an area, the higher will be its crime rate.

   a   Crowding is difficult to measure, since where one *resides* may not be where one *lives*. People are somewhat mobile, and some denizens of dense cities have periodic chances of "getting away from it all." Furthermore, the psychological dimension of *crowding* is only imperfectly gauged from measures of *density*, like the number of people per square mile. See, again, the study by Galle and his colleagues (1972) referred to earlier.

   b   Cultures of long standing may have developed particular accommodations to density that minimize crowding effects—the houseboat dwellers of Hong Kong are an example. If this were proved true, it would be necessary to qualify proposition 2 as regards *stable* populations and to apply the proposition with even greater force to areas that have recently become crowded.

3 Social Mobility It is to be expected that, when large proportions of a population climb up or fall down class ladders, the effect will be criminogenic. This does not mean that particular individuals who change their status need be more prone to criminality. The proposition refers more strongly to the correlative conditions, the culture-challenging conditions, that seem to go along with high rates of vertical mobility.

4 Relative Deprivation This subjective state is criminogenic. It feeds on that perennial emotion, envy, against which all people have tried to defend themselves. Whatever contributes to such feelings is part of the crime-making process. Such sentiments are stimulated widely today by political ideologies and disseminated by the mass media and schools. This fact says nothing about the "justice" of such stimulation.

5 Child Neglect and Misuse of Youth Any conditions or any teachings that weaken the loving and the training of offspring are part of the crime-causing system.

    a Challenges to the family, criticisms of family life, including literature and drama based on its sadness, are contributory. Saying this says nothing about the *truth* of this literature, but only about its probable *effects.*

Such challenges are contributory unless, and until, substitute institutions for the education of generations *evolve.* The term "evolve" is used because the *creation* of institutions in mass societies is difficult, if not impossible. The Israeli *kibbutzim,* of course, represent one created alternative within a relatively homogeneous socioeconomic and cultural setting.

    b Schools that shame children, or imprison them, are criminogenic.

    c Schools that provide no moral models are criminogenic. Those religious bodies that set up their own separate schools acknowledge that their formal education should include moral modeling as well as the teaching of facts and skills.

    d Societies that have little use for adolescents will have higher crime rates. The term "little use" betokens poor apprenticeship for adulthood.

6 Mass Media The mass media make a contribution to crime. These instruments have functioned, thus far, as culture-breakers and as generators of feelings of relative deprivation.

The economic motive to gain and maintain large audiences means that the "creative" people of the media must stimulate us, which often means shock us. Consequently, television, cinema, and theater stretch the limits of our morals.

More directly, the media—television and movies in particular—provide heroic models of criminals: of burglars *(The Anderson Tapes)*, of whores *(Klute[1])*, of dope peddlers *(Easy Rider)*, of bank robbers *(The Getaway; Butch Cassidy and the Sundance Kid)*, and of gangsters *(The Godfather)*.

7 The Comforting Chemicals Human beings have always attempted to alter their experience, if not steadily, at least episodically. Regularity is monotony, and monotony is a bore. The human animal sometimes seeks to elevate his experience above the normal and sometimes to depress himself toward forgetfulness. Man does this through music and drama, through poetry and dancing, and through ceremonies that celebrate the mysteries.

We also do this with the aid of comforting chemicals. The comforts run from such innocent things as chewing gum and betel nut to drinking, sniffing, smoking, and "shooting" an amazing pharmacopoeia. Once habituated to these chemical aids, we find their withdrawal painful. When the legal supply of such chemicals is cut off or restricted, an illegal market will come into being. Criminalizing the use of tobacco, alcohol, marijuana, and the more dramatic drugs of oblivion makes criminals by definition.

The public question is whether the criminal law should be employed against any or all of such chemical solace. The question is not solely a matter of the bodily harm that chronic use of these comforts may produce. Here some legal chemicals, like tobacco, have a worse record than some illegal ones like marijuana or

---

[1]"Vivienne, a pretty 22-year-old call girl, averages 3,000 to 5,000 tax-free dollars a month hustling in the San Francisco area. She started in "the life" about seven months ago, inspired by Jane Fonda's performance as a high-priced call girl in 'Klute.' 'I estimate that thousands of girls got turned on to tricking after seeing that movie,' she says" (*Newsweek*, 1973).

heroin. The question is also one of the *moral* effects of habitua-
tion to soporifics and of the *practical* effects of public intoxica-
tion.

The practical effects—drunken driving, for example—might
be penalized without forbidding the use of alcohol or marijuana.
Our moral concern intrudes, however, upon our decision to make
this separation. We are concerned lest vices[2] that are permitted
spread and change the moral tenor of our lives.

The moral question becomes a civic problem in democracies
where a libertarian tradition denies that the state has any business
protecting individuals from themselves. This tradition would
restrict crime to the damage we do others.

The question when and how the state ought to intervene in
our lives might be more readily resolved if we could calculate the
costs of ignoring vice, or suppressing it, against the benefits for
mass society. This calculation has never been attempted; perhaps
it cannot be. Meanwhile, the huge efforts to apply the criminal
law against the use of intoxicants, narcotics, and the halluci-
nogenic chemicals is, of course, criminogenic.

There is no certain advice for us. The advice that psychology might lend to social policy here is difficult to apply. Psychology
says, first, that rewards for desirable behavior are less costly
(more effective) than penalties for undesirable behavior. Persons
whose lives are "good in themselves" do not need the deadening
chemicals. However, persons who receive as much pain as
pleasure when they look at reality each morning need what
comfort they can get. The difficulty is that there is no formula for
giving joy to others. There is, moreover, no science of societal
engineering that knows how to build more rewarding societies
without risking tyranny.

Some schools of psychology provide a second piece of
advice. They would license the perennial vices and allow them to
seek their own segregated corners. To this school of thought,
leaving people alone when they damage only themselves seems
less costly than jailing them.

---

[2]"Vice has been defined as unconsciously choosing something which is bad for
yourself or for society, and sin as consciously choosing it. Vice becomes sin as soon as the
person concerned knows it is vice" (Brock, 1960:34).

It is doubtful, however, whether any of us can maintain this liberality of attitude consistently. At some point, the damage we do "only to ourselves" is seen to have a societal impact. Vice is contagious. When the medical analogy of "contagion" is adopted, it becomes questionable whether "crimes without victims" are victimless. Furthermore, when one thinks that private vices may become epidemic, he gives a different answer to the question about the "right" of the state to intrude upon the "civil liberties" of its citizens. No one has the "right" to spread smallpox, and no civil libertarian seems offended by the quarantine of Typhoid Mary.

The analogy of contagion and the epidemic has been applied, with good reason, to the spread of the use of opiates. Wilson and his colleagues argue that "heroin is so destructive of the human personality that it should not be made generally available" (1972, p. 26). They provide evidence that addiction to opiates fits the model of contagion, since the way addicts get started is by contact, through the instigation of a friend. These investigators also present data that contagion can be contained through vigorous law enforcement, that the *certainty and severity* of enforcement reduces the spread of the addiction. In their words, increasing "the 'expected costs' of an arrest to the user [reduces] the number of addicts in the city. By 'expected costs' [is meant] the probability of being arrested multiplied by the probability of being sentenced to prison and the length of the average prison sentence" (p. 19).

Containing the spread of opiates through law enforcement need not be equated, however, with jailing junkies. Quarantine is confining, but its intent is not punitive.

8 Anarchy and Authority   The Western world has recently experienced a mood of rebellion. "Authority" in itself sounds "authoritarian," and that adjective is certainly pejorative. "Expression" has increased in value as "respect" has declined. For example, Morris and Small (1971) compared the preferences for thirteen ways of life as rated by American college students in the early 1950s and in the 1970s. "Preserving the best that man has attained" dropped markedly in value during these decades, as did "social restraint" and "self-control." By contrast, in 1970 the students gave greater value to "withdrawal and self-sufficiency," "receptivity and sympathetic concern," and "self-indulgence and sensuous enjoyment."

The question here is one of limits or of what the Greeks used to think of as "balance." At one extreme there is anarchy and at the other uncritical submission to authority. The Greeks' prescription was for *sophrosyne,* a prudent moderation between self-expression and self-control. This ancient prescription is relevant to the study of criminogenesis, for people who recognize no external authority will have no internal authority. They will have no reliable self-control that limits their actions vis-à-vis others. What one wants to do will be what one does. The person who asks, "What's wrong with that?" is already infected.

9 Laws and Their Enforcement Laws without force are criminogenic. Despite our reluctance to pay its costs, force *is* effective in containing crime. Saying this does not imply that there are no limits to force. It is as Talleyrand said to Napoleon, "You can do everything with your bayonets, sire, except sit on them." But the fact that there are limits to legal sanctions (Packer, 1968) does not mean that sanctions are without effects. It is true that where there is moral control, there is less need for legal control; and it is true, as Bickel reminds us, that "law can never make us as secure as we are when we do not need it" (1972, p. 61).

This has been a theme of the theories of criminogenesis we have described—that it is in culture conflict that crime is bred. It is in such conflict between majorities and minorities that the criminal sanction is effective. There *is* a deterrent effect in the enforcement of the criminal law. It has been recorded in a wide context of behaviors—from the reduction of reckless and drunken driving (Cramton, 1969; Shumate, 1958) to the containment of the "index crimes" (Tittle, 1969) to the reduction of ritualized robbery, murder, and gangsterism (Bruce, 1969; Pantaleone, 1966) to the control of political turmoil (Feierabend and Nesvold, 1970). The conditions and the limits of the deterrent effect deserve study (Cousineau, 1972), but the *fact* of deterrence needs to be taken seriously (Andenaes, 1966; Tittle, 1969).

This fact has been obscured by the confusion of "special"

deterrence with "general" deterrence and by the intrusion of a therapeutic way of thinking upon our consideration of undesirable behavior. "Special deterrence" refers to the impact of a penalty upon the person who receives it. It is clear that some kinds of people, when punished, are not deflected from further crimes. Recidivism is a common phenomenon among those punished under the criminal law. This does not mean, however, that enforcement of the law has no *general* deterrent effect, that it has no effect in raising the threshold of temptation for most individuals. Nor does the fact of recidivism deny that law enforcement has the "indirect deterrent effect [of] stimulating and reinforcing the normative climate of the community," as Salem and Bowers put it (1970, p. 38).

A general deterrent effect is difficult to measure. It may, indeed, be impossible to isolate clearly. It is true, too, that some kinds of people, psychotically alone or fortified by peers and an ideology, are *not* deterred from some kinds of crime by fear of punishment (Ball, 1955; Taft, 1946). But it does not follow from all this that there is no general deterrent effect, or, worse, that "social science" has disproved the existence of such an effect. Much depends on the relative sizes of majorities and minorities, on the certainty and celerity of enforcement, and on the severity of the penalties a society is willing to impose.

A second source of the obscurity of deterrent effects lies in the imposition of a psychiatrically buttressed system of belief upon the definition of crime. According to this way of thinking, crime is called a "symptom." "Symptoms," of course, are to be ignored, suffered, or palliated, while physicians treat their causes. Our study of theories of criminality has shown us, however, that the causes of criminal conduct are imperfectly known. It has taught us that such causes are probably numerous, intertwined, "more than sufficient," and costly to manipulate.

The medical model that defines crime as "symptomatic" is obscurantist for another reason as well: it tends to regard criminals as sick men and never as rational ones. The idea that the causes of their "illness" should treated "is based on the belief," a former Attorney General of the United States tells us, "that healthy, rational people will not injure others. . . . Rehabilitated, an individual will not have the capacity . . . to injure another or to take or destroy property" (Clark, 1970, p. 220). Such a statement is either a tautology or an unsupported hope. Carried to its logical extremity, this therapeutic recommendation leads to such futilities as doing social work among the Mafia.[3]

IN SUMMARY

It bears repeating that values have prices and that calling conditions "crime-productive" says nothing about their possible rewards.

Physical and social mobility may be desirable in themselves. Certainly many people say so and behave as if this were so. Furthermore, some level of density is required if there is to be social activity and excitement; many people feel bored and lonely in sparse settlements.

Similarly, the sense of relative deprivation is justified morally and politically. Criminal actions that are taken in the name of reduction of deprivation are considered by some citizens to be excusable. This excuse is applied to a wide range of crimes, including even rape (Cleaver, 1968).

Mothering may once have been a virtue beyond reproach, but today it is argued that the weakening of the bonds of family and wider kinship, through which children have been acculturated, is justified because it is "liberating." So, too, among the followers of Reich (1942), there are defenders of "free schools" that allow each child to find his own morality by bumping into others.

The mass media are also valued despite their prices. They provide pleasure and information. They teach other lessons than criminal ones, and not all their heroic models break laws.

The comforting chemicals have their costs, and sometimes very high ones, but their existence throughout history and across

---

[3]On the "cure" of the Mafia in Sicily, Barzini writes, "Obviously most remedies tried were once again only partial. Some turned out to be no remedies at all, but incentives. Obviously the Mafia can exist even without poverty, illiteracy, social injustice, feudalism, *latifundia,* and foreign rulers. Like all other activities, it prospered, in fact, when backward social and economic conditions were removed" (1971, p. 368).

cultures tells us that they are not likely to be abandoned. We can work most effectively for moderation in their use and for control of their public consequences. A similar prudence is recommended in the denigration of authority and in the passage of laws without force.

We are returned to our theme, which claims that the "causes" of crime, like the "causes" of any other set of social behaviors, lie in the social fabric. The fabric is flexible. It stretches as it is altered. It can be torn, patched, and rewoven without being destroyed. What weakens one part of a culture may strengthen another.

There are limits, of course. This we believe we have learned from the histories of dead civilizations. We move uncertainly, however, like the blind philosophers, since we have not been told what these limits are. We do not know how much abrasion of the social fabric leads to its dissolution.

One conclusion is certain: we destroy cultures at our peril. Culture is an acquisition, not an endowment. It is transmitted, not invented. The best hope for containing the damage that our self-interests "naturally" inflict on each other lies in the continuity of a culture.

Bibliography

Abrams, M. 1958. "The mass media and social class in Great Britain." Paper read at the Fourth World Congress of Sociology, Stresa, Italy.

Akers, R. L. 1964. "Socio-economic status and delinquent behavior: A retest." *Journal of Research on Crime and Delinquency,* 1 (January):38–46.

Allinsmith, W. 1960. "The learning of moral standards." In D. R. Miller and G. E. Swanson (Eds.), *Inner Conflict and Defense.* New York: Holt.

Alper, T. G. 1946. "Memory for completed and incompleted tasks as a function of personality: Analysis of group data." *Journal of Abnormal and Social Psychology,* 41 (October):403–420.

American Law Institute. 1953. *Model Penal Code.* Philadelphia: The American Law Institute.

Andenaes, J. 1966. "The general preventive effects of punishment." *University of Pennsylvania Law Review,* 114 (May):949–983.

Arendt, H. 1964. *Eichmann in Jerusalem: A Report of the Banality of Evil.* New York: The Viking Press.

Arnold, W. R. 1971. "Race and ethnicity relative to other factors in juvenile court dispositions." *American Journal of Sociology,* 77 (September):211–227.

Aronfreed, J. 1963. "The effects of experimental socialization paradigms upon two moral responses to transgression." *Journal of Abnormal and Social Psychology,* 66 (May):437–448.

————and A. Reber. 1965. "Internalized behavioral suppression and the timing of social punishment." *Journal of Personality and Social Psychology,* 1 (January):3–16.

Arthur, A. Z. 1969. "Diagnostic testing and the new alternatives." *Psychological Bulletin,* 72 (September):183–192.

Ash, P. 1949. "The reliability of psychiatric diagnoses." *Journal of Abnormal and Social Psychology,* 44 (April):272–277.

Automobile Manufacturers' Association. 1966. *Automobile Facts and Figures.* New York: The Association.

Bacon, M. K., et al. 1963. "A cross-cultural study of correlates of crime." *Journal of Abnormal and Social Psychology,* 66 (April):291–300.

Bagot, J. H. 1941. *Juvenile Delinquency: A Comparative Study of the Position in Liverpool and England and Wales.* London: J. Cape.

Bailyn, L. 1959. "Mass media and children: A study of exposure habits and cognitive effects." *Psychological Monographs,* 73 (#471).

Bain, R. 1958. "Our schizoid culture and sociopathy." *Sociology and Social Research,* 42 (4):263–268.

Ball, J. C. 1955. "The deterrence concept in criminology and law." *Journal of Criminal Law, Criminology, and Police Science,* 46 (September-October):347–354.

Bandura, A. (Ed.) 1972. *Psychological Modeling: Conflicting Theories.* Chicago: Aldine.

————et al. 1961. "Transmission of aggression through imitation of aggressive models." *Journal of Abnormal and Social Psychology,* 63 (1 November):575–582.

————and R. H. Walters. 1959. *Adolescent Aggression.* New York: Ronald Press.

————and————. 1963. *Social Learning and Personality Development.* New York: Holt, Rinehart, & Winston, Inc.

Banfield, E. C. 1968. *The Unheavenly City.* Boston: Little, Brown and Company.

Barker, G. H. 1940. "Family factors in the ecology of juvenile delinquency." *Journal of Criminal Law and Criminology,* 30 (April):681–691.

Barndt, R. J., and D. M. Johnson. 1955. "Time orientation in delinquents." *Journal of Abnormal and Social Psychology,* 51 (September):343–345.

Barzini, L. 1971. *From Caesar to the Mafia.* New York: The Library Press.

Beck, B. 1967. "Welfare as a moral category." *Social Problems,* 14 (Winter):258–277.

Becker, H. S. 1963. Outsiders: *Studies in the Sociology of Deviance.* Glencoe, Ill.: The Free Press.

———.1967. "Whose side are we on?" *Social Problems,* 14 (Winter):239–247.

Behrman, S. N. 1972. "People in a diary, I." *The New Yorker,* 48 (13 May):36–94.

Beilin, H. 1956. "The pattern of postponability and its relation to social class mobility." *Journal of Social Psychology,* 44 (August):33–48.

Belson, W. A., et al., 1970. *The Development of a Procedure for Eliciting Information from Boys about the Nature and Extent of Their Stealing.* London: The Survey Research Centre, The London School of Economics and Political Science.

Bensman, J., and I. Gerver. 1963. "Crime and punishment in the factory: The function of deviancy in maintaining the social system." *American Sociological Review,* 28 (August):588–598.

Berg, I. 1971. *Education and Jobs: The Great Training Robbery.* Boston: Beacon Press.

Berkowitz, L., and J. Macaulay. 1971. "The contagion of criminal violence." *Sociometry,* 34 (June):238–260.

Berliner, J. S. 1961. "The situation of the plant manager." In A. Inkeles and K. Geiger (Eds.), *Soviet Society: A Book of Readings.* Boston: Houghton Mifflin Company.

Beynon, E. D. 1935. "Crimes and customs of the Hungarians in Detroit." *Journal of Criminal Law, Criminology, and Police Science,* 25 (January-February):755–774.

Bickel, A. M. 1972. "The 'uninhibited, robust, and wide-open' first amendment: From 'Sullivan' to the Pentagon Papers." *Commentary,* 54 (November):60–67.

Biderman, A. D., et al. 1967. *Report on a Pilot Study in the District of Columbia on Victimization and Attitudes Toward Law Enforcement.* Field Survey I.: President's Commission on Law Enforcement and Administration of Justice. Washington, D. C.: U. S. Government Printing Office.

Biggs, J., Jr. 1955. *The Guilty Mind: Psychiatry and the Law of Homicide.* Baltimore, Md.: The Johns Hopkins Press.

Bixenstine, V. L., and R. L. Buterbaugh. 1967. "Integrative behavior in adolescent boys as a function of delinquency and race." *Journal of Consulting Psychology*, 31 (October):471–476.

Black, A. H., et al. 1960. Cited in O. H. Mowrer, *Learning Theory and the Symbolic Processes*. New York: John Wiley & Sons, Inc.

Black, D. J. 1970. "Production of crime rates." *American Sociological Review*, 35 (August):733–748.

———and A. J. Reiss, Jr. 1967. "Patterns of behavior in police and citizen transactions." Section I of *Studies of Crime and Law Enforcement in Major Metropolitan Areas*. Volume II. Washington, D. C.: U. S. Government Printing Office.

———and———.1970. "Police control of juveniles." *American Sociological Review*, 35 (February):63–77.

Bloom, B. L. 1966. "A census tract analysis of socially deviant behaviors." *Multivariate Behavioral Research*, 1 (July):307–320.

Blue, J. T., Jr. 1948. "The relationship of juvenile delinquency, race, and economic status." *Journal of Negro Education*, 17 (Fall):469–477.

Blumenthal, M. D., 1972. "Predicting attitudes toward violence." *Science*, 176 (23 June):1296–1303.

Blumenthal, M. D., et al. 1972. *Justifying Violence: Attitudes of American Men*. Ann Arbor, Mich.: Institute for Social Research.

Boggs, S. L. 1965. "Urban crime patterns." *American Sociological Review*, 30 (December):899–908.

Bohlke, R. 1961. "Social mobility, stratification inconsistency and middle-class delinquency." *Social Problems*, 8 (Spring):351–363.

Boltwood, C. E., et al. 1972. "Skyjacking, airline security, and passenger reactions: Toward a complex model for prediction." *American Psychologist*, 27 (June):539–545.

Bordua, D. J. 1958–1959. "Juvenile delinquency and 'anomie': An attempt at replication." *Social Problems*, 6 (Winter):230–238.

———.1967. "Recent trends: Deviant behavior and social control." *The Annals of the American Academy of Political and Social Science*, 369 (January):149–163.

Borhek, J. T. 1970. "Ethnic-group cohesion." *American Journal of Sociology*, 76 (July):33–46.

Bottoms, A. E. 1967. "Delinquency amongst immigrants." *Race*, 8 (April):357–383.

Bowlby, J. 1952. *Maternal Care and Mental Health*. Geneva: World Health Organization.

Braginsky, B. M., et al. 1969. *Methods of Madness: The Mental Hospital as a Last Resort*. New York: Holt, Rinehart and Winston, Inc.

Brock, D. 1960. "The innocent mind: Or, my days as a juvenile delinquent." *Canadian Journal of Corrections,* 2:25–35.

Brown, S. R. 1970–1971. Review of M. L. Kohn, "Class and Conformity: A Study in Values." *Public Opinion Quarterly,* 34 (Winter):654–655.

Bruce, G. 1969. *The Stranglers: The Cult of Thuggee and Its Overthrow in British India.* New York: Harcourt, Brace & World, Inc.

Bukovsky, V. 1972. "The Bukovsky papers: Notes from Soviet asylums." *National Review,* 24 (9 June):633–636.

Burchinal, L. G. 1964. "Characteristics of adolescents from unbroken, broken and reconstituted families." *Journal of Marriage and Family Living,* 26 (February):44–51.

Burgess, A. 1962. *A Clockwork Orange.* London: Heinemann.

Burgess, R. L., and R. L. Akers. 1966. "A differential association-reinforcement theory of criminal behavior." *Social Problems,* 14 (Fall):128–147.

Burt, C. 1925. *The Young Delinquent.* New York: D. Appleton and Company. Fourth edition, 1944. London: The University of London Press.

————.1961. "Intelligence and social mobility." *British Journal of Statistical Psychology,* 14 (May):3–24.

Burton, R. V. 1963. "Generality of honesty reconsidered." *Psychological Review,* 70 (November):481–499.

————et al. 1961. "Antecedents of resistance to temptation in four-year-old children." *Child Development,* 32 (December):689–710.

Business Management. 1968. "Are your employees more dishonest than you think?" 34 (September):12–14.

Cahalan, D., et al. 1947. "Interviewer bias involved in certain types of opinion survey questions." *International Journal of Opinion and Attitude Research,* 1 (March):63–77.

Cairns, R. B. 1966. "Attachment behavior of mammals." *Psychological Review,* 73 (September):409–426.

Cameron, M. O. 1964. *The Booster and The Snitch: Department Store Shoplifting.* Glencoe, Ill.: The Free Press.

Campbell, B. A., and R. M. Church (Eds.). 1969. *Punishment and Aversive Behavior.* New York: Appleton-Century-Crofts.

The Canadian Corrections Association. 1967. *Indians and the Law.* A Survey Prepared for the Hon. Arthur Laing, Department of Indian Affairs and Northern Development. Ottawa: The Canadian Welfare Council.

Cartwright, D. S., and K. I. Howard. 1966. "Multivariate analysis of gang delinquency: I. Ecologic influences." *Multivariate Behavioral Research*, 1 (July):321–372.

Ceylon Department of Census and Statistics. 1957. *Juvenile Probationers in Ceylon.* Ceylon: Government Press.

Chambliss, W. J., and R. H. Nagasawa. 1969. "On the validity of official statistics: A comparative study of white, black, and Japanese high-school boys." *Journal of Research in Crime and Delinquency,* 6 (January):71–77

Chilton, R. J. 1964. "Delinquency area research in Baltimore, Detroit, and Indianapolis." *American Sociological Review,* 29 (February):71–83.

———and G. E. Markle. 1972. "Family disruption, delinquent conduct, and the effect of subclassification." *American Sociological Review,* 37 (February):93–99.

Cho, Sung Tai. 1967. *A Cross-Cultural Analysis of the Criminality Level Index.* Columbus, Ohio: The Ohio State University, Department of Sociology. Ph.D. Dissertation.

Christie, N. 1960. *Unge Norske Lovovertredere.* (Young Norwegian Lawbreakers) Oslo: Universitetsforlaget.

———et al. 1965. "A study of self-reported crime." In K. O. Christiansen (Ed.), *Scandinavian Studies in Criminology.* Volume 1. London: Tavistock Publications.

Church, R. M. 1963. "The varied effects of punishment on behavior." *Psychological Review,* 70 (September):369–402.

Clark, J. P., and L. L. Tifft. 1966. "Polygraph and interview validation of self reported deviant behavior." *American Sociological Review,* 31 (August):516–523.

———and E. P. Wenninger. 1962. "Socio-economic class and area as correlates of illegal behavior among juveniles." *American Sociological Review,* 27 (December):826–834.

Clark, R. 1970. *Crime in America.* New York: Simon & Schuster.

Cleaver, E. 1968. *Soul on Ice.* New York: McGraw-Hill Book Company.

Clinard, M. 1942. "The process of urbanization and criminal behavior: A study of culture conflicts." *American Journal of Sociology,* 48 (September):202–213.

———.1960. "A cross-cultural replication of the relation of urbanism to criminal behavior." *American Sociological Review,* 25 (April): 253–257.

Cloward, R. A., and L. E. Ohlin. 1960. *Delinquency and Opportunity: A Theory of Delinquent Gangs.* New York: The Free Press.

Cohen, A. K. 1955. *Delinquent Boys: The Culture of the Gang.* Glencoe, Ill.: The Free Press.

Command paper #4708. 1970. *Criminal Statistics: England and Wales.* London: Her Majesty's Stationery Office.

Connor, W. D. 1972. *Deviance in Soviet Society.* New York: Columbia University Press.

Coombs, C. H. 1967. "Thurstone's measurement of social values revisited forty years later." *Journal of Personality and Social Psychology,* 6 (May):85–91.

Cooper, C. C. 1960. *A Comparative Study of Delinquents and Non-Delinquents.* Portsmouth, Ohio: The Psychological Service Center Press.

Cousineau, D. F. 1967. *Some Current Conceptions of Rationality and the Policy Sciences.* Edmonton: The University of Alberta, Department of Sociology. M. A. Dissertation.

————.1972. "The concept of general deterrence: Critique of Theory and Research." Edmonton: The University of Alberta, Department of Sociology. Mimeographed Ph.D. dissertation proposal.

————and J.E. Veevers. 1972. "Juvenile justice: An analysis of the Canadian Young Offender's Act." In C. Boydell et al. (Eds.), *Deviant Behavior and Societal Reaction.* Toronto: Holt, Rinehart, and Winston.

Cressey, D. R. 1953. *Other People's Money: A Study in the Social Psychology of Embezzlement.* Glencoe, Ill.: Free Press. Second edition, 1971. Belmont, Calif.: Wadsworth Publishing Co., Inc.

————.1964. "Causes of Employee Dishonesty." East Lansing, Michigan: Michigan State University. Mimeographed paper presented to the Top Management Business Security Seminar, (16 April).

Crockett, H. J. 1962. "The achievement motive and differential occupational mobility in the United States." *American Sociological Review,* 27 (April):191–204.

Crook, E. B. 1934. "Cultural marginality in sexual delinquency." *American Journal of Sociology,* 39 (January):493–500.

Cuber, J., and P. Harroff. 1966. *The Significant Americans.* New York: Doubleday and Company, Publishers.

Davis, A., and J. Dollard. 1941. *Children of Bondage.* Washington: American Council on Education.

————and R. Havighurst. 1947. *Father of the Man: How Your Child Gets His Personality.* Boston: Houghton, Mifflin.

Davis, M. S. 1971. "That's Interesting!" *Philosophy of the Social Sciences,* 1 (December):309–344.

DeFleur, M., and R. Quinney. 1966. "A reformulation of Sutherland's differential association theory and a strategy for empirical verification." *Journal of Research in Crime and Delinquency,* 3 (January):1–22.

Dentler, R. A., and L. J. Monroe. 1961. "Social correlates of early adolescent theft." *American Sociological Review,* 26 (October):733–743.

DiCara, L. V. 1970. "Learning in the autonomic nervous system." *Scientific American,* 222 (January):31–39.

Dinitz, S., et al. 1962. "Delinquency vulnerability: A cross group and longitudinal analysis." *American Sociological Review,* 27 (August):515–517.

Doleschal, E. No date. *Criminal Statistics.* Rockville, Md.: National Institute of Mental Health.

Douvan, E. 1956. "Social status and success strivings." *Journal of Abnormal and Social Psychology,* 52 (April):219–223.

———and J. Edelson. 1958. "The psychodynamics of social mobility in adolescent boys." *Journal of Abnormal and Social Psychology,* 56 (January):31–44.

Duhamel, R. (Ed.). 1962. *Office Consolidation of the Criminal Code and Selected Statutes.* Ottawa: Queen's Printer and Controller of Stationery.

Durkheim, E. 1951. *Suicide: A Study in Sociology.* (G. Simpson, Ed.) Glencoe, Ill.: Free Press.

Edwards, A. L. 1957. *The Social Desirability Variable in Personality Assessment and Research.* New York: The Dryden Press.

Eliot, T. S. 1948. *Notes Towards a Definition of Culture.* London: Faber and Faber, Ltd.

Elmhorn, K. 1965. "Study in self-reported delinquency among schoolchildren in Stockholm." In K. O. Christiansen (Ed.), *Scandinavian Studies in Criminology.* Volume 1. London: Tavistock Publications.

El-Saaty, H. 1946. *Juvenile Delinquency in Egypt.* London: Faculty of Arts, University of London. Ph.D. Dissertation.

Empey, L. T., and S. G. Lubeck. 1971. *Explaining Delinquency.* Lexington, Mass.: D.C. Heath and Company.

Ennis, P. H. 1967. *Criminal Victimization in the United States: A Report of a National Survey.* A Report of a Research Study Submitted to The President's Commission on Law Enforcement and Administration of Justice. Washington, D.C.: U.S. Government Printing Office.

Epstein, R. 1964. "Need for approval and the conditioning of verbal hostility in asthmatic children." *Journal of Abnormal and Social Psychology,* 69 (July):105–109.

Erickson, M. L. 1971. "The group context of delinquent behavior." *Social Problems,* 19 (Summer):114–129.

————and L. T. Empey. 1963. "Court records, undetected delinquency and decision-making." *Journal of Criminal Law, Criminology, and Police Science,* 54 (December):456–469.

Eron, L. D. (Ed.). 1966. *The Classification of Behavior Disorders.* Chicago: Aldine.

————et al. 1971. *Learning of Aggression in Children.* Boston: Little, Brown and Company.

————et al. 1972. "Does television violence cause aggression?" *American Psychologist,* 27 (April):253–263.

Erskine, H. 1968–1969. "The polls: Recent opinions of racial problems." *Public Opinion quarterly,* 32 (Winter):696–703.

Eysenck, H. J. 1964. *Crime and Personality.* Boston: Houghton Mifflin Company.

————.1966a. *The Effects of Psychotherapy.* New York: International Science Press.

————.1966b. "Personality and experimental psychology." *Bulletin of the British Psychological Society,* 19 (January):1–28.

Fairchild, H. P. 1944. *Dictionary of Sociology.* New York: Philosophical Library.

Fancher, R. E., Jr. 1966. "Explicit personality theories and accuracy in person perception." *Journal of Personality,* 34 (June):252–261.

————.1967. "Accuracy vs. validity in person perception." *Journal of Consulting Psychology,* 31 (June):264–269.

Federal Bureau of Investigation. 1970. *Crime in the United States: Uniform Crime Reports—1969.* Washington, D.C.: U.S. Government Printing Office.

————.1971. *Crime in the United States: Uniform Crime Reports—1970.* Washington, D.C.: U.S. Government Printing Office.

Feierabend, I. K., and B. Nesvold. 1970. "Political coerciveness and turmoil: A cross national inquiry." *Law and Society Review,* 5 (August):93–118.

Ferracuti, F. 1968. "European migration and crime." In M. E. Wolfang (Ed.), *Crime and Culture: Essays in Honor of Thorsten Sellin.* New York: John Wiley & Sons, Inc.

Feshbach, S., and R. D. Singer. 1971. *Television and Aggression.* San Francisco: Jossey-Bass.

Fishbein, M., and I. Ajzen. 1972. "Attitudes and opinions." In P. H. Mussen and M. R. Rosenzweig (Eds.), *Annual Review of Psychology.* Palo Alto: Annual Reviews, Inc.

Fleisher, B. M. 1966. *The Economics of Delinquency.* Chicago: Quadrangle Books.

Forslund, M. A. 1970. "A comparison of Negro and white crime rates."

Journal of Criminal Law, Criminology, and Police Science, 61 (June):214–217.

Forssman, H., and C. F. Gentz. 1962. "Kriminalitetsförekomsten hos presumtivt ostraffade." *Nordisk Tidsskrift for Kriminalviden-skab:*318–324.

Franchini, A., and F. Introna. 1961. *Delinquenza Minorile.* Padova: Cedam.

Franks, C. M. 1956. "Conditioning and personality." *Journal of Abnormal and Social Psychology,* 52 (July):143–150.

————.1961. "Conditioning and abnormal behavior." In H. J. Eysenck (Ed.), *Handbook of Abnormal Psychology.* New York: Basic Books, Inc.

Freedman, D. 1958. "Constitutional and environmental interactions in rearing of four breeds of dogs." *Science,* 127 (14 March): 585–586.

Freud, A., and S. Dann. 1951. "An experiment in group upbringing." In R. S. Eissler et al. (Eds.), *The Psychoanalytic Study of the Child.* Volume 6. New York: International Universities Press.

Freud, S. 1958. *Civilization and Its Discontents.* Garden City, N. Y.: Doubleday & Co.

Furth, H. G. 1966. *Thinking Without Language: Psychological Implications of Deafness.* New York: The Free Press.

Gaito, J., and A. Zavala. 1964. "Neurochemistry and learning." *Psychological Bulletin,* 61 (January):45–62.

Gales, K., and M. G. Kendall. 1957. "An enquiry concerning interviewer variability." *Journal of the Royal Statistical Society,* 120 (Series A).

Galle, O. R., et al. 1972. "Population density and pathology: What are the relations for Man?" *Science,* 176 (7 April):23–30.

Gastil, R. D. 1971. "Homicide and a regional culture of violence." *American Sociological Review,* 36 (June):412–427.

Geen, R. G., and L. Berkowitz. 1967. "Some conditions facilitating the occurrence of aggression after the observation of violence." *Journal of Personality,* 35 (December):666–676.

Germani, G. 1961. "Inquiry into the social effects of urbanization in a working-class sector of Greater Buenos Aires." In P. M. Hauser (Ed.), *Urbanization in Latin America.* New York: Columbia University Press.

Gibbens, T. C. N., and R. H. Ahrenfeldt (Eds.). 1966. *Cultural Factors in Delinquency.* London: Tavistock Publications.

Gibbons, D. C. 1968. *Society, Crime, and Criminal Careers: An Introduction to Criminology.* Englewood Cliffs, N. J.: Prentice-Hall, Inc.

Ginzberg, E. 1972. "The outlook for educated manpower." *The Public Interest*, 26 (Winter):100–111.

Glazer, N., and D. P. Moynihan. 1963. *Beyond the Melting Pot*. Cambridge, Mass.: The M.I.T. Press.

Glueck, S. 1964. "The home, the school, and delinquency." In S. and E. Glueck, *Ventures in Criminology: Selected Recent Papers*. London: Tavistock Publications.

———and E. Glueck. 1950. *Unraveling Juvenile Delinquency*. Cambridge, Mass.: Harvard University Press.

———and———.1956. *Physique and Delinquency*. New York: Paul B. Hoeber, Inc.

———and———.1962. *Family Environment and Delinquency*. Boston: Houghton Mifflin Company.

———and———.1970. *Toward a Typology of Juvenile Offenders: Implications for Therapy and Prevention*. New York: Grune & Stratton, Inc.

Gold, M. 1966. "Undetected delinquent behavior." *Journal of Research in Crime and Delinquency*, 13 (January):27–46.

Goldberg, L. R., and C. E. Werts. 1966. "The reliability of clinicians' judgments: A multitrait-multimethod approach." *Journal of Consulting Psychology*, 30 (June):199–206.

Goldfarb, W. 1943a. "Effects of early institutional care on adolescent personality." *Child Development*, 14 (#14):213–223.

———.1943b. "Infant rearing and problem behavior." *American Journal of Orthopsychiatry*, 13 (April):249–265.

———:1943c. "Effects of early institutional care on adolescent personality." *Journal of Experimental Education*, 12 (#12):106–129.

———.1944a. "Effects of early institutional care on adolescent personality· Rorschach data." *American Journal of Orthopsychiatry*, 14 (July):441–447.

———.1944b. "Infant rearing as a factor in foster home replacement." *American Journal of Orthopsychiatry*, 14 (January):162–173.

———.1945a. "Effects of psychological deprivation in infancy and subsequent stimulation." *American Journal of Psychiatry*, 102 (July):18–33.

———.1945b. "Psychological privation in infancy and subsequent adjustment." *American Journal of Orthopsychiatry*, 15 (April):247–255.

Goldman, N. 1963. *The Differential Selection of Juvenile Offenders for Court Appearance*. New York: National Council on Crime and Delinquency.

Goldstein, A. S. 1967. *The Insanity Defense*. New Haven, Conn.: Yale University Press.

Goode, W. J. 1956. *After Divorce.* Glencoe, Ill.: Free Press.
———.1960. "Illegitimacy in the Caribbean social structure." *American Sociological Review,* 25 (February):21–30.
———.1966. "Family disorganization." In R. K. Merton and R. A. Nisbet, (Eds.), *Contemporary Social Problems,* Second Edition. New York: Harcourt, Brace, and World.
———.1967. "The protection of the inept." *American Sociological Review,* 32 (February):5–19.
Goodman, P. 1956. *Growing Up Absurd.* New York: Random House.
Gorbanevskaya, N. 1972. *Red Star at Noon.* New York: Holt, Rinehart, and Winston, Inc.
Gough, H., and D. R. Peterson. 1952. "The identification and measurement of predispositional factors in crime and delinquency." *Journal of Consulting Psychology,* 16 (June):207–212.
Gove, W. R. 1970. "Societal reaction as an explanation of mental illness: An evaluation." *American Sociological Review,* 35 (October):873–884.
Graham, F. P. 1970. "Black crime: The lawless image." *Harper's Magazine,* 241 (September):64–78.
Gray, P. H. 1958. "Theory and evidence of imprinting in human infants." *Journal of Psychology,* 46 (July):155–166.
Green, E. 1970. "Race, social status, and criminal arrest." *American Sociological Review,* 35 (June):476–490.
Greenspoon, J. 1962. "Verbal conditioning and clinical psychology." In A. J. Bachrach, (Ed.), *Experimental Foundations of Clinical Psychology.* New York: Basic Books, Inc.
Gregory, I. 1965. "Anterospective data following childhood loss of a parent: Delinquency and high school dropout." *Archives of General Psychiatry,* 13 (August):99–109.
Grubb, W. N. 1971. Review of I. Berg, "Education and Jobs." *Harvard Educational Review,* 41 (November):580–583.
Haan, N. 1964. "The relationship of ego functioning and intelligence to social status and social mobility." *Journal of Abnormal and Social Psychology,* 69 (December):594–605.
Haber, R. N. 1970. "How we remember what we see." *Scientific American,* 222 (May):104–112.
Hacker, E. 1941. *Kriminalstatistische und Kriminalaetiologische Berichte.* Miskolc, Hungary: Ludwig.
Hackler, J. C. 1966. "Boys, blisters, and behavior: The impact of a work program in an urban central area." *Journal of Research in Crime and Delinquency,* 3 (July):155–164.
———and J. L. Hagan. 1972. "Work, programs, and teaching machines."

Edmonton: The University of Alberta, Department of Sociology. Mimeographed manuscript.

Hagan, J. L. 1972. "The labelling perspective, the delinquent, and the police: A review of the literature." *Canadian Journal of Criminology and Corrections,* 14 (April):150–165.

Hakeem, M. 1958. "A critique of the psychiatric approach to crime and correction." *Law and Contemporary Problems,* 23 (Autumn):650–682.

Hamilton, V. 1965. Review of H. J. Eysenck, "Crime and Personality." *British Journal of Social and Clinical Psychology,* 4 (June):159–160.

Hanson, R. H., and E. S. Marks. 1958. "Influence of the interviewer on the accuracy of survey results." *Journal of the American Statistical Association,* 53 (September):635–655.

Hardt, R. G., and G. E. Bodine. 1965. *Development of Self-Report Instruments in Delinquency Research: A Conference Report.* Syracuse, N.Y.: Youth Development Center, Syracuse University.

Harlow, H., and M. Harlow. 1967. "The young monkeys." *Psychology Today,* 1 (September):40–47.

Harris, L. 1968. *The Public Looks at Crime and Corrections.* Washington, D.C.: Joint Commission on Correctional Manpower and Training.

Harris, W. J. 1972. "The militant separatists in the white academy." *The American Scholar,* 41, (Summer):366–376.

Hartshorne, H., and M. A. May. 1928. *Studies in the Nature of Character.* New York: Macmillan.

Harvey, P. 1970. "Problems in Chinatown." *Human Events,* 30 (16 May):21.

Hassan, A. 1972. In E. Pell (Ed.), *Maximum Security: Letters from Prison.* New York: E. P. Dutton & Co., Inc.

Hathaway, S. R., and E. D. Monachesi. 1957. "The personalities of predelinquent boys." *Journal of Criminal Law, Criminology, and Police Science,* 48 (July-August):149–163.

Hayner, N. S. 1946. "Criminogenic zones in Mexico City." *American Sociological Review,* 11 (August):428–438.

Healy, W., and A. F. Bronner. 1936 *New Light on Delinquency and Its Treatment.* New Haven, Conn.: Yale University Press.

Henry, J. 1963. *Culture Against Man.* New York: Random House.

Herskovits, M. J. 1941. *The Myth of the Negro Past.* Boston: The Beacon Press.

Hess, E. H. 1959. "Imprinting." *Science,* 130 (July):133–141.

———.1972. "'Imprinting' in a natural laboratory." *Scientific American,*
    227 (August):24–31.
Hewitt, L. E., and R. L. Jenkins. 1946. *Fundamental Patterns of
    Maladjustment: The Dynamics of Their Origin.* Springfield, Ill.:
    State of Illinois.
Hirschi, T. 1969. *Causes of Delinquency.* Berkeley and Los Angeles:
    University of California Press.
Hodgkiss, M. 1933. "The influence of broken homes and working
    mothers." *Smith College Studies in Social Work,* 3 (March):259–
    274.
Hoffman, A. 1971. *Steal This Book.* New York: Pirate Editions.
Holz, W., and N. H. Azrin. 1962. "Interactions between the discrimina-
    tive and aversive properties of punishment." *Journal of Experi-
    mental Animal Behavior,* 5 (#2):229–234.
Honzik, M. P. 1966. "Prediction of behavior from birth to maturity." In J.
    Rosenblith and W. Allinsmith (Eds.), *The Causes of Behavior.*
    Second Edition. Boston: Allyn and Bacon.
Hooker, E. L. 1945. *The Houston Delinquent in His Community Setting.*
    Houston, Tex.: Research Bureau, Council of Social Agencies.
Houchon, G. 1967. "Les Mécanismes Criminogénes dans une Société
    Urbaine Africaine." *Revue Internationale Criminologie et de Police
    Technique,* 21:271–292.
Hoult, T. F. 1969. *Dictionary of Modern Sociology.* Totowa, N. J.:
    Littlefield, Adams & Company.
Hubbard, D. G. 1971. *The Skyjacker: His Flights of Fantasy.* New York:
    Macmillan and Company.
Hume, David. 1758. *An Inquiry Concerning Human Understanding.*
    Reprinted, 1957. New York: The Liberal Arts Press.
Huxley, A. 1960. Brave New World. New York: Harper and Brothers,
    Publishers.
Hyman, H. H. 1953. "The value systems of different classes." In R.
    Bendix and S. Lipset (Eds.), *Class, Status, and Power.* New York:
    The Free Press.
Institute of Public Administration. 1952. *Crime Records in Police Man-
    agement.* New York: Institute of Public Administration.
Introna, F. 1963. "Aspetti degenerativi e criminologici delle migrazioni
    interne." *La Scuola Positiva,* 5:668–692.
Jaspan, N. 1960. *The Thief in the White Collar.* Philadelphia: J. B.
    Lippincott Co.
———.1970. Interview. *U. S. News and World Report,* 69 (26 Octo-
    ber):32–33.
Jayasuriya, D. L. 1960. *A Study of Adolescent Ambition, Level of*

Aspiration and Achievement Motivation. London: University of London. Ph.D. Dissertation.

Jeffery, C. R. 1959. "An integrated theory of crime and criminal behavior." *Journal of Criminal Law, Criminology, and Police Science,* 49 (March-April):533–552.

Jenkins, W. W. 1958. "An experimental study of the relationship of legitimate and illegitimate birth status to school and personal and social adjustment of Negro children." *American Journal of Sociology,* 64 (September):169–173.

Johnson, G. B. 1970. "The Negro and crime." In M. E. Wolfgang et al. (Eds.), *The Sociology of Crime and Delinquency.* Second Edition. New York: John Wiley & Sons, Inc.

Johnson, R. C., et al. 1960. "Word values, word frequency, and visual duration thresholds." *Psychological Review,* 67 (September):332–342.

Jonassen, C. T. 1949. "A re-evaluation and critique of the logic and some methods of Shaw and McKay." *American Sociological Review,* 14 (October):608–617.

Jones, J. 1972. *Prejudice and Racism.* Reading, Mass.: Addison-Wesley.

Kadish, S. H. 1967. "The crisis of overcriminalization." *The Annals of the American Academy of Political and Social Science,* 374 (November):157–170.

Kaironen, V. A. 1966. *A Study of the Criminality of Finnish Immigrants in Sweden.* Strasbourg: Council of Europe.

Kaplan, R. M., and R. D. Singer. 1972. "Psychological effects of televised fantasy violence: A review of the literature." Riverside, Calif.: University of California, Department of Psychology. Mimeographed.

Karpman, B. 1948. *The Alcoholic Woman. Case Studies in the Psychodynamics of Alcoholism.* Washington, D. C.: Linacre Press.

Kelly, E. L. 1963. "Consistency of the adult personality." *American Psychologist,* 10 (November):659–681.

Kennedy, W. A., and H. C. Willcutt. 1964. "Praise and blame as incentives." *Psychological Bulletin,* 62 (November):323–332.

Kephart, W. M. 1957. *Racial Factors and Urban Law Enforcement.* Philadelphia: University of Pennsylvania Press.

Kesey, K. 1964. *One Flew Over the Cuckoo's Nest.* New York: Compass.

Kilson, M. 1971. "An American profile: The black student militant." *Encounter,* 37 (September):83–90.

Kinsey, A. C., et al. 1948. *Sexual Behavior in the Human Male.* Philadelphia: W. B. Saunders Company.

Kitano, H. H. L. 1967. "Japanese-American crime and delinquency." *Journal of Psychology,* 66 (July):253–263.

Kobler, J. 1972. *Capone.* London: Michael Joseph.

Kobrin, S. 1951. "The conflict of values in delinquency areas." *American Sociological Review,* 16 (October):653–661.

Kohn, M. L. 1959. "Social class and parental values." *American Journal of Sociology,* 64 (January):337–351.

———and C. Schooler. 1969. "Class, occupation, and orientation." *American Sociological Review,* 34 (October):659–678.

Krash, A. 1961. "The Durham rule and judicial administration of the insanity defense in the District of Columbia," *Yale Law Journal,* 70 (#6):905–906.

Kulik, J. A., et al. 1968. "Disclosure of delinquent behavior under conditions of anonymity and nonanonymity." *Journal of Consulting and Clinical Psychology,* 32 (October):506–509.

Kutschinsky, B. 1970. *Studies on Pornography and Sex Crimes in Denmark.* Copenhagen: New Social Science Monographs.

Lachenmeyer, C. W. 1971. *The Language of Sociology.* New York: Columbia University Press.

Lander, B. 1954. *Towards an Understanding of Juvenile Delinquency.* New York: Columbia University Press.

Langer, S. 1967. *Mind: An Essay on Human Feeling.* Baltimore: The Johns Hopkins Press.

Lefkowitz, M. M., et al. 1955. "Status Factors in pedestrian violation of traffic signals." *Journal of Abnormal and Social Psychology,* 51 (November):704–706.

Leifer, R. 1964. "The psychiatrist and tests of criminal responsibility." *American Psychologist,* 19 (November):825–830.

Lemert, E. M. 1951. *Social Pathology.* New York: McGraw-Hill Book Company.

———.1962. "Paranoia and the dynamics of exclusion." *Sociometry,* 25 (March):2–20.

———.1967. *Human Deviance, Social Problems and Social Control.* Englewood Cliffs, N. J.: Prentice-Hall.

LeShan, L. L. 1952. "Time orientation and social class." *Journal of Abnormal and Social Psychology,* 47 (July):589–592.

Levitt, E. E. 1957. "The results of psychotherapy with children: An evaluation." *Journal of Consulting Psychology,* 21 (June):189–196.

Lewis, C. S. 1953. "The humanitarian theory of punishment." *Res Judicatae,* 6 (June):224–230.

Lewis, O. 1959. *Five Families: Mexican Case Studies in the Culture of Poverty.* New York, Basic Books, 1959.

————.1961. *The Children of Sanchez: Autobiography of a Mexican Family.* New York, Random House.

Lichtenstein, F. E. 1950. "Studies of anxiety: I. The production of a feeding inhibition in dogs." *Journal of Comparative and Physiological Psychology,* 43 (#1):16–29.

Liebert, R. M., and R. A. Baron. 1972. "Some immediate effects of televised violence on children's behavior." *Developmental Psychology,* 6 (May):469–475.

Life. 1972. "Are you personally afraid of crime? Readers speak out." 72 (14 January):28–30.

Lind, A. W. 1930a. "Some ecological patterns of community disorganization in Honolulu." *American Journal of Sociology,* 36 (September):206–220.

————.1930b. "The ghetto and the slum." *Social Forces,* 9 (December):206–215.

Lindesmith, A. R., and A. L. Strauss. 1956. *Social Psychology.* New York: Rinehart, and Winston, Inc.

Lorber, J. 1967. "Deviance as performance: The case of illness." *Social Problems,* 14 (Winter):302–310.

Lorenz, K. Z. 1952. *King Solomon's Ring: New Light on Animal Ways.* London: Methuen & Co., Ltd.

Lottier, S. 1938. "Distribution of criminal offenses in metropolitan regions." *Journal of Criminal Law and Criminology,* 29 (May-June):37–50.

Lovaas, O. I. 1961. "Effect of exposure to symbolic aggression on aggressive behavior." *Child Development,* 32 (#3):37–44.

Lundberg, F. 1954. *The Treason of the People.* New York: Harper and Brothers.

Mack, J. A. 1964. "Full-time miscreants, delinquent neighbourhoods, and criminal networks." *British Journal of Sociology,* 15 (Mar.):38–53.

————.1972. "The able criminal." *British Journal of Criminology,* 12 (January):44–54.

Mackie, M. M. 1971. *The Accuracy of Folk Knowledge Concerning Alberta Indians, Hutterites and Ukrainians: An Available Data Stereotype Validation Technique.* Edmonton: The University of Alberta, Department of Sociology. Ph.D. dissertation.

————.1973. "Arriving at 'truth' by definition: The case of stereotype inaccuracy," *Social Problems,* 20 (Spring):431–447.

Maller, J. B. 1932. "Are broken homes a causative factor in juvenile delinquency? IV. Discussion." *Social Forces,* 10 (May):531–533.

Malloy, M. T. 1972. "Security means lifting the phone and saying: 'Operator, get me the rent-a-cops'." *The National Observer,* 11 (14 October):1, 18.

Mannheim, H. 1948. *Juvenile Delinquency in an English Middle Town.* London: K. Paul, Trench, & Trubner.

———.1965. *Comparative Criminology.* 2 Volumes. London: Routledge & Kegan Paul.

———and L. T. Wilkins. 1955. *Prediction Methods in Relation to Borstal Training.* London: Her Majesty's Stationery Office.

Masserman, J. M. 1943. *Behavior and Neurosis.* Chicago: University of Chicago Press.

Maxwell, N. 1972. "Passing judgment: How little town reacts when banker is accused of taking $4.7 million." *The Wall Street Journal,* 82 (8 August):1, 14.

Mayer, A. J. 1972a. "Men working: Builders seek to end the ancient tradition of on-the-job larcenies." *The Wall Street Journal,* 86 (19 June):1, 12.

———.1972b. "What price justice? States face a choice: Make punishment mild or bolster legal aid." *The Wall Street Journal,* 86 (26 June):1, 14.

McCandless, B. R., et al. 1972. "Perceived opportunity, delinquency, race, and body build among delinquent youth." *Journal of Consulting and Clinical Psychology,* 38 (April):281–287.

McClintock, F. H. 1963. *Crimes of Violence.* London: Macmillan.

———and N. H. Avison, 1968. *Crime in England and Wales.* London: Heinemann Educational Books, Ltd.

———and E. Gibson. 1961. *Robbery in London.* London: MacMillan.

McCord, W., and J. McCord. 1959. *Origins of Crime: A New Evaluation of the Cambridge-Somerville Youth Study.* New York: Columbia University Press.

McDonald, L. 1969a. "Crime and punishment in Canada: A statistical test of the 'conventional wisdom'." Canadian *Review of Sociology and Anthropology,* 6 (November):212–236.

———.1969b. *Social Class and Delinquency.* London: and Faber.

McEachern, A. W., and R. Bauzer. 1967. "Factors related to disposition in juvenile police contacts." In M. W. Klein, (Ed.), *Juvenile Gangs in Context: Theory, Research, and Action.* Englewood Cliffs, N. J.: Prentice-Hall, Inc.

McEvoy, F. P. 1941. "The lie-detector goes into business." *Reader's Digest,* 38 (February):69–72.

McIntosh, M. 1971. "Changes in the organization of thieving." In S. Cohen, (Ed.), *Images of Deviance.* Baltimore: Penguin Books, Inc.

McIntyre, J. 1967. "Public attitudes toward crime and law enforcement."

Annals of the American Academy of Political and Social Science, 374 (November):34–36.

McWhirter, N., and R. McWhirter. (Eds.). 1966. *The Guinness Book of Records.* London: Guinness Superlatives, Ltd.

Medinnus, G. R. 1965. "Delinquents' perceptions of their parents." *Journal of Consulting Psychology,* 29 (December):592–593.

Medvedev, Zh. 1971. *A Question of Madness.* New York: A Knopf, Inc.

Meehl, P. E. 1954. *Clinical versus Statistical Prediction.* Minneapolis: University of Minneapolis Press.

Mehlman, B. 1952. "The reliability of psychiatric diagnosis." *Journal of Abnormal and Social Psychology,* 47 (April):577–578.

Mercer, J. R. 1965. "Social system perspective and clinical perspective: Frames of reference for understanding career patterns of persons labelled as mentally retarded." *Social Problems,* 13 (Summer):18–34.

Merrill, M. A. 1947. *Problems of Child Delinquency.* Boston: Houghton Mifflin.

Merritt, C. B., and E. G. Fowler. 1948. "The pecuniary honesty of the public at large." *Journal of Abnormal and Social Psychology,* 43 (January):90–93.

Merton, R. K. 1957. *Social Theory and Social Structure.* Revised Edition. Glencoe, Ill.: Free Press.

Metzger, L. P. 1971. "American sociology and black assimilation: Conflicting perspectives." *American Journal of Sociology,* 76 (January):627–647.

Michaels, J. J. 1955. *Disorders of Character.* Springfield, Ill.: C. C. Thomas.

Micklin, M., and M. Durbin. 1968. "Syntactic dimensions of attitude scaling techniques: Sources of variation and bias." Paper read at the annual meeting of the American Sociological Association, Boston, Mass.

Miller, N. E. 1969. "Learning of visceral and glandular responses." *Science,* 163 (31 January):434–445.

Miller, W. B. 1958. "Lower class culture as a generating milieu of gang delinquency." *Journal of Social Issues,* 14 (#3):5–19.

———.1967. "Theft behavior in city gangs." In M. W. Klein (Ed.), *Juvenile Gangs in Context: Theory, Research, and Action.* Englewood Cliffs, N. J.: Prentice-Hall, Inc.

Minear, R. 1972. *Victors' Justice: The Tokyo War Crimes Trial.* Princeton, N. J.: Princeton University Press.

Mischel, W. 1961. "Preference for delayed reinforcement and social responsibility." *Journal of Abnormal and Social Psychology*, 62 (January):1–7.

———.1969. "Continuity and change in personality." *American Psychologist*, 24 (November):1012–1018.

Mitchell, G. D. 1968. *A Dictionary of Sociology*. London: Routledge & Kegan Paul.

Molotch, H. 1969. "Racial integration in a transition community." *American Sociological Review*, 34 (December):878–893.

Monahan, T. 1957. "Family status and the delinquent child: A reappraisal and some new findings." *Social Forces*, 35 (March):250–258.

Morgenstern, O. 1963. *On the Accuracy of Economic Observations*. Princeton: Princeton University Press.

Moore, B. 1954. *Terror and Progress in the USSR*. Cambridge: Harvard University Press.

Morris, C. W. 1956. *Varieties of Human Value*. Chicago: University of Chicago Press.

———and L. Small. 1971. "Changes in conceptions of the good life by American college students from 1950 to 1970." *Journal of Personality and Social Psychology*, 20 (November):254–260.

Morris, T. P. 1957. *The Criminal Area: A Study in Social Ecology*. London: Routledge & Kegan Paul.

Moses, E. R. 1970. "Negro and white crime rates." In M. E. Wolfgang et al., (Eds.), *The Sociology of Crime and Delinquency*, Second Edition. New York: John Wiley & Sons, Inc.

Moss, R. 1972. *Urban Guerrillas*. London: Temple Smith.

Moynihan, D. P. 1965. *The Negro Family: The Case for National Action*. Washington, D. C.,: U. S. Department of Labor.

———.1969. *Maximum Feasible Misunderstanding: Community Action in the War on Poverty*. New York: The Free Press.

Mudge, E. M. 1967. *Bank Robbery in California: A 35-Year Comparison with The Rest of the United States and an Intensive Study of 1965 Offenses*. Sacramento, Calif.: Criminal Statistics Bureau.

Murphy, F. J., et al. 1946. "The incidence of hidden delinquency." *American Journal of Orthopsychiatry*, 16 (October):686–695.

Mylonas, A. D., and W. C. Reckless. 1963. "Prisoners' attitudes toward law and legal institutions." *Journal of Criminal Law, Criminology, and Police Science*, 54 (December):479–484.

The National Observer. 1971. "Women attack rape justice." 10 (9 October):1, 21.

Nettler, G. 1957. "A measure of alienation," *American Sociological Review*, 22 (December):670–677.

———.1959a. "Antisocial sentiment and criminality." *American Sociological Review*, 24 (April):202–218.

————.1959b. "Cruelty, dignity, and determinism." *American Sociological Review*, 24 (June):375–384.

————.1961. "Good men, bad men, and the perception of reality." *Sociometry*, 24 (September):279–294.

————.1968. Review, "The subculture of violence." *Social Forces*, 46 (March):427–428.

————.1970. *Explanations*. New York: McGraw-Hill Book Company.

————.1972a. "Shifting the load." *American Behavioral Scientist*, 15 (January-February):361–379.

————.1972b. "Knowing and doing." *The American Sociologist*, 7 (February):3–7.

Neumann, K. 1963. *Die Kriminalität der italienischen Arbeitskräfte im Kanton Zürich*. Zurich: Juris Verlag.

Newsweek. 1971. "The public: A hard line." 77 (8 March):39–45.

————.1972. "The booksellers' ball." 79 (26 June):86–88.

————.1973. "Sexploitation: Sin's Wages," 81 (12 February):78–79.

Normandeau, A. 1969. "Trends in robbery as reflected by different indexes." In T. Sellin and M. E. Wolfgang (Eds.), *Delinquency: Selected Studies*. New York: John Wiley & Sons, Inc.

Novak, M. 1972. *The Rise of the Unmeltable Ethnics*. New York: Macmillan.

Nuckols, R. C. 1949–1950. "Verbi!" *International Journal of Opinion and Attitude Research*, 3 (Winter):575–586.

Nye, F. I. 1957. "Child adjustment in broken and unhappy unbroken homes." *Journal of Marriage and Family Living*, 19 (November):366–361.

————and J. F. Short, Jr. 1957. "Scaling delinquent behavior." *American Sociological Review*, 22 (June):326–331.

Ortega y Gasset, J. 1932. *The Revolt of the Masses*. New York: W. W. Norton & Co.

————.1946. *Concord and Liberty*. New York: W. W. Norton, Inc.

Packer, H. L. 1968. *The Limits of the Criminal Sanction*. Stanford: Stanford University Press.

Pantaleone, M. 1966. *The Mafia and Politics*. London: Chatto & Windus.

Paranjape, W. 1970. *Some Aspects of Probation: An Exploration of Labelling Theory in Six Urban Junior High Schools*. Edmonton: The University of Alberta, Department of Sociology. M. A. Thesis.

Petersen, W. 1967. "Family structure and social mobility among Japanese Americans." *Abstracts*, American Sociological Association: 119–20.

————.1969. *Population*. Second Edition. New York: The Macmillan Company.

Peterson, D. R., et al. 1959. "Personality and background factors in

juvenile delinquency as inferred from questionnaire responses."
Journal of Consulting Psychology, 23 (October):395–399.
———and W. C. Becker. 1965. "Family interaction and delinquency." In
H. C. Quay, (Ed.), *Juvenile Delinquency.* Princeton: D. Van
Nostrand, Inc.
Peterson, J. 1972. "Thunder out of Chinatown." *The National Observer,*
11 (8 March):1, 18.
Petrie, A. 1967. *Individuality in Pain and Suffering.* Chicago: The
University of Chicago Press.
Piliavin, I., and S. Briar. 1964. "Police encounters with juveniles."
American Journal of Sociology, 70 (September):206–214.
Pittman, D. J., and C. W. Gordon. 1958. *Revolving Door: A Study of the
Chronic Police Case Inebriate.* Glencoe, Ill.: The Free Press.
Plog, S. C., and R. B. Edgerton (Eds.). 1969. *Changing Perspectives in
Mental Illness.* New York: Holt, Rinehart, and Winston, Inc.
Pokorny, A. D. 1965. "A comparison of homicides in two cities." *Journal
of Criminal Law, Criminology and Police Science,* 56 (December):479–487.
Pollak, O. 1951. *The Criminality of Women.* Philadelphia: The University
of Pennsylvania Press.
Pope, A. 1731–1735. "Moral Essays." In H. Davis, (Ed.), *Poetical Works,*
1966. London: Oxford University Press.
Porterfield, A. L. 1943. "Delinquency and its outcome in court and
college." *American Journal of Sociology,* 49 (November):199–208.
———.1946. *Youth in Trouble.* Austin, Tex.: Leo Potishman Foundation.
Porteus, S. D. 1961. "Ethnic group differences." *Mankind Quarterly,* 1
(January):#4.
Power, M. J., et al. 1972. "Neighborhood, school and juveniles before the
courts." *The British Journal of Criminology,* 12 (April):111–132.
Premack, A. J., and D. Premack. 1972. "Teaching language to an ape."
Scientific American, 227 (October):92–99.
President's Commission on Law Enforcement and the Administration of
Justice. 1967a. *The Challenge of Crime in a Free Society.* Washington, D. C.: U. S. Government Printing Office.
———.1967b. *Crime and Its Impact—An Assessment.* Washington, D. C.:
U. S. Government Printing Office.
———.1967c. *Task Force Report: Drunkenness.* Washington, D. C.: U. S.
Government Printing Office.
Price, J. E. 1966. "A test of the accuracy of criminal statistics." *Social
Problems,* 14 (Fall):214–222.
Quay, H. C., et al. 1960. "The interpretation of three personality factors

in juvenile delinquency." *Journal of Consulting Psychology,* 24 (December):555.

Rader, D. 1971. Review of "Steal This Book." *New York Times Book Review,* 120 (18 July):19.

Radzinowics, L. 1946. "Criminality by size of communities." London: University of London. Unpublished manuscript.

Reckless, W. C. 1967. *The Crime Problem.* Fourth Edition. New York: Appleton-Century-Crofts.

Reichard, G. A. 1938. "Social life." In F. Boas (Ed.), *General Anthropology.* Boston: D. C. Heath & Co.

Reiss, A. J., Jr., and A. L. Rhodes. 1961. "The distribution of juvenile delinquency in the social class structure." *American Sociological Review,* 26 (October):720–732.

Rice, S. A. 1928. *Quantitative Methods in Politics.* New York: Alfred A. Knopf, Inc.

Rieff, P. 1959. *Freud: The Mind of the Moralist.* New York: The Viking Press.

Riis, R. W. 1941a. "The repair man will gyp you if you don't watch out." *Reader's Digest,* 39 (July):1–6.

————.1941b. "The radio repair man will gyp you if you don't watch out." *Reader's Digest,* 39 (August):6–13.

————.1941c. "The watch repair man will gyp you if you don't watch out." *Reader's Digest,* 39 (September):10–12.

Rivera, R. J., and J. F. Short, Jr. 1967. "Occupational goals: A comparative analysis." In M. W. Klein (Ed.), *Juvenile Gangs in Context: Theory, Research, and Action.* Englewood Cliffs, N. J.: Prentice-Hall, Inc.

Robins, L. N., and P. O'Neal. 1958. "Mortality, mobility, and crime." *American Sociological Review,* 23 (April):162–171.

Robinson, J. P. 1970. "Public reaction to political protest: Chicago, 1968." *Public Opinion Quarterly,* 34 (Spring):1–9.

Roff, M. 1961. "Childhood social interaction and young adult bad conduct." *Journal of Abnormal and Social Psychology,* 63 (Sept.):333–337.

Rohrer, J. H., and M. S. Edmonson (Eds.). 1960. *Eighth Generation: Cultures and Personalities of New Orleans Negroes.* New York: Harper & Brothers.

Rose, A. 1962. "A systematic summary of symbolic interaction theory." In A. Rose (Ed.), *Human Behavior and Social Processes.* Boston: Houghton Mifflin Company.

Rosekrans, M. A. 1967. "Imitation in children as a function of perceived similarity to a social model and vicarious reinforcement." *Journal of Personality and Social Psychology,* 7 (November):307–315.

Rosenquist, C. M., and E. I. Megargee. 1969. *Delinquency in Three Cultures.* Austin, Texas: University of Texas Press.

Rosenthal, D. 1970. *Genetic Theory and Abnormal Behavior.* New York: McGraw-Hill Book Company.

Rossi, P. H. 1971. "The city as purgatory." *Social Science Quarterly,* 51 (March):817–820.

Rothstein, E. 1961. *An Analysis of Status Images as Perception Variables Between Delinquent and Non-Delinquent Boys.* New York: New York University. Ph.D. Dissertation.

Royal Commission. 1955. *Report of the Royal Commission on Law of Insanity as a Defence in Criminal Cases.* Ottawa: Queen's Printer and Controller of Stationery.

Rugg, D., and H. Cantril. 1942. "The wording of questions in public opinion polls." *Journal of Abnormal and Social Psychology,* 37 (October):469–495.

Ryan, E. D., and R. Foster. 1967. "Athletic participation and perceptual augmentation and reduction." *Journal of Personality and Social Psychology,* 6 (August):472–476.

———and C. R. Kovacic. 1966. "Pain tolerance and athletic participation." *Perceptual and Motor Skills,* 22 (April):383–390.

Salem, R. G., and W. J. Bowers. 1970. "Severity of formal sanctions as a deterrent to deviant behavior." *Law and Society Review,* 5 (August):21–40.

Savitz, L. 1967. *Dilemmas in Criminology.* New York: McGraw-Hill Book Company.

Schaefer, E. S., and N. Bayley. 1960. "Consistency of maternal behavior from infancy to preadolescence." *Journal of Abnormal and Social Psychology,* 61 (July):1–6.

Scheff, T. J. 1966. *Being Mentally Ill.* Chicago: Aldine.

Schelling, T. C. 1967. "Economics and criminal enterprise." *The Public Interest,* 7 (Spring):61–78.

Schiffman, H., and R. Wynne. 1963. "Cause and Affect." Princeton: Educational Testing Service, RM-63-7 (July).

Schmid, C. F. 1960. "Urban crime areas: Part II," *American Sociological Review,* 25 (October):655–678.

———and S. E. Schmid. 1972. *Crime in the State of Washington.* Olympia, Wash.: Washington State Planning and Community Affairs Agency.

Schmidt, H. O., and C. P. Fonda. 1956. "The reliability of psychiatric diagnosis: A new look," *Journal of Abnormal and Social Psychology,* 52 (March):262–267.

Schoeck, H. 1966. *Envy: A Theory of Social Behavior.* New York: Harcourt, Brace, and World, Inc.

Schuessler, K. F. 1962. "Components of variations in city crime rates." *Social Problems,* 9 (Spring):314–323.

Schultz, H. D. 1972. *Panics and Crashes.* New Rochelle, N. Y.: Arlington House.

Schur, E. M. 1965. *Crimes Without Victims: Deviant Behavior and Public Policy.* Englewood Cliffs, N. J.: Prentice-Hall, Inc.

————.1971. *Labeling Deviant Behavior: Its Sociological Implications.* New York: Harper and Row, Publishers.

Schwendinger, H. 1963. *The Instrumental Theory of Delinquency.* Los Angeles: University of California, Department of Sociology. Ph.D. dissertation.

————and J. Schwendinger. 1967 "Delinquent stereotypes of probable victims." In M. W. Klein (Ed.), *Juvenile Gangs in Context: Theory, Research, and Action.* Englewood Cliffs, N.J.: Prentice-Hall, Inc.

Scott, R. A. 1969. *The Making of Blind Men.* New York: Russell Sage.

Sellin, T. 1938. *Culture Conflict and Crime.* New York: Social Science Research Council. Bulletin #41.

————.1958. "Recidivism and maturation." *National Probation and Parole Association Journal,* 4 (July):241–250.

————and M. E. Wolfgang. 1964. *The Measurement of Delinquency.* New York: John Wiley & Sons, Inc.

———— and ————(Eds.). 1969. *Delinquency: Selected Studies.* John Wiley & Sons, Inc.

Sewell, W. H. et al., 1969. "The educational and early occupational attainment process." *American Sociological Review,* 34 (February):82–92.

Shaw, C. R., and H. D. McKay, 1931. "Social factors in juvenile delinquency." National Commission on Law Observance and Enforcement, *Report on the Causes of Crime.* No. 13. Washington, D. C.: U. S. Government Printing Office.

———— and ————.1942. *Juvenile Delinquency and Urban Areas.* Chicago: University of Chicago Press.

Sheldon, W. H. 1949. *Varieties of Delinquent Youth: An Introduction to Constitutional Psychiatry.* New York: Harper & Brothers.

Sheth, H. 1961. *Juvenile Delinquency in an Indian Setting.* Bombay: Popular Book Depot.

Shoham, S. 1966. *Crime and Social Deviation*. Chicago: Henry Regnery Company.

Shulman, H. M. 1929. *A Study of Problem Boys and Their Brothers*. Albany: New York State Crime Commission.

————.1959. "The family and juvenile delinquency." In S. Glueck (Ed.), *The Problem of Delinquency*. Boston: Houghton Mifflin Company.

Shumate, R. P. 1958. *Effect of Increased Patrol on Accidents, Diversion, and Speed*. Evanston, Ill.: Northwestern University, Traffic Institute.

Siegel, A. E. 1956. "Film mediated fantasy aggression and strength of aggressive drive." *Child Development*, 27 (September):365–378.

Siegman, A. W. 1966a. "Father absence during early childhood and antisocial behavior." *Journal of Abnormal and Social Psychology*, 71 (February):71–74.

————.1966b. "Effects of auditory stimulation and intelligence on time estimation in delinquents and nondelinquents." *Journal of Consulting Psychology*, 30 (August):320–328.

Simon, R. J., and W. Shackelford. 1965. "The defense of insanity: A survey of legal and psychiatric opinion." *Public Opinion Quarterly*, 29 (Fall):411–430.

Sluckin, W. 1965. *Imprinting and Early Learning*. Chicago: Aldine.

Smigel, E. O., and H. L. Ross (Eds.). 1970. *Crimes Against Bureaucracy*. New York: Van Nostrand Reinhold Company.

Smith, H. L., and H. Hyman. 1950. "The biasing effect of interviewer expectations on survey results." *Public Opinion Quarterly*, 14 (Fall):491–506.

Smith, K. J. 1965. *A Cure for Crime*. London: Duckworth.

Smith, R. A. 1961. "The incredible electrical conspiracy." *Fortune*, 63 (April):132–137 and *passim;* (May):161–164 and *passim.*

Soares, L. M., and A. T. Soares. 1969. "Social learning and social violence." *Proceedings*, 77th Annual Convention of the American Psychological Association. Washington, D. C.: American Psychological Association.

———— and ————.1970. "Social learning and disruptive social behavior." *Phi Delta Kappan*, (October):82–84.

Solhaug, M. L. 1972. "Accuracy of 'bad men' stereotypes: A comparison of autostereotyping by lawbreakers with stereotyping by more lawful others." Edmonton: The University of Alberta, Department of Sociology. M.A. thesis prospectus.

Sollenberger, R. T. 1968. "Chinese-American child rearing practices and juvenile delinquency." *The Journal of Social Psychology*, 74 (February):13–23.

Solomon, R. L. 1964. "Punishment." *American Psychologist,* 19 (April):239–253.

Sontag, L. W. 1963. "Somatopsychics of personality and body function." *Vita Humana,* 6 (Nos. 1-2):1–10.

Sorel, G. 1908. *Reflections on Violence.* Reprinted 1950. Glencoe, Ill.: The Free Press.

Sorokin, P. A. 1959. *Social and Cultural Mobility.* Glencoe, Ill.: The Free Press.

Spinley, B. M. 1964. *The Deprived and the Privileged.* London: Routledge & Kegan Paul.

Spitz, R. A. 1946. "Hospitalism: A follow-up report." In R. S. Eissler et al. (Eds.), *The Psychoanalytic Study of the Child.* Volume 2. New York: International Universities Press.

Srole, L., et al. 1962. *Mental Health in the Metropolis: The Midtown Manhattan Study.* Volume 1. New York: McGraw-Hill Book Company.

Staats, A. W. 1968. *Learning, Language, and Cognition.* New York: Holt, Rinehart, and Winston, Inc.

Staats, C. K., and A. W. Staats. 1957. "Meaning established by classical conditioning." *Journal of Experimental Psychology,* 54 (July):74–80.

Stacey, B. G. 1965. "Some psychological aspects of inter-generation occupational mobility." *British Journal of Social and Clinical Psychology,* 4 (December):275–286.

Stein, A. H., et al. 1971. "Television content and young children's behavior." In J. P. Murray et al. (Eds.), *Television and Social Behavior.* Volume 2. *Television and Social Learning.* Washington, D. C.: United States Government Printing Office.

Stein, K. B., et al. 1968. "Future time perspective: Its relation to the socialization process and the delinquent role." *Journal of Consulting and Clinical Psychology,* 32 (June):257–264.

Stember, H., and H. Hyman. 1949–1950. "How interviewer effects operate through question form." *International Journal of Opinion and Attitude Research,* 3 (Winter):493–512.

Stephenson, R. M., and F. R. Scarpitti. 1968. "Negro-white differentials and delinquency." *Journal of Research in Crime and Delinquency,* 5 (July):122–133.

Stinchcombe, A. L. 1964. *Rebellion in a High School.* Chicago: Quadrangle Books.

Stott, D. H. 1966. *Studies of Troublesome Children.* London: Tavistock Publications.

Straus, M. A. 1962. "Deferred gratification, social class, and the achievement syndrome." *American Sociological Review*, 27 (June):326–335.

Sudnow, D. 1966. *Passing On*. Englewood Cliffs, N. J.: Prentice-Hall.

Surgeon General's Scientific Advisory Committee on Television and Social Behavior. 1972. *Television and Growing Up: The Impact of Televised Violence*. Washington, D. C.: U. S. Government Printing Office.

Sussman, F. B. 1959. *Law of Juvenile Delinquency*. Revised Edition. New York: Oceana Publications, Inc.

Sutherland, E. H., and D. R. Cressey. 1970. *Criminology*. Eighth Edition. Philadelphia: J. B. Lippincott Company.

Sveri, K. 1960. *Kriminalitet og Older*. Stockholm: Almquist and Wiksell.

Szasz, T. S. 1957. "Commitment of the mentally ill: 'Treatment' or social restraint?" *Journal of Nervous and Mental Disease*, 125 (April-June):293.

————.1958. "Politics and mental health: Some remarks apropos of the case of Mr. Ezra Pound." *American Journal of Psychiatry*, 115 (December):508.

———— .1961. *The Myth of Mental Illness: Foundations of a Theory of Personal Conduct*. New York: Paul B. Hoeber, Inc.

————.1963. *Law, Liberty, and Psychiatry: An Inquiry into the Social Use of Mental Health Practices*. New York: The Macmillan Company.

Taft, D. R. 1946. "The punishment of war criminals." *American Sociological Review*, 11 (August):439–444.

Tannenbaum, F. 1938. *Crime and the Community*. Boston: Ginn and Company.

Tappan, P. W. 1947. "Who is the criminal?" *American Sociological Review*, 12 (February):96–102.

Teele, J. E., et al. 1966. "Teacher ratings, sociometric status, and choice-reciprocity of anti-social and normal boys." *Group Psychotherapy*, 19 (September-December):183–197.

Terman, L. M., and M. H. Oden. 1947. *Genetic Studies of Genius, IV. The Gifted Child Grows Up*. Stanford, Calif.: Stanford University Press.

———— and ————.1955. *Genetic Studies of Genius, V. The Gifted Group at Mid-Life*. Stanford, Calif.: Stanford University Press.

Terry, R. M. 1967. "Discrimination in the handling of juvenile offenders by social-control agencies." *Journal of Research in Crime and Delinquency*, 4 (July):218–230.

Theis, S. van S. 1924. *How Foster Children Turn Out.* NewYork: State Charities Aid Association.

Thomas, A. E. 1972. "Community power and student rights." *Harvard Educational Review,* 42 (May):173–216.

Thomas, A., et al. 1970. "The origin of personality." *Scientific American,* 223 (August):102–109.

Thomas, W. I. 1923. *The Unadjusted Girl.* Boston: Little, Brown and Company.

Thompson, G. G., and C. W. Hunnicutt. 1944. "The effect of repeated praise or blame on the work achievement of 'introverts' and 'extroverts'," *Journal of Educational Psychology,* 35 (May):257–266.

Thompson, H. S. 1966. *Hell's Angels: A Strange and Terrible Saga.* New York: Random House.

Thompson, P. G. 1971. "Some factors in upward social mobility in England." *Sociology and Social Research,* 55 (January):181–190.

Thurstone, L. L. 1927. "Method of paired comparisons for social values." *Journal of Abnormal and Social Psychology,* 21 (January):384–400.

Time. 1964. "To catch a thief." 84 (2 October):14.

————.1968. "The thin blue line." 92 (19 July):39.

————.1972a. "Con-man of the year: The fabulous hoax of Clifford Irving." 99 (21 February):16–25.

————.1972b. "Time citizens panel: The sour, frustrated and volatile voters." 99 (8 May):22–23.

Tittle, C. R. 1969. "Crime rates and legal sanctions." *Social Problems,* 16 (Spring):409–423.

Toby, J. 1950. "Comment on the Jonassen-Shaw and McKay controversy." *American Sociological Review,* 15 (February):107–108.

————.1957. "The differential impact of family disorganization." *American Sociological Review,* 22 (October):505–512.

————.1969. "Affluence and adolescent crime." In D. R. Cressey and D. A. Ward (Eds.), *Delinquency, Crime, and Social Process.* New York: Harper & Row, Publishers.

Toro-Calder, J., et al. 1968. "A comparative study of Puerto Rican attitudes toward the legal system dealing with crime." *Journal of Criminal Law, Criminology, and Police Science,* 59 (December):536–541.

Trasler, G. 1962. *The Explanation of Criminality.* London: Routledge & Kegan Paul.

Tryon, R. C. 1967. "Predicting group differences in cluster analysis: The social area problem." *Multivariate Behavioral Research,* 2 (October):453–476.

Turner, R. H. 1969. "The public perception of protest." *American Sociological Review,* 34 (December):815–831.

———.1972. "Deviance avowal as neutralization of commitment." *Social Problems,* 19 (Winter):308–321.

Turner, S. 1969. "The ecology of delinquency." In T. Sellin and M. E. Wolfgang (Eds.), *Delinquency: Selected Studies.* New York: John Wiley & Sons, Inc.

United Nations. 1953. *Comparative Survey on Juvenile Delinquency.* Part V: Asia and the Far East. New York: United Nations.

———.1958a. *Comparative Survey of Juvenile Delinquency. Part I: North America.* New York: United Nations.

———.1958b. *Estudio Comparado Sobre Delinquencia Juvenil. Parte III. America Latina.* New York: United Nations.

———.1960. *Second United Nations Congress on the Prevention of Crime and the Treatment of Offenders.* Report Prepared by the Secretariat. New York: United Nations, Department of Economic and Social Affairs.

———.1965a. *Third United Nations Congress on the Prevention of Crime and the Treatment of Offenders.* Report Prepared by the Secretariat. New York: United Nations, Department of Economic and Social Affairs.

———.1965b. *Comparative Survey on Juvenile Delinquency.* Part V: Middle East. New York: United Nations.

———.1970. *Demographic Yearbook 1969.* New York: Statistical Office of the United Nations.

U. S. Department of Health, Education and Welfare. 1963. *Illegitimate Births: United States, 1938-1957.* Washington, D. C.: U. S. Government Printing Office.

U. S. Department of Transportation. 1971. *Department of Transportation News.* (26 July). Washington, D. C.: U. S. Government Printing Office.

U. S. News & World Report. 1970a. "Why streets are not safe: Special report on crime." 68 (16 March):15–21.

———.1970b. "U. S. faces 'choice between anarchy and repression'." 68 (15 June):45–46.

———.1970c. "Growing concern over 'crisis in morality'." 68 (29 June):56–60.

———.1970d. "What's bothering Americans: A nationwide survey." 69 (5 October):32–36.

————.1970e."Booming industry—Home safeguards." 69 (26 October):35.

————.1970f. "Crime expense now up to 51 billions a year." 69 (26 October):30–34.

————.1972. "Newsgram." (21 August):8.

Van den Haag, E. 1968. "On deterrence and the death penalty." *Ethics,* 78 (July):280–288.

Vandivier, K. 1972. "The aircraft brake scandal." *Harper's Magazine,* 244 (April):45–52.

Vislick-Young, P. 1930. "Urbanization as a factor in juvenile delinquency." *Publications of the American Sociological Society,* 24 (May):162–166.

Voss, H. L. 1963. "Ethnic differentials in delinquency in Honolulu." *Journal of Criminal Law, Criminology, and Police Science,* 54 (September):322–327.

————.1966. "Socioeconomic status and reported delinquent behavior." *Social Problems,* 13 (Winter):314–324.

Waldfogel, S. 1948. "The frequency and affective character of childhood memories." *Psychological Monographs,* 62 (#4):1–39.

Waldo, G. P., and T. G. Chiricos. 1972. "Perceived penal sanction and self-reported criminality: A neglected approach to deterrence research." *Social Problems,* 19 (Spring):522–540.

Walker, N. 1971. *Crimes, Courts and Figures: An Introduction to Criminal Statistics.* Harmondsworth, England: Penguin Books Ltd.

Wall Street Journal. 1972. "And somebody stole our carpet and chairs." 86 (19 June):12.

Wallerstein, J. A., and C. J. Wyle. 1947. "Our law-abiding law-breakers. " *Federal Probation,* 25 (April):107–112.

Wallis, C. P., and R. Maliphant. 1967. "Delinquent areas in the county of London: Ecological factors." *British Journal of Criminology,* 7 (July):250–284.

Walters, R. H. 1967. "Nurturance and the intensity and timing of punishment." Public Lecture. Edmonton: The University of Alberta.

————and L. Demkow. 1963. "Timing of punishment as a determinant of response inhibition." *Child Development,* 34 (#1):207–214.

————et al. 1962. "Enhancement of punitive behavior by audio-visual displays." *Science,* 136 (June):872–873.

————et al. 1965. "Timing of punishment and the observation of consequences to others as determinants of response inhibition." *Journal of Experimental Child Psychology,* 2 (March):10–30.

Ward, R. H. 1971. "The labeling theory: A critical analysis." *Criminology*, 9 (August-November):268–290.

Warner, W. L. 1953. *American Life: Dream and Reality*. Chicago: University of Chicago Press.

———and J. Abegglen. 1955. *Big Business Leaders in America*. New York: Harper & Bros.

———and P. S. Lunt. 1941. *The Social Life of a Modern Community*. New Haven: Yale University Press.

Weiner, N. L., and C. V. Willie. 1971. "Decision by juvenile officers." *American Journal of Sociology*, 77 (September):199–210.

Weissman, H. H. (Ed.) 1969. *Justice and the Law in the Mobilization for Youth Experience*. New York: Association Press.

Wertheimer, M. 1955. "Figural aftereffect as a measure of metabolic deficiency." *Journal of Personality*, 24 (September):56–73.

West, D. J. 1969. *Present Conduct and Future Delinquency*. London: Heinemann Educational Books Ltd.

Wheeler, S., et al., 1968. "Agents of delinquency control: A comparative analysis." In S. Wheeler (Ed.), *Controlling Delinquents*. New York: John Wiley & Sons, Inc.

Whiting, J. W. M., and I. L. Child. 1953. *Child Training and Personality*. New Haven: Yale University Press.

Wiers, P. 1939. "Juvenile delinquency in rural Michigan." *Journal of Criminal Law and Criminology*, 30 (July-August):148–157.

Wilensky, H. L. 1964. "Mass society and mass culture: Interdependence or dependence?" *American Sociological Review*, 29 (April):173–197.

Williams, H. D. 1933. "A survey of pre-delinquent children in ten middle western cities." *Journal of Juvenile Research*, 17 (July-October):163–174.

Willie, C. V., and A. Gershenovitz. 1964. "Juvenile delinquency in racially mixed areas." *American Sociological Review*, 29 (October):740–744.

Willing, M. K. 1971. *Beyond Conception: Our Children's Children*. Boston: Gambit, Inc.

Wilson, J. Q. 1968. "The police and the delinquent in two cities." In S. Wheeler (Ed.), *Controlling Delinquents*. New York: John Wiley & Sons, Inc.

———et al. 1972. "The problem of heroin." *The Public Interest*, #29 (Fall):3–28.

Wirth, L. 1929. *The Ghetto*. Chicago: The University of Chicago Press.

Witkin. H. 1965. "Psychological differentiation and forms of pathology." *Journal of Abnormal Psychology*, 70 (October):317–336.

————et al. 1962. *Psychological Differentiation.* New York: John Wiley & Sons, Inc.

Wolf, P. 1962. "Crime and social class in Denmark," *British Journal of Criminology,* 13 (July):5–17.

————.1965. "A contribution to the topology of crime in Denmark." In K. O. Christiansen et al. (Eds.), *Scandinavian Studies in Criminology.* Volume One. London: Tavistock Publications.

Wolfgang, M. E. 1958. *Patterns in Criminal Homicide.* Philadelphia: University of Pennsylvania Press.

———— 1966. "Race and crime." In H. J. Sklare (Ed.), *Changing Concepts of Crime and Its Treatment.* London: Pergamon.

————and F. Ferracuti. 1967. *The Subculture of Violence: Towards an Integrated Theory in Criminology.* London: Tavistock Publications.

————, R. M. Figlio, and T. Sellin. 1972. *Delinquency in a Birth Cohort.* Chicago: The University of Chicago Press.

Yarrow, M. R., et al. 1968. *Child Rearing: An Inquiry into Research and Methods.* San Francisco: Jossey-Bass, Inc., Publishers.

Zax, M., et al. 1968. "Follow-up study of children identified early as emotionally disturbed." *Journal of Consulting and Clinical Psychology,* 32 (August):369–374.

Zeitlin, L. R. 1971. "A little larceny can do a lot for employee morale." *Psychology Today,* 5 (June):22–26, 64.

Zeigarnik, B. 1927. "About the memorizing of completed and incompleted actions." *Psychologische Forschung,* 9:1–86.

Zigler, E., and L. Phillips. 1965. "Psychiatric diagnosis and symptomatology." In O. Milton (Ed.), *Behavior Disorders.* New York: Lippincott.

Index